WHAT YOU MUST DO FOR YOUR COUNTRY

WHAT YOU MUST DO FOR YOUR COUNTRY

CLAUDE GENDREAU

DEDICATION

To Jean for her understanding and encouragement, to Gretchen for her assistance and to all the people who will do their part to set the country on a sustainable course.

TABLE OF CONTENTS

PROLOGUE

A mericans are the beneficiaries of a great country thanks to the hard work, the sacrifices, and the heroism of this and previous generations. For decades, Americans have enjoyed an enviable standard of living. They have had the satisfaction of living in the country widely viewed as the best for working, living, recreating, and growing old. They have basked in the pride of being citizens of the most powerful and the most influential nation on earth. A large population, expansive land mass, abundant natural resources, temperate climate, and strategic location relative to the rest of the world have sustained Americans' high living standards and the country's preeminent role on the world scene.

Americans must now realize they are in the process of squandering that heritage. The inefficient use of the country's resources—oil and other energy sources, water, land, and lumber and other building materials, human resources, and capital—diminishes the competitiveness of the U.S. economy. Inefficiencies worsen the reliance of Americans on imported goods. Some of the imported goods have a strategic importance: oil. The inefficient use of energy for transportation and for heating, cooling, and lighting our homes and commercial buildings unnecessarily enlarges the country's environmental footprint at a time when the international community's concern about climate dictates that polluters pay a price for degrading a common asset.

It is not too late to salvage the American heritage. We need to stop building houses that are twice the size of those built forty years ago to house families that are smaller than they were in 1970. We must get out of our SUVs and other gas-guzzlers and drive less. The average American family drives nine thousand miles per year more now than it did in 1969. It is imperative that we start retaining some of the $400 billion a year that we send to foreign oil producers every year. Slashing oil, natural gas, and electricity consumption is also necessary to align our energy use with that of other economies against which the United States is competing.

Cutting consumer spending is equally important. Americans account for nearly one-third of total global consumption spending. Purchasing consumer goods manufactured abroad in excess of products we export transfers another

$400 billion a year to foreign countries, which denies entrepreneurs the funds to grow the U.S. economy and empowers our competitors. We need to seek out products made in the United States to create employment for our fellow Americans. Building our manufacturing base is important to restore a positive trade balance. The United States has not had a single year of positive current account balance since 1969, a situation that had occurred only occasionally during the preceding forty years.

The United States has major strengths that need to be exploited more fully. It is still the largest economy in the world, by far. It has the third-largest population, one that will continue to grow while the population of most other competing economies will be stagnant or decrease. It has the fourth-largest land mass, almost equal to Canada's and China's, so the population can continue to expand without the country feeling crowded. It benefits from a temperate climate and fertile soil. The country is blessed with an abundance of natural resources, including one of critical importance: water. It has the advantage of almost limitless sources of renewable energy. It has a mature infrastructure, world class universities, a solid democratic system, an effective legal system, and a dynamic society.

This book points out some of the weaknesses of the American life-style and offers suggestions about adopting a way of life that is more suited for today's world, one that could inspire others around the world to become better inhabitants of the planet.

It writing this book, I have been inspired by great thinkers. I give special credit to Douglas Farr, author of *Sustainable Urbanism: Urban Design with Nature*; Andres Duany, Elizabeth Plater-Zyberk, and Jeff Speck, authors of *Suburban Nation, The Rise of Sprawl and the Decline of the American Dream*. Credit also goes to Lester R. Brown, *Plan B 4.0, Mobilizing to Save Civilization*; David JC McKay, *Sustainable Energy Without the Hot Air*; Thomas L. Friedman, Hot, Flat, and Crowded; Stanley I. Hart and Alvin L. Spivak, *The Elephant in the Bedroom*; James Howard Kunstler, *The Geography of Nowhere* and *The Long Emergency*; Nicholas Stern, *The Global Deal*; Charles J. Kibert, *Sustainable Construction, Green Building Design and Delivery*; Fred Krupp and Miriam Horn, *Earth: The Sequel*; Michael Pollan, *The Omnivore's Dilemma*; Jeffery D. Sachs, *Common Wealth*; Fareed Zakaria, *The Post-American World*; Laura Stec with Eugene Cordero, *Cool Cuisine*; Al Gore, *Our Choice*; Felix Rohatyn, *Bold Endeavors*; Roger Pielke, Jr., *The Climate Fix*; and Arianna Huffington, *Third World*

America. I strongly recommend you read their books for an in-depth study of the specific issues they address. Many more people shaped my thinking, most of them writing about current events, science, politics, and economics in daily, weekly, or monthly publications.

I want to introduce this book to you by quoting two great leaders:

> *"The difference between what we do and what we are capable of doing would solve most of the world's problems."* Mahatma Gandhi

> *"Don't ask what your country can do for you. Ask what you can do for your country."* John F. Kennedy

PART ONE:
SQUANDERING OUR RESOURCES

Chapter 1: Suburban Sprawl

RICHARD MOE, president of the National Trust for Historic Preservation, defines sprawl as "low-density development on the edges of towns—poorly planned, land-consumptive, auto-dependent, and designed without respect to its surroundings."[1] Sprawl is one of the most wasteful uses of land ever devised. It also represents one of the greatest misallocations of American wealth, human capital and natural resources. Low-density development, typical of suburbia, results in inefficient use of all infrastructures, including streets, sanitation and storm-water systems, potable-water systems, and electricity, phone, and internet-transmission lines. Those are all investments that service few people per mile of infrastructure.

Land-consumptive, auto-dependent, low-density development typical of subdivisions in exurbia. (Photo: The Author)

The wasteful use of resources does not end when the last pallet of sod is laid down. The cost of maintaining those streets and underground utilities; the expenses of policing those large areas; the expenses of providing education to suburban children, including the cost of busing them to schools continues to be a financial burden on suburbanites and a drain on the country's and the earth's resources. In the words of James Howard Kunstler, author of *The Long Emergency*, "America finds itself nearing the end of the cheap-oil age having invested its natural wealth in a living arrangement, suburban sprawl, which has no future. Suburbia has a tragic destiny." Kunstler further remarked that

---

1 Lockwood, Charles, National Geographic, September 1999, 82–92

"suburbs represent the greatest misallocation of resources the world has ever known." He added, "Now that Americans worry about global warming, the acres of bungalows and freeway exit ramps seem not just pointless but shameful."[2] William E. Rees, urban planner, professor of Community and Regional Planning at the University of British Columbia, Canada, could not agree more. "Since World War II, politicians and planners have shaped cities with no regard for resources use or ecological concerns. Today's land-grabbing, auto-dominated, fuel-inefficient metropolises have evolved into parasitic black holes, sucking in excessive megatons of energy and materials from all over the globe and spewing out volumes of (often toxic) waste."[3]

"Now that Americans worry about global warming, the acres of bungalows and freeway exit ramps seem not just pointless but shameful". James Howard Kuntsler
(Photos: IStock Photo # 1569497, 10431532)

Not surprisingly an important measure of the country's economic strength is the number of housing starts.[4] Our inefficient housing arrangement, until the collapse of the housing market in 2008, employed more than 10 million people building large, single-family homes, constructing streets and sidewalks in corn fields, laying down sod, etc. We were lulled into thinking that our economy could grow forever building houses designed to enlarge our egos, not to house our families. **In 1970, the size of the average American house was 1,385 square feet. The size of a typical new home in 2000 was 2,140 square**

---

2 Kuntsler, James Howard, The Long Emergency, 2005

3 William E. Rees; Scientific American, Earth 3.0, Volume 19, Number 1, 2009, 18

4 Andres Duany, Elizabeth Plater-Zybeck and Jeff Speck; Suburban Nation, 2000

feet, a 54 percent increase in size while the average household decreased in size from 3.14 to 2.52 persons.⁵ According to data from the Environmental Protection Agency (EPA), the average four-bedroom house in the United States in 2009 was roughly 2,800 square feet.⁶

Deerfield, IL - Traditional homes in urban setting. In 1970 the size of the average American house was 1,385 square feet. In 2009, the average size of a four-bedroom house was roughly 2,800 feet. (Photo: The Author)

Large houses and suburban living represent a diversion of capital to non-productive assets, reducing America's competitiveness in the world. "Much of America's manufacturing output is destined for new homes and buildings, from bricks to bulldozers, and a lot goes into cars."⁷ It also contributes to America's oversized carbon footprint. Douglas Farr, author of *Sustainable Urbanism*, pointed to the ecological burden of our housing arrangement

---

5 Douglas Farr, Sustainable Urbanism: Urban Design with Nature, 2008

6 Jeffrey Ball, The Wall Street Journal, June 26, 2009

7 The Economist, "Manufacturing's Futures," October 3, 2009, 36-38

when he wrote: **"The American dream of a large house on a large lot in the suburbs is what's most responsible for cooking the planet."**[5] The so-called energy-efficient single-family residence cannot match the energy efficiency of average multifamily housing units. Single-family homes also are more costly to maintain, adding to the financial burden of our housing arrangement.

"The American dream of a large house on a large lot in the suburbs is what's most responsible for cooking the planet." Douglas Farr (Photo: The Author)

Suburban sprawl fostered the reliance on the car. Because few suburbanites can walk or take public transportation to their place of work, they spend an inordinate amount of time and energy commuting. In 2000, the U.S. Census Bureau determined that 3.5 million Americans subjected themselves to "extreme commutes," defined as travel times to and from work of three hours or more each day. Because they live far from shopping areas, restaurants, the entertainment district, and their place of worship, families need multiple cars, 244 million of them. Of course suburbanites need big cars to match their living room comfort since they spend a good part of their lives in their cars. The number of cars sold is another important barometer of the country's economic health. Several hundred thousand workers were busy manufacturing cars to be purchased by all those suburbanites. Other tens of thousands of workers were erecting gas stations on farmland along highways to refuel those cars. None of those activities produced goods that we could export in exchange for those we needed to import.

Congestion on roads costs $78 billion annually in the form of 4.2 billion lost hours and 2.9 billion gallons of wasted gasoline. In 2000, 3.5 million Americans spent three hours or more commuting each day to and from work. (Photo: IStock Photo #11994853)

We were lulled into believing that we could continue to grow our economy by expanding sprawl, building McMansions, and manufacturing cars. We let manufacturing that was fundamental to innovation leave the country. There are not a lot of productive assets left that offer us the same kind of economic strength that America had at the end of World War II when the United States represented basically every product and technology that existed. Data from the National Association of Manufacturers show that of the fifteen large manufacturing economies, U.S. manufacturers are the least geared toward exports.[7]

While we were busy transforming corn fields into suburbs and exurbs and building cars to take those homeowners to work or the sports centers to cheer for their favorite teams, we allowed our infrastructure to deteriorate. We are still living off the infrastructure investments of the Roosevelt and Eisenhower years. "We haven't built anything in years," exclaimed Arnold Schwarzenegger, former governor of California, on *Meet the Press*, January 10, 2010.[8] U.S.

8 Arnold Schwarzenegger: Meet the Press, January 10, 2010

spending on infrastructure as a percent of the gross domestic product (GDP) is the lowest in the industrial world. The United States invests a mere 2.4 percent of its GDP on infrastructure, compared with 5 percent in Europe and 9 percent in China.[9] Much of it is spent on sprawl. Railways are old. America's only "high-speed" train runs between Boston and Washington, D.C., on inadequate tracks. Public transportation within cities needs to be expanded and modernized. The electrical grid is fast becoming inadequate. If America does not act, said Robert Yaro of the Regional Planning Association (RPA), a body that plans for New York, New Jersey, and Connecticut, "it will have the infrastructure of a third-world country within a few decades. Economic growth will be constricted and the quality of life will be diminished."[9] Already America's inadequate infrastructure is costing Americans billions of dollars each year in lost productivity and affecting their quality of life.

* Domestic flight delays cost $32.9 billion in 2007, according to researchers at UC Berkeley.
* Congestion on roads costs $78 billion annually in the form of 4.2 billion lost hours and 2.9 billion gallons of wasted gasoline.[9]
* The power infrastructure is outdated: For every kWh of electricity used 2.2 kWh are lost on average during transmission. Power outages cost the economy $150 billion a year.
* Important ports, such as New York and Los Angeles (L.A.), are choked.
* The freight rail hub south of Chicago is so clogged that trains take longer to move through Chicago than to travel from L.A. to Chicago.

Profligate Consumerism

Our inordinate spending on consumer goods constitutes another misallocation of our resources while giving the country a false sense of economic health.[10] For more than three decades after World War II, private consumption as a percentage of GDP remained constant between 61 and 63 percent. In 1983, consumption started to rise and in 2007 reached a record $9.7 trillion, 70 percent of the United States' $13.8 trillion GDP. Between 2000 and 2007 the average American increased personal consumption by 44 percent. It accounted

9 The Economist, "Infrastructure," June 28, 2008, 36

10 The Economist, A Special Report on Business in America, May 30, 2009, 3-18

for 77 percent of America's economic growth, and consumer spending became the main indicator of the country's economic health. Excessive personal consumption supported economic activities that produced nonperforming assets. Using another metric, debt relative to income, one can appreciate the unsustainability of consumer spending. Household debt between 2000 and 2007 grew from 94 percent of income to 133 percent of income.[11] In the 1980s, Americans saved about 9 percent of their income. It fell to 5 percent in the 1990s. In 2005, the saving rate dropped to a mere 0.5 percent of earnings before rebounding to 3.9 percent in the last quarter of 2009. For comparison, households in the Euro zone save 9 percent of their income on average.[12]

Gurnee Mills Shopping Mall – Consumer spending by Americans accounts for 28 percent of the world total. (Photo: The Author)

Economic growth has been driven by an unsustainable consumer boom supported by borrowing. The total credit card debt has increased 50 percent since 2002, increasing by $6.8 trillion.[13] Consumers borrowed against their properties. Between 2003 and 2006 they borrowed almost $2 trillion via home-equity loans and mortgage refinancing.[11] From 2000 thru 2007 U.S. purchases amounted to $97 trillion, exceeding gross domestic production by $4.5 trillion. The excess purchases were mostly by consumers and were financed by borrowing, almost all

11 The Economist, "American Consumers Off Their Trolleys," May 9, 2009, 75-77

12 Leo Abruzzese, "The Buck Stops Here" The Economist, The World in 2009, p. 40

13 Kimberly Palmer: U.S. News & World Report, August 18/August 25, 2008, 41-45

of it secured by houses.[14] Consumption spending by Americans accounted to 28 percent of the world total.[15] The consequence of this debt burden is that Americans now spend 14 percent of their income on debt service. Since Americans are borrowing 80 percent of the world's surplus savings, a great portion of the interest on their debt is being paid to foreigners, further strengthening the economic and geopolitical power of America's competitors in world markets. The Chinese, the main beneficiaries of our frivolous purchases and of our debt service, are starting to worry about our ability to continue down that path. Chinese Premier Wen Jiabao, addressing the World Economic Forum in Davos-Klosters, Switzerland, January 28, 2009, blamed the financial crisis on "an unsustainable model of development characterized by prolonged low savings and high consumption."

The free-spending life-style that spread across America was fostered by retailers' gimmicks and misguided fiscal policies. "Virtually every Pavlovian trigger discovered in the human brain is now pulled by advertisers. Partly as a result, material consumption in our society has reached absurd levels, declining slightly only in the teeth of the worst economic downturn since the Great Depression."[16] We were encouraged to live above our means. Banks issuing credit cards to marginal borrowers were part of the problem. More than 8 billion credit card solicitations poured into Americans' mailboxes in 2006 alone.[11] **Had Americans not spent so frivolously, charging up their credit cards, more Americans would have been able to afford the higher monthly payments of adjustable mortgages.** Innovative credit schemes also played a role as financial institutions devised new ways for Americans to borrow against their residences.[10] Had Americans not used their homes as ATM machines, piling new debt onto their homes, a cyclical reduction in real estate value would not have caused the value of so many homes to drop below the amount of the mortgages they carried.

Our elected officials bear a lot of the responsibility for Americans' reckless spending. They want you to spend. That's their way of pumping the economy. An example is the stimulus package voted into law by our legislators in the spring of 2008, which returned to taxpayers an amount up to $600 each to encourage consumption. After 9/11, President Bush exhorted Americans to "go out and spend." Americans binged on "dead assets," items that did not pro-

---

14 Charles R. Morris, Businessweek, August 4, 2008, 73-74

15 Robert J. Samuelson, Newsweek, May 10, 2010, 24

16 Al Gore, Our Choice, 2009

duce any wealth—televisions, electronic gadgets, clothing, and furniture, most of which was manufactured abroad and had little or no resale value. Spending on consumer goods was at the expense of investments in productive assets that could have created wealth.

The perception that consumer spending is good for the economy has not changed in the aftermath of the economic crisis of 2008–2009. Secretary of the Treasury Tim Geithner was asked about his assessment of the health of the economy on *Meet the Press* April 18, 2010. He affirmed that the economy was recovering. One of the reasons he gave to support his claim was that consumers were starting to spend more of their income.

Responsible consumption would have gone a long way toward eliminating or alleviating many of the problems facing this country. **Buying smaller, more affordable homes; driving smaller, more fuel-efficient cars; and buying fewer discretionary goods would have averted the housing debacle that triggered our economic crisis.** Had people not succumbed to wasteful consumption patterns, loading up their credit cards, most of them would have been able to meet their mortgage obligations, sparing the country the housing crisis.

There are encouraging signs. A survey found that people ranked being in control of their finances and having a green life-style higher as signs of success than having a luxury car, and viewed having a paid-off mortgage as more of a status symbol than having a big home.[13] Anti-consumption ways have a positive effect on the environment as well, but Russell Simon, a twenty-six-year-old communications manager, feels that a more frugal life-style goes beyond that. "It's about uncluttering my mind, uncluttering my space, and allowing me to focus on things that matter."[13]

Frugality is becoming more fashionable. *U.S. News and World Report* chronicled an example of an enlightened life-style.[13] Cindee Mazzanti, a self-employed fifty-seven-year-old living in upstate New York, started downsizing in 2001. She sold her home, used the equity to pay off her debts, and purchased a smaller home without a mortgage. She traded her big SUV for a thrifty Ford Focus. Her monthly living expenses shrank from $5,600 to $1,200. Without debt, she says, she feels free. That's one homeowner who did not lose her house to foreclosure. It is time to embrace a simpler, less wasteful, more sustainable life-style.

Throttling back on unnecessary purchases can be rewarding in ways we might not anticipate. It has been demonstrated that children who make some of their own toys develop their creativity. During a year of buying only "necessities,"

Judith Levine, who wrote about her experience in *Not Buying It: My Year Without Shopping*,[17] related that the greatest value came from the experiences that filled the time she once spent shopping. We should be spending more of our time and money stocking our minds rather than our drawers, closets, and shelf spaces. One thing that happens when one ratchets down on consumption is that one finds other satisfactions, not the least being able to afford one's mortgage payments.

Environmental Cost

The economic cost of sprawl and free-spending habits is tangible. The environmental cost of our life-style is not obvious to most of us but it is starting to matter. Excessive consumption depletes scarce commodities. Oil is an example of a finite commodity that is being depleted by our spend-free habits. More than two million of the twenty million barrels of oil that we consume each day are used for purposes other than transportation. It is a component of many of the products we use daily—tires, plastic toys, plastic containers and bags, synthetic fabric, and more. There is oil embedded in the cotton of your clothes in the form of fertilizer used to grow the cotton plant, unless you bought clothes fabricated with organic cotton. Oil powered the tractors that cultivated and harvested the cotton. It is in everything we purchase, if only as diesel or gasoline used to bring those products to the retailers in your neighborhood.

Unbridled consumerism contributes to the emission of unnecessary tons of greenhouse gases in ways that are not a priori evident. Our splurging on all those imported goods built Asia's export economy, causing surging demand for energy to the point that China is putting in operation a new power plant almost every week. A great portion of China's greenhouse gas emissions comes from the power plants supplying its industries that are manufacturing goods for American consumers. **A full 23 percent of China's greenhouse gas emissions can be attributed to the manufacture of goods exported to the West, according to Tyndall Center for Climate Change Research in England. Researchers at Carnegie Mellon University estimate that share at 33 percent.**[18]

What is not taken into consideration are the emissions that result from the building boom created by the profits garnered by the countries (mostly Asian) that manufacture all of the products that we import. The trillions of dollars

---

17 Judith Levine: Not Buying It: My Year Without Shopping, Free Press, New York, 2006

18 David Biello, Scientific American Earth 3.0, Volume 18, Number 5, 2009, 34–40

that we sent to China and other Asian countries drove the migration of peasants to cities, turning hamlets into mega cities. Shenzhen, China, is a city of thirteen million people. It sports wide streets and thousands of concrete-and-steel apartment and commercial buildings. Two decades ago it was a small village. That is part of the carbon footprint of all the toys purchased for our kids; toys that will be used a few times before they are abandoned and replaced by new ones. It's part of the carbon footprint of the shoes and T-shirts that fill our closets. It's part of the carbon footprint of the electronic gadgets that we keep updating at an alarming rate. Unbridled industrialization, especially in emerging economies, is polluting waterways and aquifers. According to the World Bank, around 90 percent of the rivers in China near urban areas are severely polluted, adding to the environmental cost of our profligate consumption.

Shenzhen, China – American consumers fueled the meteoric growth of this and other Chinese cities. In 2007 shoppers spent $321 billion on Chinese-manufactured goods. (Photo: IStock Photo #14936689)

Our insatiable appetite for Asian-manufactured goods has raised the purchasing power of Asian workers, engendering an expansion of their domestic economy. An income of $5,000 a year is the threshold for affording a private car. There must be a lot of Chinese making $5,000 a year because a lot of Chinese are buying cars in Shanghai, Beijing, Guangzhou, Shenzhen, and the rest of China, straining crude-oil supplies and emitting climate-changing greenhouse gases.

The overuse of private transportation also carries an environmental cost beyond the twenty pounds of CO_2 emitted by each gallon of gasoline used. The trillions of dollars we sent to the countries of the Gulf Cooperation Council (GCC) for that oil was used to build islands in the Arabian Sea and erect thousands of massive, concrete-and-steel buildings in Kuwait, Dubai, and Abu Dhabi at great cost to the environment. Without America's price-supporting, insatiable appetite for oil, I doubt that a building more than twice the height of our Empire State Building, the 2,300-foot Burj Khalifa that opened in Dubai January 4, 2010, or the 3,284-foot Burj Mubarak al Kabir skyscraper to be completed in 2016 in Kuwait at an estimated cost of $7.37 billion would be constructed.[19] The world has us to blame for much of the Arab world's greenhouse gas emissions. We have ourselves to blame for making possible the erection of landmark buildings in foreign countries that dwarf the Empire State Building, a landmark that made Americans proud and drew tourists from all over the world for decades.

Burj Khalifa Skyscraper, Dubai – Americans import 12 million barrels of oil each day. In 2009, Americans spent $416 billion on imported oil. (Photo: IStock Photo #14003716)

19 Popular Science, March 2009, 37

Our profligate consumerism also depletes another precious resource: water. It takes around 117 cubic feet of fresh water to produce a single, 200-micron semiconductor wafer.

Urbanization is also a factor in water consumption. City dwellers use more water than rural people. Almost all of the two billion people who will be added to the world's population between now and 2030 will be third-world city dwellers.[20] The Food and Agricultural Organization (FAO) estimates that the world will require about 60 percent more water for agriculture to feed those two billion people, or 1,500 Km^3 per year, the equivalent of today's worldwide consumption outside of Asia.

Garbage Issues

The amount of waste a country generates tends to grow with its economy and its urban concentration. The richer the people, the more they consume, the more they discard. Americans produce over 1,500 pounds of municipal waste per person each year. The average for member countries of the Organization of Economic Cooperation and Development (OECD) countries is a little over 1,200 pounds. Brazilians produce about 650 pounds and the Chinese about 250 pounds. Electronic waste (e-waste) is an unintended consequence of consumers being able to afford the ever more sophisticated high-tech gadgetry. The Environmental Protection Agency (EPA) estimates that 2.6 million tons of e-waste is produced in the United States each year.[21]

Our gargantuan appetite for discretionary goods is causing the expansion of landfills. "Out of sight, out of mind" is not an acceptable way of treating garbage anymore. It is the source of about 4 percent of the world's greenhouse gases, mostly in the form of methane. Organic waste is particularly offensive to the atmosphere. Together the dumps emit more of the greenhouse gas methane than any other human-related source, according to Melinda Wenner.[22] They have a greenhouse-gas impact equal to one-fifth of that produced by the nation's coal-fired power plants. Dumps are also a source of toxic chem-

---

20 The Economist, "Water. Sin aqua non," April 11, 2009, p. 59-61

21 Kent Garber: U.S. News & World Report, December 31, 2007/January 7, 2008

22 Melinda Wenner: Scientific American Earth 3.0, December 9, 2009, 10

icals that find their way into our aquifers and streams. There is no surer way to reduce waste than cutting back on our purchases.

Non-biodegradable wastes even find their way into our oceans. It is estimated that perhaps 100 million tons of garbage is floating in the Pacific Ocean between California and Hawaii. The United Nations Environmental Program (UNEP) estimates that as much as 6.4 million tons of waste ends up in the sea each year. Every square kilometer of the Pacific Ocean has an average of 13,000 pieces of plastic floating on it and many more times that number have settled to the floor of the ocean.[23]

The increased volume of waste going into landfills causes a myriad of other problems, not the least of which is the cost of managing waste. Industrialized countries spend some $120 billion a year handling municipal waste, alone.

Finding space for landfills is also problematic and trucking garbage to faraway sites uses a lot of oil and adds to traffic woes. A fleet of trucks carries Floridians' garbage to Indiana. Some of the garbage collected in Illinois heads for Iowa. Municipal waste generated by residents of Toronto, Canada, ends up across the border in Michigan.

The increase in the amount of rubbish worldwide is expected to come from the developing countries, paralleling the rise in their urban population and the affluence of their citizens. India's city dwellers are projected to generate 130 percent more waste and China's over 200 percent more by the year 2030.[23] Their rubbish is also our concern because it pollutes the atmosphere that we share and causes climate changes that affect all of us. Consumer spending and garbage generation go hand in hand.

Waste Reduction Measures

William McDonough and Michael Baumgart in their book *Cradle to Cradle* propose a new approach to the manufacturing industry. The authors advocate "designing products using components that can be recovered to be utilized as technical biological nutrients eliminating the concept of waste." The cradle-to-cradle concept is the antithesis of cradle-to-grave. The concept leapfrogs the current approach of recycling, which often turns specialized products, computers, and other electronic devices into products of low sophistication that eventually are discarded. McDonough and Baumgart suggest

---

23 The Economist, A Special Report on Waste, February 28, 2009, 3-18

that discarded carpeting be returned as carpeting, tires be returned as tires. They recommend that items that are replaced by more sophisticated ones be reused by people who don't require the more sophisticated devices. When I was growing up, the milkmen collected empty milk bottles. The bottles were returned to their original purpose, according to the cradle-to-cradle principle. Oberweiss, a Chicago-area dairy product distributor, is still recycling glass milk bottles to the benefit of the environment.

Individuals need to do their part. The catch phrase often mentioned regarding waste is "reduce, reuse, and recycle." "Refrain" should be substituted for reduce. Refrain from buying so much stuff that you can do without. That's the first step to reducing one's contribution to the garbage problem. Reuse is gaining in popularity with economic hardship. There are drives to collect and distribute used shoes and toys and to return to use unwanted cell phones.

Communities are embracing recycling and individuals are participating. Some municipalities do a better job than others. Los Angeles recycles 65 percent of its waste. **San Francisco keeps some 70 percent of its waste out of landfills, one of the highest rates in the world.** The City Council hopes to eventually achieve "zero waste."[23] In 2009, San Francisco supplied residences with compost bins and made it illegal to put food and yard waste in the garbage. Only a handful of communities compost food scraps but twenty-two states ban leaves and yard waste from landfills. Food scraps, yard waste, and other biodegradable garbage make up one-fourth of the nation's trash. Those items could be turned into nutrient-rich compost by worms and microorganisms for use by gardeners and farmers while sparing the atmosphere of large quantities of methane. Waste food, because it contains all its energy, is a promising source of biogas. Restaurants, hotels, and food-processing plants need to be incentivized to turn waste food into energy. Numerous sewage plants have begun processing food scraps in the past year.[24]

Many companies are already showing the way toward responsible behavior. Subaru of Indiana is a great example. Its manufacturing plant achieved the remarkable goal of zero landfill waste by careful planning and sophisticated recycling, a responsibility that was outsourced to Allegiant Global Services, a firm that specializes in waste management.[25] Wal-Mart, the world's biggest retailer, set up an ambitious program in 2005 with a long-term goal of becoming

24 The Economist, "Renewable Energy. The Seat of Power, January 2, 2010, p. 59–60

25 Brad Kenney, Industry Week, July 2008, 36–43

a zero-waste, renewably powered enterprise. The company installs green roofs, uses LED lights, and introduces other energy-saving measures. But its most significant contribution will most likely be the implementation of its sustainability index. By 2012, all of its suppliers, more than 100,000 of them, mostly in Asia, will have to meet standards of social and environmental responsibility to continue to supply Wal-Mart. That could have a ripple effect throughout the Asian manufacturing sector resulting in enormous benefit for the planet. Another large retailer, Target, is touting the environmental benefits of its waste-reduction measures. It claims to have diverted 80,000 tons of construction material from landfills in 2009 and recycled 950 million pounds of cardboard from its stores and distribution centers. It further burnished its environmental credentials by reusing 370 million garment hangers.

■ Chapter One: What You Must Do For Your Country:

* ✹ Choose an urban life-style. It is especially suited to the 75 million baby boomers who are about to retire
* ✹ Support zoning ordinances and other measures that maximize housing density. Support measures that discourage the building of large homes
* ✹ Adopt a more frugal life-style. Cut back on discretionary spending
* ✹ Recycle

PART TWO: ENERGY

Chapter 2: Global Energy Consumption

"What we do about energy may be the most important question the country faces." Michael Moyer and Amanda Schupak, Popular Science, November 2008

"Energy will be a key factor in the new world order." Mikhail Khordorkovsky, The World in 2007

Americans, until recently, have not had to concern themselves with the amount of their energy use. The two main sources of their energy, oil and coal, have been abundant and cheap except for two short periods in the 1970s when the flow of oil was politically restricted and prices shot up. Our life-style evolved in an environment of disregard for energy conservation.

Consequently, our use of energy has been out of line with the rest of the world's. **Western Europeans enjoy a similar standard of living to ours on half the energy we use.** America's total energy consumption in kilograms of oil equivalent per head per year amounts to 7,921 kg versus 4,457 kg for France, 4,218 kg for Germany, 4,173 kg for Japan, and 3,906 kg for the United Kingdom. When measured against developing countries, the comparison is even more startling. Chinese get by on 1,242 kg equivalent per person, Brazil, 1,114 kg, and India uses a mere 0.531 kg per capita.[26] Yet, the Energy Information Administration estimates that our energy consumption will rise by more than 40 percent by 2030. While the amount of energy use continues to grow in the United States, it is declining in Europe. In 2007, Germany's energy consumption decreased by 5.6 percent while its economy grew by 2.6 percent.

---

26 The Economist's Pocket World in Figures 2008 Edition, "Energy. Largest Consumers," 56

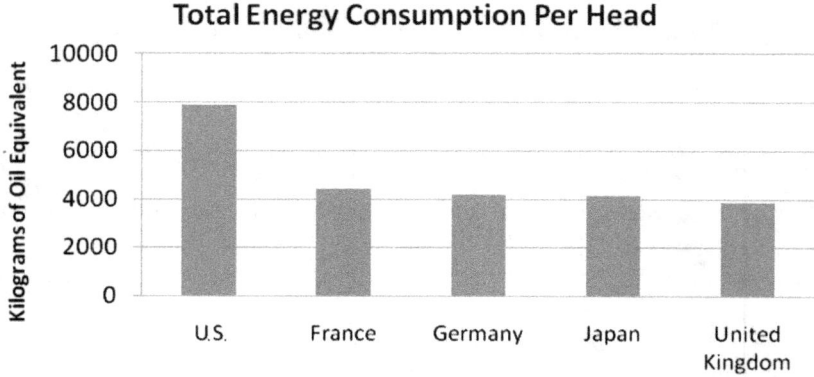

Figure1: Total Energy Consumption per Head per Year in Kilograms of Oil Equivalent; Source: The Economist Pocket World in Figures, 2008

Our wasteful ways are even more remarkable when it comes to oil consumption. **We use almost 25 percent of the world's daily oil production—20 million of 84 million barrels—to support our life-style.** China, the second-largest economy in the world, with a population that is more than three times ours, uses 7 million barrels per day. Japan and Germany, the third- and fourth-largest economies use 5.3 and 2.5 million barrels a day, respectively. France with 61 million people uses less than 2 million barrels a day. Those figures underscore our vulnerability to oil shortages and the impact of high oil prices on our economy and our life-style.

When America's use of energy is measured using yet another yardstick, the amount of energy used per unit of GDP, we also find that we use more energy than any other industrialized nation. The European economy needs 20 percent less energy than the United States to produce one unit of GDP, according to UBS, a Swiss bank.

A life-style supported by an inordinate amount of energy becomes less sustainable when competition for energy is causing prices to escalate. It appears even less sustainable when oil, one of its two main sources of energy, risks becoming a scarce commodity in the not so distant future. It is certainly problematic when fossil fuels account for a full 80 percent of our total energy needs and burning fossil fuels is considered a threat to the earth's ecosystem.

Drivers of Energy Consumption

Increased competition for energy is not about to relent. The main drivers of energy consumption are well entrenched. Expanding population, industrialization and improved purchasing power in developing countries, urbanization, and changing dietary habits are megatrends that will not be reversed in favor of less energy consumption for a long time. The International Energy Agency (IEA) expects energy demand to increase nearly 50 percent by 2030, fueled mostly by the expanding economies of the developing countries.

Energy consumption is increasing worldwide with the expanding population. In 1800, the world population totaled 1 billion people. It took 130 years to add one more billion individuals. In the following seventy-five years, the world population increased by four billion to reach six billion in 2005. By 2012 the earth will be populated by seven billion people and by 2050, nine billion people will be sharing the earth. The number of cows, sheep, and pigs to support the dietary needs of those people and the number of their pets is also on the rise, all consuming energy.

The more people the more minds driving innovations. One hundred and twenty-five years ago there were no cars and no aircraft burning fuel. There were no clothes washer-dryers, no dishwashers, no hot water heaters, no refrigerators, and no air-conditioners. There were no televisions, no computers or other electronic devices drawing power from the utility companies. There were no elevators or escalators. No wonder the demand for energy keeps growing.

Energy consumption is also spurred by affluence. During the past fifteen years, a new middle class has made its presence felt, especially in emerging markets, creating new aspirations. Higher income also feeds a culture of "wants" over one of "needs." Why not own a television, a second or even a third one if one can afford it? Why not own a dishwasher, an air-conditioner, or a dehumidifier? All draw power. This new middle class is loosely defined as people having about one-third of their income left for discretionary spending after providing basic food and shelter. In the developing world, the middle class has expanded from being one-third of the population in 1980 to about half today. For the first time in history, more than half the world's population is considered middle class.

Most developing countries find that when GDP per person reaches about $5,000, people start switching from motorcycles to cars. A car tends to be the first big purchase a family makes once its income rises about $5,000 a year in purchasing-power parity.[27] [28] As recently as a century ago few people could afford cars even in the developed countries. At the turn of the last century there were 8,000 cars in the United States. Less than a hundred years ago, in 1912, there were still only 902,000 cars on America's roads. **In 2008, there were 244 million cars in the United States alone and there were 700 million cars worldwide.**[27, 28]

Competition for oil, one of our main sources of energy, is set to accelerate. There is a huge, unsatisfied demand for cars in four big emerging markets— China, India, Brazil, and Russia. Because of those expanding markets, global car sales in 2008 established an all-time record of 59 million units in spite of a decline of about 5 million units in the United States.[28] Consider the fact that fewer than 200 residents of Russia per 1,000 potential drivers own a car. In Brazil, that number is about 130. In China it is less than 40. In India there are only 10 cars per 1,000 potential drivers. In America, 900 people per 1,000 of driving age own a car. The dream of hundreds of millions of people in the developing world is to own a car just like Americans do. CSM Worldwide Inc., a market research firm, expects auto sales to nearly triple to 4.6 million units a year in India by 2014 up from 1.6 million units in 2007. Tata Motors Ltd., India's largest automobile company, started accepting deposits in May 2009 for the Nano, its newest model. It had to set up a lottery to determine who got to buy the first 100,000 cars since it had millions of orders![29] **In 1976 Chinese vehicle production was running at 150,000 a year. In 2010 it reached 15 million units.** It was only twenty-five years ago—in 1984—that the first private vehicle appeared in Beijing. Economists at the International Monetary Fund (IMF) have calculated that the number of cars in the world will grow from 700 million in 2009 to 2.9 billion by 2050, roughly a fourfold increase. Ponder for a moment the impact of 2.9 billion cars on the earth's resources and on the environment. Americans better find ways to reduce their fuel consumption and slash oil imports because oil is going to get scarce and expensive.

---

27 The Economist, "Detroitosaurus Wrecks," June 6, 2009, p. 9

28 The Economist, "A Special Report on Cars in Emerging Markets," November 15, 2008, 3–20

29 Eric Bellman, The Wall Street Journal, March 24, 2009

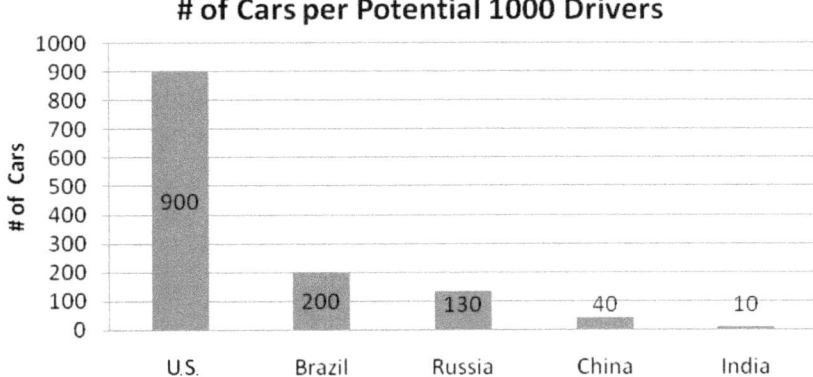

Figure 2: Number of Cars per Potential 1,000 Drivers; Source: The Economist, November 15, 2008

Improved purchasing power also leads to more energy-intensive dietary habits. Affluent people eat more meat and processed foods and drink more bottled water and sodas. In 2000, global meat consumption was 230 million tons. It is expected to double by 2050. Meat and poultry consumption was 222 pounds per person the in United States in 2006. Chinese consumption of beef, pork, and poultry has increased 140 percent between 1990 and 2008. Agriculture is a very energy-intensive activity. The production of animal protein is an especially inefficient process and one that is responsible for 18 percent of all greenhouse gas emissions.

In America, affluence created additional demand for energy. It led to the popularity of the single-family home and suburban living. It also contributed to a 54 percent increase in the size of the typical American house between 1970 and 2000. Since World War II the American dream has consisted of building bigger houses far apart from each other where corn used to grow and stuff them with ever more furniture and appliances. Those are important factors contributing to the energy intensity of the American life-style.

Chapter 3: Transport-related Energy: Oil

The year 2009 marked the 150th year of the crude oil age. Oil was first noticed in pools on the ground in northwestern Pennsylvania where locals soaked it up in rags and rung it into bottles. Originally, people used it as a substitute for whale oil to fuel their lamps. In August 1859, Edwin L. Drake and his crew drilled a seventy-foot well near Titusville, Pennsylvania, and hit a gusher. Fifteen months later, there were seventy-five wells pumping oil out of the ground in the surrounding areas, marking the beginning of a new era. Two years later the area was yielding three million barrels a year. By 1860 at least twenty oil refineries had been built in the state, producing mostly kerosene for use in lamps. By the end of the century oil fields had been found in thirteen other states, including New York and California. In 1901, thanks to the advent of new drilling techniques, a gusher was uncovered near Beaumont in southern Texas. The oil rush spread to Oklahoma, Louisiana, and northern Texas, sharply increasing supplies.[30]

Meanwhile demand for kerosene dropped as Thomas Edison's 1882 invention, the electric light bulb, started to replace kerosene lamps. By 1902, eighteen million light bulbs were in use in the United States. Fortunately for the likes of the Rockefellers, the car industry started its rapid expansion. By 1910, gasoline was the main product of oil distillation. The market for crude was quickly expanding globally. California was exporting most of the crude to Asia.[30]

Petroleum discoveries were also happening in other parts of the world. Huge deposits were found near Baku, the capital of Azerbaijan, in the early 1870s. Ten years later, two hundred refineries were in operation around the city, which was then under the control of Russia. In 1908 came the discovery of the largest reservoir in the Middle East in Persia, which is now Iran. In 1938, large oil fields were discovered in Saudi Arabia and Kuwait. The year 1948 witnessed the largest oil find, Al-Ghawar in Saudi Arabia. To this day it is the largest oil field.[30]

---

30 Science Illustrated, "Oil. From the first drop to the last," July/August, 2009, 59–69

The United States again was at the forefront of oil exploration when, in the later part of the 1890s, exploration moved offshore. Summerland oil field off the coast of California was the first offshore well. In 1949 the Soviet Union pioneered modern-age offshore drilling by creating a platform almost twenty-eight miles into the Caspian Sea. Soon after, oil rigs started appearing in the deep waters of the Gulf of Mexico.[30]

Already scientists and oil industry executives are expressing concern that new discoveries are not keeping pace with fading existing oil fields, not a comforting situation when the United States uses 25 percent of all the oil extracted from the earth.

Peak Oil

"Humanity's way of life is on a collision course with geology—with the stark fact that the earth holds a finite supply of oil." Tim Appenzeller, National Geographic, June 2004

Unlimited access to affordable oil has been underpinning the American economy and supporting our life-style for decades. Yet, in the face of threats posed by rising oil prices and dwindling supplies, we are lackadaisical about taking steps to counter those threats. We take the view that new discoveries will keep up with increasing demand or that innovation will keep pushing the envelope of what is recoverable. That view may be naïve.

Peak oil used to refer to the time when the world oil production would start declining. It is known as "Hubert's Peak" after M. King Hubert, a geologist who predicted in 1956 that America's oil production would begin to decline in the early 1970s. To his credit, production from the forty-eight contiguous states peaked around 1970. The debate is ongoing about when the global "Hubert's Peak" will occur.[31]

As Chevron Company stated, **"It took us 125 years to use the first trillion barrels of oil. We'll use the next trillion in 30."**[32] As early as April 2006, in a special report on the oil industry published in *The Economist*, the author made the case that what really matters to the world economy is not when

---

31 The Economist, "A Survey of Oil. The Bottomless Beer Mug," April 30, 2005, 16–20

32 The Economist, "Special Report. The Oil Industry, April 22, 2006, 65-67

conventional oil production peaks but whether we have enough affordable and convenient fuel from any source to power our current fleet of cars, trucks, buses, and airplanes.

Peak oil is now more aptly defined as the time when production will be inadequate to meet demand. Mr. Christophe de Margerie, a senior oilman and a chief executive of Total, the most valuable French company, is one of many oil executives who define peak oil as the situation "when supply cannot meet demand." There is mounting evidence that the world will face that reality soon, a lot earlier than was envisioned a few years ago.[33] Mr. de Margerie pointed out, "The output of existing fields is declining by five to six million barrels per day every year. That means that oil firms have to find lots of new fields just to keep production at today's levels." In 2007 he said, "The world would never be able to increase its output of oil from the current level of 85 million barrels a day to 100 million barrels a day, let alone the 116 million barrels a day that energy analysts predict will be needed by 2030."[33]

According to Neil King Jr. and Peter Fritch in their *Wall Street Journal* article dated May 22, 2008, about the International Energy Agency (IEA) assessment of production capacity, "Future crude supplies could be far tighter than previously thought. Last summer the IEA said its analysis of projects known to be in the works suggested that the world could face a shortfall by 2015 of as much as 12.5 million barrels a day unless there was a sharp drop in expected demand."[34]

While forecasters expect demand to continue to rise, production is declining. A Cambridge Energy Research Associates study concluded, "The depletion rate of the world's 811 biggest fields is around 4.5 percent a year."[35] The IEA on November 6, 2008, released a summary of the annual study of about eight hundred oil fields. The IEA work echoed the gloomy forecast of oil industry executives. It estimated that the combination of rising demand and production declines in existing fields will require oil companies to add 64 million barrels a day in capacity by 2030, more than six times Saudi Arabia's current production. Nearly half that will be needed in the next eight years, the report warned.[35] Nobuo Tanaka, the IEA's executive director, said, **"Even if oil demand was**

---

33 The Economist, "Face value. Totally different," January 12, 2008, 61

34 Neil King , Jr. and Peter Fritch, The Wall Street Journal, May 22, 2008

35 Guy Chazan, The Wall Street Journal, November 7, 2008

to remain flat to 2030, 45 million barrels per day of gross capacity would need to be built by 2030 just to offset oil fields decline."[36] Merrill Lynch analysts concurred. They concluded that "they must find another Saudi Arabia's worth of oil every two years just to maintain production at today's levels."[37]

Declines are occurring at many of the main oil fields. Non-OPEC fields, such as Alaska, the North Sea, and the Gulf of Mexico saved the western oil companies and helped check OPEC's market power but now they are entering a phase of rapid market decline. Some of the biggest fields in the North Sea, Alaska, and the Gulf of Mexico are now declining at rates approaching 18 percent a year. Sharp declines in North Sea output turned the UK into a net importer of oil in 2005. In 1999 it was the world's sixth-biggest source of oil and gas. In 2008 it was twelfth. Since the peak of 1999, production in 2009 had fallen 40 percent and the target output of 3mb/d in 2010 seemed unrealistic.[38] Cantarell, in the Gulf of Mexico, was once the world's largest offshore oil field. Now it's running out. In 2004 it produced 2.1 million barrels a day making up 60 percent of Mexico's output. In July 2008 Mexico's government released figures showing that output at Cantarell oil field had fallen by one-third over the previous year. The output in 2009 was only 600,000 barrels a day and twenty-three of Mexico's thirty-two oil fields were in decline. Indonesia, the world's fourth-most-populous country, used to be an oil-exporting member of OPEC. Now Indonesia is a net oil importer.

The leading oil exporting country for decades, Saudi Arabia is not a bottomless well either. Matthew Simmons' research, referred to by *The Economist* in a July 12, 2008, article, concluded, "Saudi Arabia's biggest oil fields were already past their peaks, required ever more expensive technological fixes to prop up production, and would soon enter a period of inevitable and rapid decline." OPEC production fell in 2008 even as prices of oil were setting record after record. According to Simmons, the debate between the proponents and the critics of "peak oil" boils down to an argument about timing. He thinks the decline will come too soon and be too sharp for the world to adapt in time.[39]

---

36 Guy Chazan, The Wall Street Journal, November 13, 2008, A8

37 The Economist, "Briefing. The outlook for the oil price," May 23, 2009, 73–75

38 The Economist, "Oil and gas. Drying up," May 31, 2008, 59

39 The Economist, "Face Value. The Only Way is Down," July 12, 2008, 77

Sadad al-Husseini, an engineer geologist who, until 2004, was second-in-command of Aramco, the most powerful oil company in the world, argues that the world will have to work hard just to keep its oil production where it is. It is not reassuring that geoscientists have not found much oil since the late 1960s, since the discoveries in Alaska, the North Sea, and Siberia. "**Conservation, not new oil discoveries, will be the primary source of overall energy availability going forward,**" said Sadad al-Husseini. Oil magnate T. Boone Pickens says Husseini's views dovetail with his own.

Many oil executives insist that much of today's oil woes are actually created: environmental restrictions and stingy foreign governments keep valuable reserves locked up.

In light of this situation, a somewhat different notion of peak oil has emerged, dubbed "peak nationalism." The world oil supply would increase markedly if "Exxon Mobil and Royal Dutch Shell had freer access to Russia, Venezuela, and Iran. In short, the world is facing not peak oil but the pinnacle of nationalism."[40] According to Energy Intelligence Research, 85 percent of the world's oil reserves were held by state-controlled companies in 2003, most of those countries, at a minimum, having unfriendly relationships with the United States. We should be very uncomfortable knowing that Russia, Iran, Iraq, Saudi Arabia, Venezuela, Kuwait, Libya, and the United Arab Emirates held 75.4 percent of the world's proven oil reserves in 2009.[41]

Nationalism is already evident among major producers. Foreign companies operating in Russia's oil fields complain of prohibitively high costs of doing business in Russia. When all government levies are added, "The states cream off as much as 92 percent of the profits." Executives at TNK-BP have argued that rising costs will make many investments in Russia unprofitable unless the tax regime is changed. Robert Dudley, head of TNK-BP Ltd., left Russia after what he called "sustained harassment of the company and myself" when Russian authorities declined to issue him a new work visa. BP owns half of TNK-BP. Nigeria is another example of nationalism. It is not only the insurgents who are making Nigeria a less-than-hospitable operating environment for oil companies. It is Nigeria's government. In May 2008, President Umaru Yar'Adua instructed his government to recoup $1.9 billion from Exxon Mobil and Royal Dutch Shell in revenue and taxes on offshore projects, accusing oil compa-

---

40 Jim Appenzeller, National Geographic, June 2004, 84–109

41 The Economist, "Oil," Pocket World in Figures, 2011 Edition, 55

nies of reaping excessive profits and benefiting from agreements made with long disregarded military regimes. Analysts who have seen the documents say Yar'Adua's administration is rewriting the rules and applying them retroactively. Supply and demand imbalances are sure to fan the flames of nationalism in the future. Let's not forget: The guys with the oil make the rules.

Regardless of the cause of global oil shortages, be they political or geologic, the economic toll will be just as high and will be felt mostly by Americans. Nationalism and politics will likely always be a part of the equation, but we need to keep in mind that oil is a finite commodity. **"The real threat to our economy and to our well being twenty years from now may not be the policies of the Middle East, but global shortage of oil."**[40] In *The Elephant in the Bedroom*, Stanley I. Hart and Alvin L. Spivak warn of the dangers Americans face as supplies dwindle. "We need to envision the implications of running out of oil. We need a wake-up call as a society."[42]

Some argue that a more imminent threat to our economy and our lifestyle comes from the escalating cost of extracting oil. Analysis by Tom Morgan and Tullett Prebon reported by *The Economist*, October 23, 2010, estimates that oil found in the 1930s delivered around 100 units of energy per unit invested. In the 1970s, it dropped to 30 units for every unit invested while current finds offer a return of 16 to 20 units per unit invested. To the extent that conventional sources are declining, the higher cost of new sources is expected to continue to drive up the price of oil, a serious risk to an economy that imports 12 million barrels of oil each day.

Dependence on Foreign Oil Spells Vulnerability

"For our economy, our security, and our environment, we must free ourselves from foreign oil." Steven Chu, U.S. Secretary of Energy[43]

"America and the world depend on oil from many countries that do not share our values, regimes that are even hostile to the United States and its allies, coun-

---

42 Stanley J. Hart and Alvin Spivak, The Elephant in the Bedroom, 1993, (Pasadena, CA 91116: New Paradigm Books)

43 Steven Chu, Newsweek, April 13, 2009, 44

tries that threaten our own national security." Jennifer Granholm, former gov-ernor of Michigan[44]

"Simultaneously, the worsening military conflict in Afghanistan and continu-ing struggle to stabilize Iraq are both ongoing reminders of the security threats that will likely continue to emanate from the Persian Gulf region so long as the United States and the rest of the global economy are so dependent on oil—the largest reserves of which are controlled by sovereign states in the Middle East."
Al Gore, Our Choice, 2009

P eople looking at our national security from vantage points that most of us don't have feel strongly that we need to end or drastically reduce our dependence on foreign oil. Chu, our secretary of energy, is convinced of the need for energy independence from the standpoint of our economic security, national security, and our environment.

Americans need to wake up to the consequences of their profligate gaso-line consumption. The environmental degradation is getting increasingly more attention but the economic and geopolitical implications deserve more consideration. A statement by none other than America's former number one enemy, the late Osama bin Laden, contained in a letter to Mullah Omar, the leader of the Afghan Taliban, should galvanize our determination to end our dependence on foreign oil. **Bin Laden wrote, "Whoever has dominion over the oil has dominion over the economies of the world."** [45]

Those "whoever" are the countries with the largest reserves. At the end of 2008 the top five countries by oil reserves were: Saudi Arabia, Iran, Iraq, Kuwait, and Venezuela, all OPEC members. [46] Figure 3 shows the to-tal for each country. Those "whoever" are the countries producing the most oil. The top five producers in 2009 outside the United States were: Russia, Saudi Arabia, Iran, China and Canada.[41] Figure 4 shows the total for each country.

---

44 Jennifer M. Grandholm, Newsweek, April 13, 2009, 45

45 The Economist, "A Special Report on The Arab World," July 25, 2009, 3

46 Hassan Hafidah and Guy Chazan, The Wall Street Journal, December 10, 2009

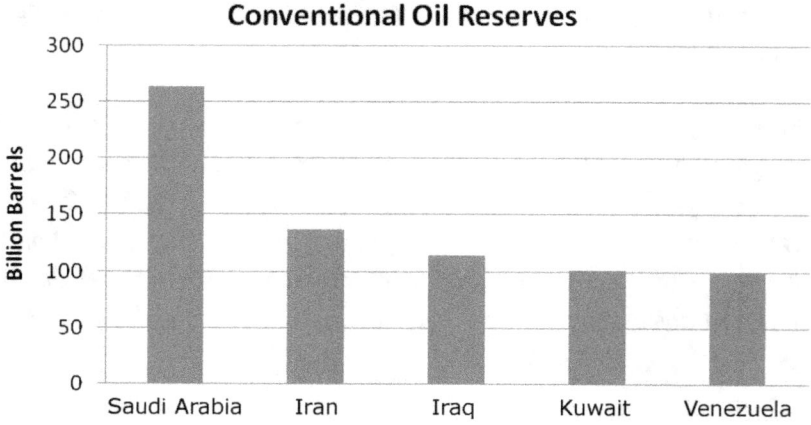

Figure 3: Conventional oil reserves in billion barrels in 2008; Source: Hassan Hafidh and Guy Chazan, The Wall Street Journal, December 10, 2009.

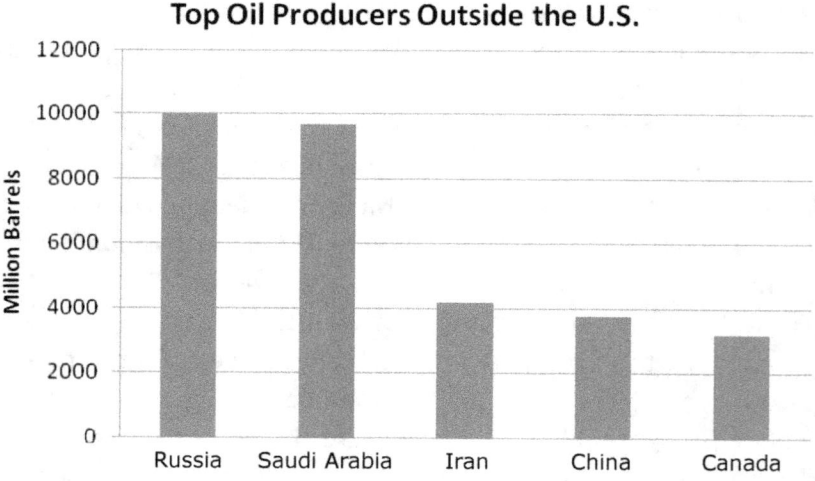

Figure 4: Top oil producers outside the United States in 2009 in millions of barrels per day; Source: The Economist, Pocket World in Figures, 2011 Edition.

Approximately one-third of our imported oil comes from OPEC countries. The U.S. government's Energy Information Administration projected in 2004 that in twenty years the Persian Gulf will supply between half and two-thirds of the oil in the world market, the same percentages as before the 1973 oil embargo, conferring those few countries enormous pricing power and political clout.[40]

The great majority of those countries don't have our economic or our national security at heart. Saudi Arabia, the leading country of the OPEC cartel, imposed oil embargoes on shipments to the United States twice and has repeatedly led OPEC countries in production cuts to support oil prices. The oil embargo of 1973 to retaliate against Western backing of Israel caused oil prices to triple and resulted in a global recession. Recently, Saudi Arabia rejected U.S. appeals to improve ties with Israel to help restart Middle East peace talks. Ali a-Naimi, Saudi Arabia's oil minister, recently warned that rising oil prices may soon derail the budding economic recovery. At an OPEC meeting in the spring of 2009, the oil minister pointed out that low oil prices always sowed the seeds of a future price rise.[37] We also need to keep in mind that Saudi Arabia was the home of fifteen of the nineteen terrorists who participated in the 9/11 attack on the Twin Towers of the World Trade Center. It is the country of the late Osama bin Laden, a country that has a record of funding terrorists.

Russia has been America's main antagonist for most of the last fifty years and is still resentful of the rise of America's power, the breakup of the USSR engineered by President Reagan, and the fact that it lost the Cold War. Natural gas-rich Russia feels that it can use Gazprom, its giant energy company, as an instrument for its geopolitical strategies by threatening to turn off supplies to neighboring countries heavily dependent on them. [47] Russia supplies 42 percent of the European Union (EU) gas imports. Russia cut gas supplies to Ukraine in January 2006, causing gas supplies to drop by more than one-third in central Europe, affecting eighteen of the twenty-seven EU countries.[48] In July 2008, Russia reduced its gas supplies to the Czech Republic by half. The cut came just after the Czechs agreed to host American missile defense radar. [49] As recently as May 2009, Russia was again trying to blackmail Europe over gas supplies. Prime Minister Vladimir Putin told the EU that the Ukraine must get help in the form of an emergency loan of $4.2 billion to pay for gas to fill its Soviet-era storage tanks if Europe wants to avoid cutoffs. Ukraine's Prime Minister Yulia Tymoshenko reiterated the threat, telling EU officials that $5

47 The Economist, "Oil, politics and corruption," September 20, 2008, 18–20

48 The Economist, "Ukraine, Russia and gas. Energetic blackmail," July 4th 2009, 48–49

49 The Economist, "The world this week" July 19, 2008, 11

billion was needed to avert a fresh gas crisis. Russia and Iran have plans backed by Qatar, which dominates the world liquefied natural gas (LNG) market, to create a gas cartel analogous to the OPEC oil cartel. Already a secretariat is being set up in Doha. [50] The United States should feel very uneasy to be so dependent on oil imports knowing that Russia and Saudi Arabia, currently the number one and number two world oil producers, have used embargoes and other forms of blackmail to impose their will on other countries.[48]

Iran has threatened the annihilation of Israel, a close American ally, and Iran's Qods Force is training and arming terrorists to fight and kill Americans in Iraq. Hezbollah is fighting Iran's proxy war against Lebanon's pro-American government. Iran is supporting Hamas and its terrorist activities against Israel. Iran's Mahmoud Ahmadinejad's rhetoric against America is well known and his ambition to develop nuclear weapons constitutes a growing threat to world peace. Iran has consistently argued against doing anything to moderate the rise in crude oil prices and holds the second-largest reserve of oil in the world. Iran has hinted that it would retaliate against any hostile act by impeding the flow of oil. It is ironic—even unsettling—that consideration has been given to cut off Iran's gasoline imports to force Iran to abandon its nuclear ambitions. Iran's vulnerability is its dependence on imported gasoline for 40 percent of its needs even though it is a major exporter of oil. [51] To think that we can bring that country to its knees by forcing its main gasoline suppliers to stop shipping it gasoline should sound an alarm. America could be on the receiving end of such an embargo. Have we forgotten that OPEC used that weapon successfully against the United States at a time when we depended on oil imports for only 41 percent of our needs? It resulted in a deep recession. Today we rely on oil imports for about 60 percent of our needs.

Venezuela's president, Hugo Chavez, has always believed in oil as a tool of geopolitics to be used against American imperialism. In the special report "Energy Security" in *The Economist*, January 7, 2006, the author points out that we live in a producers' world that no one has exploited more gleefully than Hugo Chavez.[51] Chavez's rants against President Bush at the UN and his diatribes directed at our country are all too familiar. In 2004 Chavez declared, "The world should forget about cheap oil." [52] Venezuela's oil riches are a huge prop to his influence in South America where he is doing all he can to undermine

---

50 The Economist, "Face value. Turning up the gas," 64

51 Orde F. Kittrie, The Wall Street Journal, "How to Put the Squeeze on Iran," November 13, 2008, A19

52 The Economist, "A Survey of Oil. Oil in troubled waters," April 30, 2005, 3–8

U.S. interests. Chavez's nationalization of American oil companies and of other countries' companies operating in Venezuela and threats to halt exports to the United States are not comforting. In 2006, Venezuela increased oil royalties by 75 percent on companies that had invested there, doubled their taxes, and even took over fields from Total and Eni. Chavez gives top priority to forging anti-American political alliances with Iran, Syria, and Russia. *The Economist* reported in 2009 that Chavez had spent $4.4 billion on Russian fighter jets, military helicopters, and rifles, and had ordered ninety-two Russian tanks and anti-aircraft missiles. [53] It was also reported that he had sealed an agreement of nuclear cooperation with Iran's Mahmoud Ahmadinejad. Venezuela is our third-largest supplier of oil and Americans fill up their cars at Venezuela-owned retail stations—Citgo in the Midwest, Florida, and other parts of the country.

The vulnerability of our economy to imported oil is twofold: The country's economy would grind to a halt in the event of an embargo. Additionally, the economy is weakened by the daily drain of American wealth. Since 13 million of the 20 million barrels that we use every day are imported, the transfer of wealth abroad amounts to more than $1.0 billion every day. In 2008 America's net imports of oil and gas came to $416 billion, 60 percent of the trade deficit.[54] That is an unsustainable transfer of American dollars to the sheiks of Arabian countries, Hugo Chavez's Venezuela, and a few other foes of America. It is an expense that our economy cannot withstand for extended periods of time. That money is not available to create American jobs and American wealth. It is not available to generate tax revenues for our federal, state, and local governments to build our infrastructure, support social programs, and fund research and development. We have been lulled into believing that much of that money comes back to the United States to generate economic activity. The reality is that much of it will never return to America. It is tied up in skyscrapers in Kuwait, Dubai, Abu Dhabi, and Saudi Arabia. It was spent erecting a building in Dubai that is more than twice as tall as our Empire State Building, dwarfing a landmark building that helped project America's boldness to the world, one that underscored the power of our market economy for decades.

Our armed forces are feeling the vulnerability of dependence on fuel imports. The military is the country's single largest user of oil. In 2008, the military was consuming 340,000 barrels a day, a quantity equal to about 2.5 per-

---

53 The Economist, "Venezuela's foreign policy. Dreams of a different world" September 19, 2009, 49

54 The Economist, "Energetic progress," April 3, 2010, 10–11

cent of all imported oil.[55] In 2008 American forces consumed more than one million gallons of fuel each day in Afghanistan and a similar quantity in Iraq. It takes as much as five gallons of fuel to deliver one gallon to a forward operating base (FOB) in Afghanistan and more than one hundred gallons for each gallon delivered to an outpost that has to be resupplied by helicopter. Interestingly, in those two conflicts about 40 percent of fuel is used to run electricity generators. Military planners are addressing that problem by implementing conservation measures and turning to renewable energy sources. In July 2006, General Richard Zilmer, then marine general in charge of American forces in Western Iraq, sent out an urgent request for solar panels and wind turbines to reduce the need for liquid fuels. The payback is measured in lives saved. For every 1 percent of fuel not used, 6,444 fewer soldiers have to be involved in fuel-convoy operations, an activity that accounts for as much as half of the casualties in Iraq and Afghanistan. [56]

Empowerment of Oil Producers

Vulnerability also comes in the form of increased competition from the oil exporters that are developing their petrochemical industries and using their riches to advance their geopolitical power. It is said that sovereign wealth funds had accumulated $3.3 trillion at the beginning of 2008 and were expected to be $10 trillion strong by the year 2015. **In 1998, the energy share of global spending was 1.1 percent. Ten years later, energy accounted for 7.4 percent of global spending.**

The United States indirectly contributes to the transfer of wealth from other oil-importing countries to oil exporters filling the coffers of countries that are unfriendly and even hostile to America. Our indulgence in oil – 25 percent of the world's output – is raising the price that all other importing countries are paying for oil and enriching countries like Iran, Russia, Libya, Venezuela, and Nigeria in addition to the Gulf Cooperation Council (GCC) countries. All told, the importing world is handing over $1.8 trillion to oil producers every year. [57]

---

55 Dreazen, Yachi J., The Wall Street Journal, May 21, 2008, 1

56 Edward Humes, Sierra, July/August 2011, 27-33

57 Terry Jones, Investor's Business Daily, June 19, 2008, A10

The transfer of wealth to oil-rich countries not only weakens the United States; it props up regimes that have a history of misusing their wealth. In a communiqué reported in *U.S. News and World Report,* Fouad Ajami exposed what he calls "petrocracy," pointing out that the modern global economy itself has been restructured in favor of the oil producers. "A handful of sheiks in Abu Dhabi now dispose of a sovereign wealth fund that approximates a trillion dollars." [58] Falling output in countries outside OPEC means that Saudi Arabia, Iran, and Iraq will assume an ever larger portion of the world supply.[59] Senator John McCain was quoted in *The Investor's Business Daily* as saying, "In effect our petro-dollars are underwriting tyranny, anti-Semitism, the brutal repression of women in the Middle East, and dictators and criminal syndicates in our own hemisphere. Thanks to our need for oil, the United States has become the number one supporter of many of the world's most questionable petro tyrannies, some of which are avid supporters of terrorism."[57]

It is telling that American presidents for almost four decades have made it an important part of their agenda to reduce the country's reliance on imported oil. The case for energy independence was first made by President Richard Nixon in November 1973, three weeks after the Arab oil embargo. He introduced "Project Independence" and pledged that the United States would within seven years, "meet our energy needs without depending on any foreign energy source." Not only did it not happen but the real surge in imports started in the late 1970s.[60]

Gerald Ford, president from 1974 to 1977, pushed the target date of Nixon's energy independence from 1980 to 1985. When Jimmy Carter became president, he declared energy independence to be "the moral equivalent of war" and proposed a plan to be free of foreign energy by 1990.

George W. Bush, U.S. president from 2000 to 2008, set a goal in his 2007 State of the Union message of slashing the nation's reliance on Middle Eastern oil by 75 percent by 2025, chiefly by conservation, developing our ethanol industry, and using new technology. He announced an Advanced Energy Initiative calling for a 22 percent increase in funds for clean energy research by the Department of Energy.

---

58 Fouad Ajami, U.S. News & World Report, December 31, 2007/January 7, 2008, 31

59 Neil King, Jr. and Spencer Swartz, The Wall Street Journal, November 7, 2008, A10

60 Daniel Yergin, The Wall Street Journal, January 23, 2007

On June 18, 2008, President Bush asked Congress to:

1. Expand oil production by increasing access to the Outer Continental Shelf (OCS).
2. Extract oil from oil shale.
3. Expand oil production by permitting exploration in the Arctic National Wildlife Refuge in Alaska (ANWAR).
4. Increase our refining capacity.

The Obama administration has not made it a priority to take steps to decrease oil consumption. Energy issues are on the agenda but the main focus of his administration is expanding wind and solar energy and upgrading the country's power infrastructure. So far the administration has not come forward with any plan to drastically reduce oil consumption. We never hear of any increase, let alone a steep increase, in gasoline tax. Granted, President Obama increased CAFE standards slightly ahead of the previous timetable, but considering the number of cars added to our roads every year, such small incremental changes will only slow the rate of increase in our fuel consumption and therefore, our dependence on foreign supplies. Our legislators deplore our dependence on foreign oil but few, if any, have the political will to introduce effective measures to significantly reduce that reliance.

To their credit, some of our legislators have recognized the insecurity of being so dependent on foreign energy. Speaking at the August 2006 Purdue University Energy Summit, Senator Richard Lugar, a key Senate leader, cited projections that the United States will require 50 percent more energy within the next twenty-five years. He warned that Americans will face "severe economic and national security consequences" if they fail to wean themselves from "dangerously unsustainable" dependence on foreign oil. He made the point that petroleum is at the center of existing Middle East and South American tensions and argued that given projected energy demands by large, expanding economies like China and India, oil increasingly "will become a magnet for international conflict." He termed the U.S. domestic energy strategy "a major national security failure."

Our economic security alone is a compelling reason for slashing our oil consumption. Former Vice President Al Gore put it bluntly. "So long as the United States spends close to half a trillion dollars per year for foreign oil, the U.S. current account deficit will be impossible to manage, and the value of the dollar will become increasingly vulnerable. **The U.S. current account deficit is being driven by ridiculously high dependence on foreign oil toward what the Peterson Institute for International Economics—founded by former Secretary of Commerce Peter G. Peterson—describes as an 'economic catastrophe in the making'.**"[16] Every day America burns 20 million barrels of oil. Oil accounts for 40 percent of all the energy that we use and we depend on foreign oil for nearly 60 percent of our needs. These are not comforting statistics considering who controls that oil. The former vice president continued, "The longer the global economy is hostage to energy reserves located in what is arguably the most unstable region in the world, we will continue to experience periodic price hikes like the one that drove the price of oil to $145 a barrel in the summer of 2008."[16] Was it pure coincidence that the worst economic downturn that America experienced since the Great Depression came on the heels of the rapid ascension of oil prices to $145 a barrel?

Our dependence on foreign oil has influenced foreign policies for years. In the opinion of Alan Greenspan, retired chairman of the Federal Reserve, the war in Iraq was "largely about oil." [61] Many credible analysts foresee a new "energy cold war" as the United States and China square off over the planet's last reserves. The Chinese life-style is increasingly energy intensive. In 2009 Chinese yearly car production overtook our own supply of new cars. China is using its vast foreign currency reserves to buy energy companies and controlling stakes in oil fields. It is scouring the world, including South America, Africa, and Australia, in search of oil and other natural resources. China is forging relationships with oil-rich countries, ignoring human rights issues and even UN sanctions, in an effort to gain control of as much oil production as possible through its Chinese National Offshore Oil Corporation (CNOOC). Chinese oil companies have secured deals for oil in Africa, Uzbekistan, and even signed a $70 billion oil and gas deal with Iran.[7] This is not comforting news for America. It underscores the urgency for Americans to reduce their dependence on oil.

Competition for oil is also mounting from other parts of the world. In 2006, the Japanese government called on industry to increase its ownership of foreign energy projects to cover 40 percent of the country's needs, up from 15 percent at that time. In January 2009 Nippon Oil acquired rights to oil fields in Papua, New Guinea. Inpex, Japan's largest oil-development company, has purchased rights to oil in South America and Australia. Nippon Oil and Inpex

---

61 The Economist, "The Undertaker's Story," September 22, 2007, 99

are part of a consortium that is vying for rights to a project in Iraq. In the event of a crisis, it's obvious who would get access to the output of those wells. Japan has already contracted to receive 60 percent of the liquefied natural gas (LNG) produced by Russia's Sakhalin II project. Fortunately, the United States can count on one reliable source of oil, Canada. But that foreign supply raises environmental concerns.

It's no wonder that Presidents Nixon, Carter, Ford, and Bush all set targets for energy independence. None succeeded. Let's hope that President Obama will have the fortitude to implement measures that will curtail our use of oil, for the sake of our ecosystem, our economy, our security, and our political clout. Drastically reducing fuel use would have more benefit for the United States than any other single measure. So far the president has not sent any encouraging signal.

The Benefits of Degrading the Value of Oil

R. James Woolsey, director of the Central Intelligence Agency (CIA) from 1993 to 1995 and a founding member of Set America Free, a Washington D.C.-based coalition devoted to reducing oil dependence, feels that merely lessening our dependence on foreign oil would not solve the national security problem. His main concern is how energy use affects national security "because so much of the oil we import comes from countries that hate us." He talks about independence from oil, not just foreign oil. Woolsey advocates a major effort to do to oil what refrigeration did to salt at the end of the nineteenth century: destroy oil's monopoly. Once refrigeration destroyed salt's monopoly, it stopped mattering whether a country had large salt reserves. Countries didn't go to war over salt mines anymore. His commitment to reducing oil consumption goes as far as modifying his Toyota Prius into a plug-in hybrid that bears a bumper sticker that reads, "Bin Laden Hates this Car."[62] The exhortation of a former CIA director should not be taken lightly in matters of national security. We need to do to oil what the light bulb did to kerosene.

Reduction in our oil imports would carry immense benefits for the United States' economy and geopolitical power. It is important that we keep in check the value of oil from a geopolitical standpoint primarily because we don't have a lot of it and the countries that have a lot of it are mostly countries that don't

---

62 Stephen D. Solomon, Scientific American, Volume 18, Number 4, December 2008, 50–53

share our values; countries that don't wish us well and that often misuse their oil and gas riches. It has already been pointed out that we have only 3 percent of the world's oil reserves. The countries with the top proven reserves at the end of 2008 as a percent of the world total were Saudi Arabia, 21.0 percent; Iran, 10.9 percent; Iraq, 9.1 percent; Kuwait, 8.1 percent; Venezuela, 7.9 percent; United Arab Emirates (UAE), 7.8 percent; Russia, 6.3 percent; and Libya, 3.5 percent.[63] None of those countries are friends of the United States.

High oil revenues don't even benefit the people of oil-exporting countries. High oil prices are contributing to the "curse of oil." "Society shrivels in the oil lands; the state grows more confident, casting aside popular will." Sudden wealth, enjoyed by the Saudis because of high prices in the 1970s, brought social strains in Saudi Arabia and helped create the fundamentalist backlash that produced, among other things, al Qaeda.[64] Today, oil windfalls create another risk. They empower Iran, the revolutionary Shia state that the conservative Sunni Saudis view as their main rival for regional influence.

Degrading the value of oil boils down to a supply-and-demand equation. We either use less of it or expand its supply. Emphasis must be placed on reducing demand for the added benefits of stretching supplies and lessening the impact on our economy and our life-style of eventual dwindling supplies and sharp price increases.

Demand Destruction

H istory shows that curbing demand can be a powerful check on the OPEC cartel. After the oil embargo of 1973–1974, the developed world introduced policies to promote energy conservation. In Europe and Japan they took the form of energy taxes. America chose to regulate the car industry through the Corporate Average Fuel Economy (CAFE) law. The result was an increase of over two-fifths in the miles per gallon of new cars, undermining OPEC's pricing power for a decade.

Conservation measures cost little or nothing and can be implemented without any delays. We would do ourselves a lot of good by slashing our oil consumption and would do all the other oil importing countries a favor by applying downward pressure on oil prices. Americans need to realize that they

---

63 The Economist, "Oil," Pocket World in Figures, 2010 Edition, 55

64 The Economist, "Saudi Arabia: The Puzzle of Oil Production," June 21, 2008, 59

are the world's main counterweight to the oil producers. World oil prices are greatly influenced by American consumption. The journalist Michael Kinsley pointedly stated, "We have only ourselves to blame for high oil prices." [65]

The rest of the world also has us to blame. How long will gasoline users around the world tolerate our inordinate use of a common resource without resenting us? In the words of Stanley Hart and Alvin Spivak, "How long will the tolerance of other nations endure?"[42] We need to keep in mind that **we make up less than 5 percent of the world population yet we use 25 percent of all the oil.**

In an advertising piece in The Economist, July 8, 2006, Chevron states, "The average person wields incredible power when it comes to conserving energy. It is the lowest-cost new source of energy we have at hand." [66] Amory Lovins, one of the world's most famous apostles of energy efficiency is quoted as saying, "Demand is the sum of a lot of negligible individual actions. When there are a lot of individuals, it isn't negligible."[67]

There are numerous ways for us to immediately start saving oil. Since almost 50 percent of our total oil consumption is refined into gasoline used for personal transportation, emphasis must be placed on changing driving habits: driving less, driving slower, and adopting numerous small measures that will amount to a lot of savings when practiced by millions of individuals. Longer term, it means driving more fuel-efficient vehicles. As usual, compliance on a grand scale will require public policies favoring conservation and efficiency.

Smarter Use of the Family Car

One solution to our profligate oil consumption is to drive less. Since 1983, the number of miles cars travel has grown at least eight times the population growth rate. According to the Pew Center on Global Climate Change and reported by Douglas Farr, in 2001, the average American family drove 21,500 miles per year. That was an increase of more than 9,000 miles from 1969, even though the American family shrank from 3.2 members to 2.6 members.[5]

We can reduce our use of the car by living close to our workplaces and civic centers. We can live in areas serviced by public transportation. Some

65 Michael Kinsley, Time, July 7, 2008, 64

66 The Economist, "Americans Spend Over One Million Dollars in Energy Every Minute," July 8, 2006, 5

67 Jeffrey Ball: The Wall Street Journal, August 7, 2009

envision a time when workers will be freed from their offices by technology and allowed to work from home.[68] Some studies indicate that more than one-quarter of the U.S. workforce could eventually participate in this new work pattern. IBM is facilitating that trend. Roughly 40 percent of the company's workforce now works at home or remotely from a client's location. Demographer Wendell Cox suggests that by 2015 more people will be working at home full time than taking mass transit, "making it the largest potential source of energy savings on transportation."[69] That seems overly optimistic, since only 4 percent of Americans worked from their homes in 2007, according to the Bureau of Transportation Statistics.[68]

Short of moving to decrease car dependence or finding a job that allows for laboring from home, there are many ways that can lower our use of the car. We need to challenge ourselves to see how long we can go on a tank of gasoline. The most effective way to stretch a tank of gasoline is to drive less. Plan your errands carefully to combine purposes. Grocery shop on your way home from work. Shop for the entire week. Shop from a grocery list that you develop daily. Don't wait until the last minute to finalize your list; you will forget a staple.

Ride your bicycle to get around in your neighborhood. According to an article in Sierra, March/April 2008 issue, a human on a bicycle is more efficient (in calories expended per pound per mile) than any other form of transportation, including walking, which takes three times as many calories as cycling. We need to make greater use of bicycles for the purpose of transportation and for family activities. Going on a bicycle excursion with the family or neighbors uses no fuel, is healthy, and can take the place of driving to the movie theater or the mall.

Enjoy activities closer to home. Watch the fireworks in your local community instead of driving forty miles to watch similar fireworks in you area's metropolis. Forego distant holiday weekend trips. Celebrate Memorial Day, the Fourth of July, or Labor Day with your neighbors or spend the weekend exploring the large city nearest to your hometown. What a show of support it would be for our troops who are risking and losing their lives and limbs, their ability to walk or their eyesight in Iraq if we all stayed home on Memorial Day weekend! What a meaningful way to honor the more than four thousand

68 Matthew Philips: Newsweek, May 24–31, 2010, 51–52

69 Joel Katkin, Newsweek, October 19, 2009, 42–43

Americans who lost their lives in oil-rich Iraq for the benefits of their fellow American drivers. Empty highways over a long weekend would be a great way to demonstrate solidarity with our troops, and an opportunity to experience a simpler and more responsible life-style. It would also save many Americans from accidental death and greatly benefit the environment. It would send a loud message to OPEC.

In addition to driving less you can extend your gasoline purchases by practicing "eco-driving" techniques. **Driving slower is a small inconvenience but one that has a marked impact. Speed counts a lot because the resistance to an object moving through air increases by the square of the speed of that object.** In the February 2006 issue of *Car and Driver* magazine, Patrick Bedard reported on the influence of speed on fuel consumption. The test consisted of repeating the same 13.7-mile stretch of interstate at constant speeds of 40, 50, 60, 70, and 80 miles per hour (mph). Runs were made both ways to eliminate the variables of wind and elevation changes. The car was already at the test speed at the starting point and maintained its speed until it passed the finish line.[70] The results reflected two-way averages with only the driver on board. The findings were as follows reported in miles per gallon (mpg):

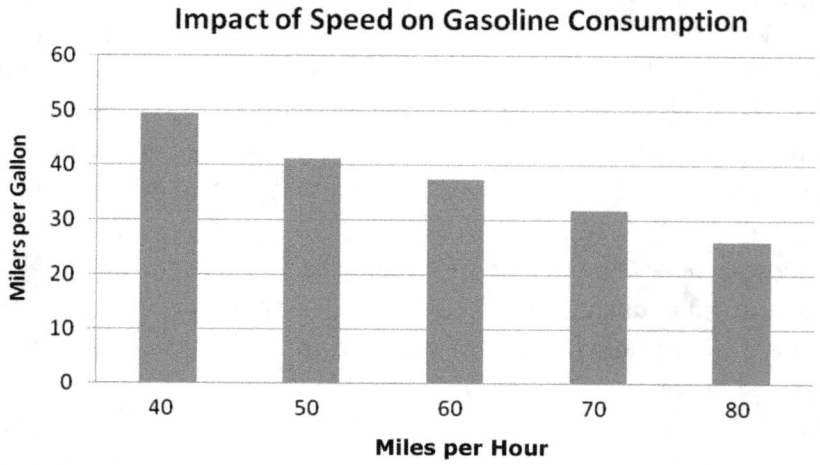

Figure 5: Impact of Speed on Gasoline Consumption; Source: Car and Driver, February 2006

---

70 Patrick Bedard, Car and Driver, February 2006, 26

In 1974, in response to the Arab oil embargo, President Richard Nixon signed the Emergency Highway Energy Conservation Act, which prohibited the Federal Highway Administration from approving highway projects in any state having a maximum speed limit over 55 mph. The law was modified in 1987 to allow 65 mph speed limits, and it was repealed in 1995. The 55 mph law resulted in approximately a 10 percent decline in oil use and the subsequent collapse of oil prices. A 10 percent drop in gasoline consumption carries the same benefits as removing 24 million cars from our roadways.

Recent administrations have not seen fit to impose such measures, but responsible Americans should drive slower, preferably no faster than 55 mph. Fuel conservation also reduces CO_2 emissions and that of other pollutants. Driving slower is a small sacrifice when compared with the sacrifices of our troops deployed in Iraq and of their families. Small reductions in highway speed when multiplied by the 2.7 trillion car-miles driven each year in the United States would amount to huge savings. Chevron claimed in an advertising piece in the July 8, 2006, edition of *The Economist* that "If everyone reduced their driving speed from 65 mph to 55 mph, we'd save three million gallons of gas a day."[66] One trucking company reduced the maximum speed of its trucks by adjusting the governor from 65 mph to 62 mph for a savings of three million gallons of fuel per year and sparing the atmosphere of thirty thousand tons of CO_2.

Other smart driving habits also can make a difference. Keep your engine below 2,500 rpm when accelerating. Use your vehicle's kinetic energy. Allow for gradual deceleration. Drive with an awareness of what is ahead so you can anticipate traffic slowdowns or stops, adjusting your speed to minimize the need to brake and the need to stop. Reducing breaking is an important energy saver and also spares your brakes. Jeffrey Ball refers to those fuel-saving measures as "eco-driving." He chronicles the experience of a young woman who applied the techniques described herein to boost her pickup truck's fuel consumption to 21 mpg from 15 mpg, a 40 percent improvement.[71] **EPA officials claim that changing driving style can increase fuel economy by more than 20 percent.** Trials in Europe, Japan, and the United States support that claim. Driving slower provided the greatest benefit. Using cruise control also results in savings, increasing fuel efficiency by up to 14 percent. Consider a manual transmission when shopping for your next car. A car equipped with a stick shift delivers better fuel economy than the same vehicle equipped with

---

71 Jeffrey Ball, The Wall Street Journal, April 17, 2009

an automatic transmission. A report in the October2008 *Consumer Reports* claimed a 2 mpg to 5 mpg advantage and reported savings on the purchase cost of the vehicle.[72]

Fuel-efficiency gauges can reduce consumption by an average of 10 percent. To promote eco-driving, Nissan, a Japanese car maker, has decided to install them in all its cars.[73] Other automakers are promoting eco-driving. Ford Motors and Pro Formance Driving Events, a professional-driving company in Phoenix, Arizona, conducted eco-driving classes with forty-eight Phoenix-area drivers. The result was a 24 percent average fuel economy. Eco-driving techniques are taught in driver education classes in Germany. Students learn to watch the tachometer and shift into higher gears before the engine speed reaches 2,000 rpm. They are taught to maintain a sufficient distance between their car and the one in front to avoid unnecessary breaking. They learn to coast if an upcoming light is red, allowing time for it to turn green so they will not have to stop.[71] Even hybrids need to be driven gingerly to take advantage of their technology. According to Ball, hybrid-car manufacturers receive numerous complaints from buyers who are not getting nearly the mileage the cars' advertisements claim.[71]

Other measures can also increase gas mileage. Avoid carrying unnecessary luggage, including full tanks of gas. A gallon of gasoline weighs about 6 lbs. Every additional 100 pounds of weight increases fuel consumption 2 percent or more. Test results reported by Michael Austin in *Car and Driver's* December 2008 issue indicated a 4.2 percent decrease in mpg when adding 100 pounds of cargo and driving the test car at 75 miles per hour. The decrease in mpg was reduced to 1.4 percent at 55 mph. So think of losing weight as well as driving slower!

Check your car's air filter. Replacing a dirty air filter (at a small cost) can increase gas mileage by as much as 10 percent. Inflate your car's tires to the recommended pressure. During the 2008 presidential campaign, Senator McCain and others ridiculed Senator Obama for recommending that drivers maintain proper inflation of their car tires. That recommendation was appropriate, since about 15 percent of the energy required to move your car down the road goes to overcoming resistance, which is the friction of the tires against the road surface. Maximize fuel economy by inflating your tires to the recommended pressure. If you ever rode a bicycle, you should know from personal

---

72 Consumer Report, "Save Gas and Money with a Stick Shift," October 2008, 39–42

73 The Economist, "Power Plays," March 8, 2009, 16

experience how much easier it is to pedal a bicycle that has pumped-up tires. Under-inflated tires reduce fuel efficiency by as much as two miles per gallon. Properly inflated tires alone could save Americans more than four million gallons of gasoline each day.

The California Energy Commission recommends that you turn your car's engine off if you are going to be parked for more than thirty seconds. Order your lunch at the inside counter of your favorite fast-food chains instead of inching your way to the take-out window. Your will save time and gasoline, reduce pollution and get a little exercise. The same applies when picking up your prescription at the pharmacy. People operate their cars on idle between five and ten minutes every day.[74] **For every two minutes a car is idling, it uses the same amount of fuel it takes to go about one mile.** Waiting for a train at a railroad crossing is another opportunity to save fuel and the atmosphere. When you restart your engine, don't step down on the accelerator. Keep in mind that little things add up to significant savings. UPS truck routes have been redesigned to avoid left turns. In 2007 the company estimated that the route-planning method saved three million gallons of petrol by reducing idling time.

For every two minutes a car is idling, it uses the same amount of gasoline it takes to go about one mile. (Photo: The Author)

---

74 The Economist, "Indian Fuel Prices. Too Hot to Touch," December 1, 2007, 90

Since many drivers fail to grasp the imperative of fuel conservation, public policies are needed for large scale adoption of fuel-sparing measures. Former Vice President Dick Cheney agreed. "Conservation may be a sign of personal virtue, but it is not a sufficient basis, all by itself, for a sound, comprehensive energy policy".[75]

Fuel Tax

Motorists have enjoyed a subsidized ride for a long time. The general funds of the federal, state, and local governments pay for highway-related expenses. Fuel taxes, revenues from tolls and parking meters are woefully inadequate to cover the prohibitive costs of building roadways, maintaining streets and highways, policing them, lighting them, installing, and operating traffic signals, landscaping, managing storm water, mitigating wetland encroachments, providing noise abatement, and compensating for the loss of property tax revenues from rights of way.[42] A subsidy that gets little attention is the cost of U.S. military expenditures attributable to maintaining the flow of Middle East oil. A 2008 study referred to by Al Gore estimates a price between $27 billion and $73 billion per year, of which $6 billion to $25 billion is attributable to petrol demand for U.S. cars and trucks.[16] Those costs don't even take into consideration the hundreds of billion dollars spent on fighting the Iraq War, the lost lives and limbs, and the cost of caring for our war veterans. Would Americans be in Iraq if we were less dependent on foreign oil?

Those subsidies, many of them hidden, raise questions of inequity. Duany made the point in Suburban Nation: "Subsidized automobile use is the single largest violation of the free market principle in the U.S. fiscal policy."[4] The appropriation of tax dollars to the highway departments and the Pentagon from the general fund mean that the cost of driving is also imposed on those who don't drive. **Duany estimated that fuel subsidies amount to about $3.50 for each gallon of fuel burned.**[4] The fuel tax would need to be much higher if the cost of mitigating the environmental impact of refining and burning all that fossil fuel were passed on to motorists and other users of refined oil products. The total fuel tax would need to be around $9, according to Hart and Spivak, the authors of The Elephant in the Bedroom.[42]

Those subsidies distort market forces. They favor the private transportation system over the public system. They also influence driver preference for the type of vehicle they purchase. Would big sedans, SUVs, pickup trucks and

---

minivans be so popular without subsidies? Duany is equally critical of the subsidy bias in favor of trucks.[4] The trucking industry benefits from the same favorable treatment as car owners do, helping to keep the trucking industry competitive with rail even though "trucks consume fifteen times the fuel for the equivalent job."

The United States is not the only country to shield its motorists from the true cost of driving. "Only one-third of forty-eight developing countries studied by the International Monetary Fund (IMF) let the market set fuel prices."[76] For example, in 2007 the government of Indonesia (the fourth most populous country in the world) has spent more holding down the prices of fuel than it spent on health and education combined."[76] India's government subsidizes kerosene and liquefied petroleum gas (LPG). All told, India's fuel subsidies might cost as much as $17.5 billion, according to Lombard Street Research, a British firm of economists. That amounts to as much as 2 percent of the country's GDP. Governments that subsidize gasoline consumption, including our own government through hidden subsidies, are driving a demand that will be difficult if not impossible to destroy.

Some governments are realizing the need for market forces to play a greater role in setting fuel prices. Since 2007, China, in response to Western criticism, has been aggressively raising its fuel prices. China acted responsibly. By the summer of 2009 the average price for petrol in China was more than 20 percent higher than it was in the United States.[53] How long will it be before China blames the United States for the rise in global oil prices by not taking steps to discourage consumption?

Other countries are reducing their oil subsidies. Indonesia raised prices at the pump by 28 percent on May 24, 2007.[77] In 2008, the Malaysian government increased its heavily subsidized gasoline prices by 41 percent. India has been raising its retail prices of gasoline and diesel fuels. By 2010, the price of gasoline at the pump in India was $4.92 per gallon when the average price in the United States was $2.55 a gallon. In 2008, Thailand cut some fuel subsidies sending bicycle sales soaring.[78] Governments are acting to reduce the burden of subsidies on their budgets and to foster frugality. Because of fewer government subsidies, forecasters have lowered their estimate of the rate at which Asian oil demand will rise to 2.7 percent versus earlier estimates of 3.3 percent.

---

76 The Economist, "Electric Cars. A Netscape Moment?", February 6, 2010, 71-72

77 Andrew Barton and Neal King, The Wall Street Journal, June 20, 2008

78 Patrick Barta, The Wall Street Journal, July 9,2008

European countries for decades have been exposing their drivers to the truer cost of using public roadways. Even Canada, a country rich in oil, has seen fit to have its drivers more appropriately bear the cost of providing them with roads to drive on. **The United States, a country that champions market economy, is the only major country that subsidizes the personal transportation industry to the extent that it does**. The United States is the only major country to act so irresponsibly when it comes to moderating oil consumption. Our gasoline is the cheapest of the industrialized world. Not surprisingly, our fleet of cars is the least fuel-efficient in the world. How long will the rest of the world tolerate the irresponsibility of our leaders?

A fuel tax that more closely reflects the cost of providing services to motorists is essential to promote conservation. Americans have responded to rising fuel prices by cutting back on the use of their cars. *USA Today* reported on June 19, 2008, that Americans had driven 30 billion fewer miles from November 2007 to April 2008 than they did during the same period in 2006–2007 as gasoline prices were marching towards $4 a gallon. (The national average price for a gallon of 87 octane gasoline reached $4 on June 6, 2008, which was the most expensive gasoline on record in the United States at that time, even when adjusted for inflation.)[79] The decline in miles driven amounted to 1 percent, the largest decrease since the supply shortages in 1979–1980 following the Iranian revolution. Increasing gasoline prices continued to suppress driving. In August, the Department of Transportation revealed that in the previous nine months, Americans had driven 53.2 billion fewer miles than they did in the same period the previous year. The greatest drop in gasoline usage occurred in September, a 6.2 percent drop. At the end of 2008, the Energy Information Administration reported a year-on-year decline of 2.2 percent for gasoline consumption—enough to have a dramatic effect on crude oil prices.[80] In June 2008, Americans used an average of 20.342 million barrels of oil a day, down 400,000 barrels a day when compared to June 2007.

Not surprisingly the return to lower gasoline prices as a result of the cheapest oil prices seen in four years reversed those trends. In November 2008, gasoline consumption started turning up. Data compiled by MasterCard Advisors showed an increase of 0.3 percent in gasoline purchases the first week of November when compared with the same period the previous year, the first time

---

79 Joe Lorio, Automobile, September 2008, 14-16

80 The Wall Street Journal, January 2, 2009

that had happened since April 2008.[81] This occurred in spite of the mounting economic woes. The trend continued into 2009 with January consumption averaging 0.8 percent over the previous year.

Fuel Efficiency

Car buyers need to consider the impact of their choice of vehicle on the country's energy security, the country's economy, the country's geopolitical clout and the environment when selecting a car.

Acting responsibly is very important since the useful life of the average car is between eight and ten years. **The selection of your next car will have an impact on the price of crude oil, on America's trade balance, and on America's carbon emissions for almost a decade.** A great opportunity exists to make a difference. Americans have bought fewer cars since the beginning of the economic crisis. It is imperative that when they return to the car dealers' showrooms they make enlightened choices. A lot will ride on their decisions.

Tri State Auto Auction - The new car you purchase will still burn gasoline nine years later. (Photo: The Author)

81 Ana Campoy, The Wall Street Journal, December 11, 2008

The reluctance to downsize is often rationalized by the security risk of driving smaller vehicles in the event of a collision. Ponder for a moment the level of risk that our young men and women take every day they serve our country in conflicts that are usually over oil. Consider the possibility that your decision to buy a smaller car will make it a little easier for the not-so-brave to follow suit. Someone has to show the way. The time will come when few large vehicles will be seen on our roads anyway. Higher fuel economy standards will necessitate a substantial downsizing of passenger vehicles to maximize the benefits of new power-train technologies and compensate for smaller engines. It's time to get out of our SUVs and small trucks to commute to work or take our pets to the veterinarian, visit the dentist, attend parent-teacher conferences, or drive to the mall.

The most enlightened car owners are already taking advantage of technological advances. More than one million Priuses have been sold in the United States since the car's advent in 1997. A few American-made vehicles offer such a power train and many more will soon appear in the dealers' showrooms. Hybrid power trains utilizing lithium-ion batteries and other future energy-storing devices as the primary source of power assisted by small, internal-combustion engines are already in advanced planning stages. A few cars powered exclusively by batteries are already on our roads. Tesla, a California-based company founded by Elon Musk, has been selling an electric-motor-powered roadster for more than a year and will be offering a sedan in 2012. Better Place, founded by Shai Agassi, a former software entrepreneur, is planning to set up in the Los Angeles area to service the all-electric vehicles market. [82] Carlos Ghosn, who runs both Renault and Nissan, recently declared, "We must have zero-emission vehicles. Nothing else will prevent the world from exploding."

Toyota Prius, Ford Fusion Hybrid - Cars currently available in the United States can travel more than 40 miles on one gallon of gasoline. (Photos: The Author)

82 The Economist, "Electric Cars. A Netscape Moment?" February 6, 2010, 71–72

Battery-operated cars will not replace the internal-combustion engine vehicles in the near future, but upgrades in the efficiency of those engines are already taking place. Engines are becoming smaller without sacrificing power aided by turbocharging and supercharging. The trend toward fewer cylinders and more transmission speeds and smaller, lighter cars promises more miles per gallon.

High gasoline prices incentivize people to purchase fuel-efficient vehicles. The sale of SUVs and large vehicles fell 22.2 percent and 31.0 percent, respectively, from April 2007 to April 2008. The sale of pickup trucks and minivans fell 16.8 percent and 19.8 percent, respectively, during the same period while the sale of midsize and small cars increased 0.3 percent and 7.1 percent, respectively.[83] For twenty-six years in a row, the Ford F-series pickup truck had been the best-selling vehicle in America, a run that ended in May 2008 as gasoline prices were ramping up.[79] In May, sales of the F-series pickup fell to fifth place when year-on-year sales for that month dropped 30.6 percent. Honda Civic sales increased 33.3 percent to propel the gas-miser to top place. Significantly, that change in driver preference preceded the economic downturn. Four-dollar-a-gallon gasoline appears to have been the tipping point. There were fewer miles driven and sales of fuel-efficient vehicles were up.

Predictably, lower gasoline prices prompted a resurgence in demand for pickup trucks and SUVs. U.S. sales of hybrid vehicles fell along with the price of gasoline. In the final months of 2008, sales of hybrids plunged. Prius purchases fell off 48 percent in November while sales of hybrid Civics suffered a 68 percent decline. Cars for which there were waiting lists a year ago were being offered at a discount, and Toyota delayed the opening of a new Prius factory in America.

There is concern that fuel-economy targets mandated by law will be difficult to meet if gasoline is cheap. Car buyers will lack the incentive to buy small, gas-miser vehicles or spend more to purchase the more expensive hybrid and other high-tech vehicles. Mike Jackson, chief executive of Auto Nation Inc., has long advocated a higher federal gasoline tax to ensure that gas prices stay above $4 a gallon to drive demand for fuel efficient cars, otherwise there will be "a huge disconnect between the vehicles available and what consumers will want."[84] There is general agreement that a tax on fuel to boost the price of gasoline back to the $4 a gallon range is needed to support investments in fuel-efficient vehicles and in alternative energy power trains.

---

83 Matthew Dolan and Josée Valcourt, The Wall Street Journal, May 2, 2008, B–4

84 Dashka Slater and Paul Rauber, Sierra, March/April 2009, 25

Chevy Volt – Car buyers will lack the incentive to buy the more expensive hybrids as long as low gasoline taxes subsidize drivers of gas guzzlers (Photo: The Author)

Additional Benefits of Higher Fuel Taxes

A tax would also have the benefit of generating revenue. In 2008, motorists consumed 144 billion gallons of gasoline and truckers 60 billion gallons of diesel. A $1 per gallon tax on fuel would hopefully reduce that amount but it would still likely generate more than $175 billion. Those funds could underwrite the wide range of infrastructure projects needed to help bring the country into the twenty-first century. Polly Trottenberg, the assistant secretary for Transportation Policy, was quoted as saying the United States has a structural imbalance of tens of billions of dollars between what the federal fuel tax is expected to raise over the next six years and the $450 billion to $500 billion that transportation experts say will be needed for maintenance, repairs, and new projects.

Investments in roadways would generate much-needed jobs with wide-ranging benefits for the economy. Drivers would get some return on their investment by traveling on better roads. According to the American Society of Engineers' Infrastructure Report Card of 2009, "Americans spend 4.2 billion hours a year stuck in traffic at a cost of $78.2 billion a year—$710 a year for each motorist."

A tax on gasoline would reduce the number of barrels of oil imported and lower the cost of each barrel, two measures that would stem the flow of the hundreds of billion dollars that leave the country every year. **It is puzzling that our legislators are scrambling to find billions of dollars to inject into the American economy to stop its downward spiral, yet they have no plan to stem the flow of dollars to the oil-exporting countries.** Crude oil imports account for the lion's share of America's current account deficit of more than $700 billion a year. In 2009, oil imports drained $416 billion from the U.S. economy.

Governments need to create a safe environment for entrepreneurs who are willing to invest in ways to reduce our dependence on fossil fuel and its inherent ills. In a 2008 article titled "From Geeks to Greens," *The Economist* chronicled examples of executives pursuing opportunities in clean energies.[85] It underscored the fact that **the private sector creates jobs, but private enterprise depends on public policies to create a stable environment for investors.** When it comes to green investing, public policy risk may matter as much as technology risk.

The gasoline/diesel tax, by curbing consumption, would apply downward price pressure on oil products used off road. The competitiveness of freight trains relative to the trucking industry would be improved. Burlington Northern Santa Fe railroad CEO Matthew K, Rose, estimates that, of the $500 billion that is spent each year to haul U.S. freight, $300 billion is spent on shipments between cities.[86] Rails get only 13 percent of that business according to Rose, even though freight trains can move one ton of cargo 457 miles on one gallon of diesel, a fifteen-fold efficiency advantage over trucks. For the sake of reducing America's fuel consumption, it is important to implement policies that favor the more efficient freight transportation system. It would limit the rise in road congestion "since one freight train can carry as much as 280 lorries

85 The Economist, "From Geeks to Greens," The Wall Street Journal, March 1, 2008, 65–66

86 Mark Clothier, Bloomberg Businessweek, May 16-May 23, 2011, 19-20

can."[87] It would lessen the pressure to expand the roadway system, saving public funds. It would bring reductions in diesel consumption, applying pressure on oil prices. Yet government money continues to favor the trucking industry over the rail system. Transportation consultant Fletcher Hall, quoted by Martin Ross in a *FarmWeek* article September 10, 2007, labeled the 2005 Federal Highway Package "probably the biggest pork barrel rolled out of Washington in a long time." Providing a more level playing field for the freight industry would ensure large benefits in the long term, since the U.S. freight volume is expected to double by the year 2035 according to Hall.

Low gasoline taxes allow the less efficient trucks to compete with freight trains even though trucks consume fifteen times the fuel for the equivalent job. (Photo: The Author)

Applying downward pressure on oil prices is important for many industries. Manufacturers of drugs, chemicals, fertilizers, plastics, rubber, asphalt, etc. all depend on oil. Lower oil prices would favor many of our industries and ultimately consumers of their products. It would reduce our armed forces' fuel

87 Stephen Power and Christopher Conkey, The Wall Street Journal, May 19, 2009

costs. The U.S. military is the country's largest single user of oil, consuming 340,000 barrels of oil daily, which is 1.5 percent of the country's total usage and 10 percent of the entire domestic market in aviation fuel. Our military's fuel expenses cost taxpayers $6 billion in 2007, up from $2 billion in 2005.[88]

Lower oil prices would cut the energy bills of many homeowners. Eight million American homes depend on oil for heat. Lower oil prices would reduce our farmers' production expenses. Their cost is greatly influenced by the price of oil-rich fertilizers and the price of petrol to power their tractors and combines. Because U.S. farmers are exempt from taxes on the fuel they use off road, reduction in crude oil prices lowers their cost of production. It is well known that high oil prices contribute to high food prices here and abroad. High fuel prices raise the cost of seeds and fertilizer, resulting in the idling of some acreage in developing countries because farmers cannot afford the up-front cost of planting their crops. High food prices have sparked riots around the world and malnutrition for tens of millions of people. One study estimates that high food prices have caused at least 300 million people to swell the ranks of those living below the poverty line, erasing the progress that had been made the last ten years. High food prices in America are contributing to a decrease in living standards for the less affluent Americans. Reasonably priced oil is an important factor in the affordability of food for the one billion people who live on $1 per day and the 1.5 billion who live on $1 to $2 a day.

Reductions in fuel consumption would have geopolitical benefits. Condoleezza Rice, secretary of state in the Bush administration, bemoaned oil's unsavory effect on foreign affairs. In a *Chicago Tribune* special report, Paul Salopek quoted Rice as telling Congress: "I can tell you that nothing has really taken me aback more as secretary of state than the way the politics of energy is—I will use the word "warping" diplomacy around the world. It has given extraordinary power to some states that are using that power in not very good ways for the international system, states that would otherwise have very little power."[89]

Reducing oil prices and oil imports would rein in the power of countries that use petrodollars to sustain geopolitical influence beyond the limits of their societies. Petrodollars underpin the rising power of Russia, Iran, the Middle East, and Venezuela. The governments of Iran, Kuwait, and Saudi Arabia

---

88 Yochi, J. Dreazen, The Wall Street Journal, May 21, 2008, 1

89 Paul Salopek, Chicago Tribune, "Twilight of the Oil Age," July 30, 2006, Sect 2, page 1–14

realize at least 80 percent of their revenue from oil. Energy policy has many foreign policy ramifications.

Putting a lid on fuel consumption would help America meet its goal of carbon emissions reduction, which would be a significant benefit for the planet and for America's image. More than 20 percent of America's carbon emission is attributable to roadway traffic. The oil we burn in transportation in the United States releases nearly 2 billion tons of carbon dioxide in the atmosphere each year. Each gallon of gasoline that we burn produces about twenty pounds of CO_2.

There is even evidence that a gasoline tax to raise gas prices could have health benefits. A study from Washington University in St. Louis suggests that 8 percent of the rise in obesity since the 1980s is attributable to low gas prices, which led to less walking and biking. Fred Krupp, president of the Environmental Defense Fund and coauthor of the book, *Earth: The Sequel*, believes that 13 percent of the weight gain of Americans is attributable to low gas prices. [90] Increased bicycle ridership as a result of expensive gasoline last spring and summer supports the results of those studies. In Broward County, Florida, 35,000 people typically put their bicycles on a bus bike rack every month. In May 2008, 68,000 did so. Elizabeth Preston of the League of American Bicyclists reported, "Bicycle ridership is skyrocketing." Rising healthcare expenditures is one of the main challenges facing the country. While obesity costs our healthcare system $150 billion a year, no consideration has been given to a gasoline tax increase to help reduce obesity and its burden on our government. Michael Milken, the discredited-bond-trader-turned-philanthropist and founder of the Milken Institute, stated during a CNBC special segment conducted by Maria Bartiromo on the future of healthcare on July 27, 2009, "If we could get Americans to reduce their weight to the same as they weighed in 1991, we could save $1 trillion."

Underfunding of the nation's transportation infrastructure is putting our lives at risk. In a report issued in 2005 the American Society of Civil Engineers (ASCE) predicts a dangerous future. Twenty-seven percent of the nation's 590,750 bridges are "structurally deficient or functionally obsolete". The Transportation Construction Coalition (TCC) determined in 2009 that poor maintenance of roads contributed to $217 billion in car crashes annually. According to the TCC, 53 percent of road fatalities each year are somehow related to poor road conditions. In 2010, 33,000 Americans were killed on United States roads,

---

90 Fred Krupp and Miriam Horn: Earth: The Sequel, W. W. Horton & Company, New York, 2008

amounting to 15 deaths per 100,000 people, a road fatality rate 60 percent above the OECD average, according to a report published in the April 30th, 2011 edition of *The Economist*.

Eighteen Years Without a Tax Increase

The total lack of initiative on the part of our legislators to raise the price of gasoline is puzzling. The federal tax on gasoline has remained a measly 18.4 cents per gallon and the tax on diesel 24.2 cents a gallon since 1993. Yet the cost of acquiring land for roadways, the cost of building and maintaining streets and roads has escalated. The lack of adequate funding for roads is costing Americans wasted time and fuel in traffic jams. It is costing injuries and lives.

Politicians argue that a tax on fuel amounts to a regressive tax. That is a weak argument. Wealthy individuals spend more on fuel driving large sedans, cruising their yachts, and flying than do less affluent people. Besides, a tax on fuel is a self-imposed tax. Much of our driving is unnecessary. If people don't want to pay the higher price, they can take public transportation, carpool, move closer to their job, or find work closer to where they live. They can better plan their errands. They can vacation closer to home. They also have the option of driving more fuel-efficient cars. Several models of cars for sale in 2010 achieve twice the fuel efficiency of most SUVs and many of the cars on the roads. Gasoline prices probably would have to double before people would be forced to spend more on gasoline because most of us could halve our fuel consumption by driving less and driving more-efficient vehicles. Perhaps a more-important reason for the lack of political will to raise fuel taxes is the clout of the oil industry lobby and the automakers' lobby.

One should not discount the possibility that a fuel tax increase would be substantially offset by lower oil prices, making the producers pay a share of the tax. The highly respected journalist Michael Kinsley said, "It's interesting to consider what the price of oil would be today if it had been higher in the past. Suppose for example, that President George W. Bush had used the political gift certificate he was granted on September 11, 2001, when he could have asked Americans to do almost anything in the name of fighting terrorism, to impose a $1.50 'War on Terror' tax on a gallon of gas."[65] Would that not have been the smartest way to retaliate against the countries that funded those responsible for the attacks?

Missed Opportunities

"Either we raise the price of oil or OPEC will." Ken Rogoff, professor at Harvard and former chief economist of the IMF.[91]

What an opportunity there was to apply a $1 tax on every gallon of fuel used in this country when gasoline prices had come down from more than $4 a gallon to less than $2 per gallon in 2009. A $1 tax per gallon would generate nearly $175 billion per year, the equivalent of almost 12 percent of the country's 2011 projected fiscal deficit of $1.5 trillion. Those funds would stay in the country instead of being invested in indoor ski slopes in the desert outside Dubai and in skyscrapers that dwarf our iconic buildings. Those funds would be available for roadway projects making our roads safer while creating jobs. The benefits would be so tangible that American workers would be more accepting of future increases in gasoline taxes. It's better to pay $1 more per gallon of gasoline and have a job than pay less and be unemployed. It's better to pay more for gasoline and spend less time in traffic. It's better to pay more for gasoline and have safer roads. Sadly the country squandered a great opportunity to send America on a better path. The opportunity still existed at the beginning of 2011 to raise gasoline taxes while gasoline retails for about $3 per gallon. Unfortunately, the political will was missing.

The inability of our legislators to stop subsidizing gasoline represents a grave distortion of our market economy and a deplorable failure of leadership. How can our legislators be so wimpy? Our neighbors to the north, the Canadians, pay about 25 percent more for their gasoline as a result of higher taxes and Canada hasn't shut down. A Canadian province has even found the need to add an additional tax. On July 1, 2008, the province of British Columbia added a tax on gasoline to help defray the cost of mitigating CO_2 emissions. The revenue will be returned in reduced income and business taxes. Gasoline prices are even higher in Europe. **European governments collect taxes**

---

91 The Economist, "A Survey of Oil. Not so shocking," April 30, 2005, 4

equivalent to more than \$4 U.S. per gallon in most countries. That has not affected their quality of life or their competitive position vis-à-vis the United States.

Fuel Efficiency Standards

S ince the shift to fuel-efficient vehicles will not happen on a grand scale solely out of driver enlightenment, public policies have an important role to play in promoting efficiency. Corporate Average Fuel Economy (CAFE) standards are the U.S. means of assuring a certain level of efficiency.

CAFE was formed in 1975 in response to the 1973–1974 Arab oil embargo. It required each automaker's new car fleet to average a minimum of 18.0 mpg. The new law produced an improvement of over two-thirds in the average fuel efficiency of new American-made cars. Between 1977 and 1985, the volume of America's net oil imports fell by nearly half even as its economy grew by one quarter.[91]

By 1996 the passenger car minimum was set at 27.5 mpg. Loopholes abounded. Since light trucks were held to lower standards (22.2 mpg), manufacturers used a loose definition of light trucks to label some of their SUVs as light trucks, eliminating their impact on the passenger-car fleet average. American carmakers exploited that market-distorting loophole by churning out squadrons of SUVs. Light trucks (pickup trucks, SUVs, and minivans) accounted for about 50 percent of sales for several years. Consequently, our personal-transportation fleet averages less than 25 mpg, the lowest in the world. The International Council on Clean Transportation rated the fuel efficiency of the largest fleets of cars in the world. Europe scored best followed by Japan, China, and Canada. The United States came out a distant last.[92]

---

92 Reed McManus, Sierra, January/February, 2008, 19

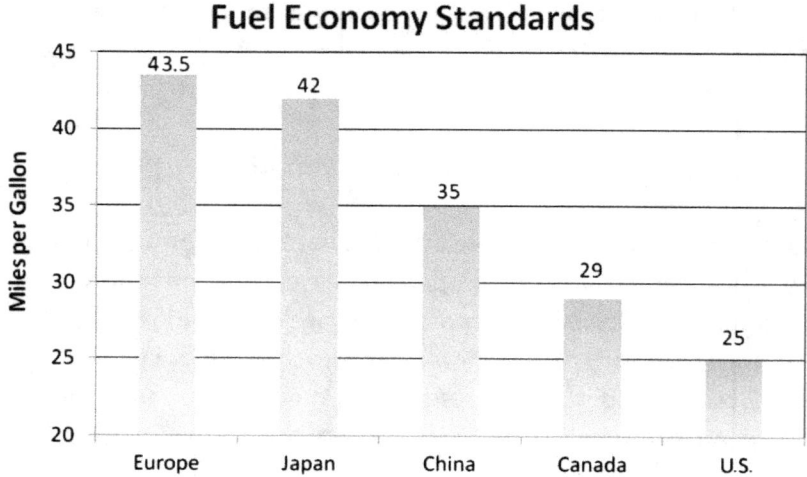

Figure 6: Fuel Economy Standards; Source: The International Council on Clean Transportation

The energy bill passed by the Bush administration at the end of 2008 required that cars and light trucks be treated as one category by the automakers and achieve a combined fuel efficiency of 35mpg by 2020.[93] The new benchmark amounted to an improvement in gas mileage of about 40 percent over the previous standards. On May 29, 2009, President Obama, surrounded by auto industry executives, government officials, and political leaders, announced slightly more ambitious targets: 35.5 miles per gallon by 2016 – 39.5 mpg for cars and 30.0 mpg for light trucks.[93] Those standards announced with fanfare will be less than standards currently in effect in China. Japan, and the European Union. Against the backdrop of future fuel standards already mandated by the European Union, the change is even less impressive. The EU's maximum CO_2 emissions for 2020 translated into miles per gallon will result in European manufacturers achieving 58.8 mpg for gasoline-powered cars and 65.3 mpg for diesel-powered cars – the difference accounts for the fact that diesel fuel emits about 18 percent more CO_2 than gasoline does – the world's strictest fuel-efficiency standards.[92]

One must also consider the fact that CAFE standards don't reflect the realities of everyday driving. For example, a car rated at 35 mpg by CAFE standards might get only 26 mpg in the real world. The EPA Fuel Economy Estimates

93 Dennis Simanaitis, Road and Track, August 2009, p 84–88

affixed to the window of new cars more accurately reflect actual operation performance. Those numbers are typically about 25 percent lower than the numbers used in CAFE calculations.[93] Considering that at best our new cars will achieve a 33 percent increase in fuel efficiency in 2017 over today's fleet's performance of 26.6 mpg and that new cars will account for about 6 percent of all the cars on the road that year, the new standards of efficiency will spare about 636,000 barrels of oil a day in 2017, a small fraction of the 10 million to 12 million barrels we import every day. (We use about 19 million barrels a day but only roughly 16 million goes toward powering cars and trucks.) If one considers that not all new cars will replace old ones, since two million Americans reach driving age each year, higher fuel standards will only slow the increase in fuel consumption, not reduce it.

America needs to adopt stronger measures to decrease its reliance on imported oil and reduce its noxious emissions. Regulators, led by the Environmental Protection Agency, will decide in September 2011 future mileage standards. The Agency is considering increasing efficiency requirements by 6 percent a year with the goal of achieving 62 mpg by 2025. Americans must show their support for efficiency standards that would greatly benefit the country's energy security, trade balance, geopolitical clout and environmental credentials.

The other public policy measure put forth by our federal legislators is the alternative fuel legislation referred to as the Energy Policy Act.

Alternative Transportation Fuels

Gasoline engines have the flexibility to adapt to a variety of alternative fuels, such as ethanol, butanol, natural gas, propane, and even hydrogen.[94] Alternative liquid fuels are being used in other parts of the world to mitigate the risks of dependence on oil. Brazilians and other South Americans are making extensive use of ethanol to replace gasoline. In Brazil it accounts for 50 percent of all fuel used for transportation. Europeans use compressed natural gas (CNG) to power many of their cars. In the United States there are only 120,000 vehicles running on CNG. Honda markets a CNG-powered vehicle in New York and California. The Honda Civic GX retails for about $7,000 more than the comparable gasoline-powered Civic. It is rated America's "greenest

---

94 Patrick Bedard, Car and Driver, December 8, 2008, 94–96

vehicle." Most gasoline vehicles can be modified to run on CNG. Conversion kits cost $3,700 to $5,500 to modify a gasoline engine to run on CNG.[95]

The refueling infrastructures need to be expanded if this form of propulsion is to become common. Nationwide, there are fewer than one thousand refueling stations that offer CNG to the public. California is the only state with more than one hundred locations. It is also possible to set up your own refueling station. One manufacturer, Fuelmaker Corporation, sells an in-home refueling system called "Phill." Using a standard residential gas line, it can refill a CNG car's tank overnight. It costs about $4,000 and may qualify for tax incentives. Natural gas is a cleaner-burning fuel than gasoline or diesel, reducing a whole panoply of emissions: carbon dioxide, carbon monoxide, nitrogen oxide, and particulate matter. A study by the California Energy Commission found that using natural gas instead of gasoline reduced global warming pollution by 20–30 percent. [96]

Aside from higher CAFE standards, promotion of biofuel represents the only plan the U.S. government has to reduce the country's reliance on oil. The Energy Policy Act of 2005 requires that a gradually increasing volume of ethanol be used as fuel to reduce the amount of gasoline we burn. It also mandates the use of a certain quantity of biodiesel.

Biofuels

B iofuels refers to energy derived from vegetation or animals. Ethanol, biodiesel, and methane are all biofuels. Ethanol occupies center stage in the biofuel world but, in fact, wood produces twice as much renewable energy in America than does ethanol. As far as transportation is concerned, ethanol is by far the main biofuel, followed by biodiesel. Both are being promoted as alternatives to petroleum fuels.

Ethanol used as fuel is also known as gasohol, which refers to a mixture of up to 10 percent ethanol and 90 percent gasoline. It is commonly called E-10. All vehicle engines are engineered to burn gasohol, a mixture that has been widely used in the Midwest for many years. E-85 fuel consists of 85 percent ethanol and 15 percent gasoline. It can be used only in flex-fuel vehicles. GM already has 3 million flex-fuel vehicles (E-85-capable) on

95 Cassandra Sweet, The Wall Street Journal, August 13, 2008, B3B

96 Henry Caroselli, Automobile, December 2008, 80–81

the road. The total number of flex-fuel vehicles in operation in the United States exceeds 5 million, but less than 1 percent of filling stations offer E-85, most of them confined to the Midwest farm states. In 2007, Ford, General Motors, and Chrysler pledged that 50 percent of their production would be flex-fuel vehicles by 2012, if crucial E-85 infrastructure emerges. As of October 2008, there were only 1,802 gas stations offering E-85 fuel, not enough to meet the infrastructure goals the automakers called for in 2006.[97] In October 2008, Congress extended the alternative refueling stations tax credit to help offset the cost of installing new E-85 pumps. In Brazil, 77 percent of new vehicles are flex-fuel vehicles and ethanol accounts for more than 50 percent of all the fuel burned.

E-85 service station - Only 5 to 26 percent of the energy in today's corn-based ethanol is new. The other 74-95 percent represents the recycling of fossil-fuel energy. (Photos: The Author)

Biofuels have advocates in high places. Congress is a staunch supporter. The 551-page Energy Policy Act of 2005 mandates the use of ethanol as part of the fuel mixture that we put in our cars. The renewable fuel standards (RFS) were signed into law in December 2007. They called for motor biofuel use to stair-step annually, reaching 11.1 billion gallons in 2009, 20.5 billion gallons in 2015, 30 billion

97 Martin Ross, FarmWeek, October 27, 2008, 5

gallons by 2020, and 36 billion gallons by 2022.[98] The plan limits corn-based ethanol contributions toward the 36 billion gallon goal to 15 billion gallons. The rest, 21 billion gallons, must be made up by cellulosic ethanol and biodiesel. The U.S. ethanol capacity in 2008 was on target at roughly 10.96 billion gallons.[98]

President George W. Bush was a strong backer of ethanol, touting this homegrown fuel every time he delivered his message of energy self-reliance. President Barack Obama, a former senator from the agricultural state of Illinois, is a staunch supporter of biofuels. U.S. Agriculture Secretary Tom Vilsack, a former governor of Iowa and past chair of the Governor's Ethanol Coalition, is a believer in biofuel.[99] Not surprisingly, the agricultural community supports the strong lobby of the biofuel industry.

The United States is not alone in promoting the use of ethanol as a fuel for transportation. The British government had a plan to ensure that 5 percent of Britain's transport runs on fuel made from plants by 2010.

Biofuels' Credentials

Biofuel supporters make the following claims: Biofuels are renewable and are homegrown. They reduce our dependence on oil. They emit less greenhouse gas than petroleum. Those are all laudable attributes but as you will find out, not all are justified.

There is no question that ethanol and other biofuels qualify as renewable energy. Corn, sugarcane, sugar beet, wheat, and all the cellulosic crops that are capable of producing ethanol and the crops from which biodiesel is extracted can grow in the same field or in rotation year after year. They have been for many decades.

Biofuels are homegrown. The United States, one of the main producers of corn and soybeans in the world, has vast expanses of land on which to grow crops that could yield cellulosic ethanol. The United States is already the largest producer of ethanol in the world.

The other biofuel credentials touted by the promoters of the biofuel industry are reduced dependence on foreign oil and decreased greenhouse gas emissions. Those claims have been challenged and deserve more scrutiny.

98 FarmWeek, "The RFS: New targets, new fuels, December 24, 2007, 2

99 Martin Ross, FarmWeek, December 20, 2008

The claim that biofuels reduce U.S. dependence on oil is hard to defend. There are many variables to consider. The same input of oil and gas-rich fertilizer; the same input of herbicides, pesticides, and other chemicals; and the same amount of diesel fuel used to sow the crops, to cultivate the fields, and to harvest the crop can produce a record crop or a meager one. The size of the harvest greatly influences the amount of ethanol yield per acre. The average U.S. corn yield is around 150 bushels per acre, delivering around 400 gallons of ethanol per acre. (One 56-pound bushel of corn yields 2.8 gallons of ethanol.) The size of the crops varies with the quality of the soil in a consistent way but it also depends on the vagaries of the weather. Scorching heat at the time of pollination can greatly reduce the size of the crop just as timely showers can boost yield. The same acre of land can produce fifty bushels of corn one year and two hundred bushels the next year—the only variable being the weather. That explains the range of results when evaluating ethanol as a substitute for petrol or as a savior of the atmosphere. What is clear is that no one should entertain the notion that one gallon of ethanol displaces one gallon of gasoline even under the best of circumstances. A recent study published by the University of California at Berkeley concluded, **"Only 5 to 26 percent of the energy in today's corn-based ethanol is new. The other 74 to 95 percent represents the recycling of fossil-fuel energy."**[100] A *FarmWeek* report on a University of Nebraska-Lincoln study gives a slightly more favorable account, crediting the corn-ethanol energy balance with 1.5 to 1.6 times more energy per unit produced by ethanol than is used to grow the corn and convert it to fuel. The author stressed the importance of this conclusion, stating that it was "potentially crucial to the future development of an industry facing growing social and policy scrutiny."[101]

Others have been more critical of the energy balance of ethanol. Some studies have concluded that making ethanol from corn requires more energy than is contained in the finished product. The fertilizers are oil-based. The tractors that prepare the ground that apply fertilizers, plant the crops, cultivate the land to control weeds, and apply chemicals to control diseases are all powered by diesel fuel. Harvesting is also fuel-intensive. Combines the size of small houses advancing through the cornfields, followed by dump trucks to collect the kernels, is an energy-intensive operation. Trucking the corn to

---

100 Patrick Bedard, Car and Driver, July 2006, 112–120

101 Martin Ross, FarmWeek, September 29, 2008

elevators also adds to the fuel cost. Finally, a little more diesel must be charged to each gallon of ethanol. Ethanol must be transported from the corn-processing plant to its destination by truck or by rail, since it cannot be distributed via pipelines because it picks up water and has corrosive properties.[100] Dr. Jan Krieger of Krieger and Associates and the University of Colorado looked at life cycle analyses of conventional and unconventional fuels, a field-to-wheel comparison. While only 5 percent of its energy is needed to produce a gallon of gasoline from oil, corn-based ethanol requires 98 percent of its energy. The reality is that a gallon of ethanol contains a lot of crude oil in the form of fertilizer, chemicals, diesel fuel, and gasoline.

Biofuels don't fare well when their greenhouse gas-sparing claims are scrutinized. As we already found out, each bushel of corn "contains" a lot of fossil fuel in the form of fertilizer, chemicals, and diesel fuel. In addition, the distillation of corn into ethanol once the corn gets to the processing plant requires a lot of heat. That heat is usually generated by natural gas and some coal— two fossil fuels. An article in the September/October 2007 issue of Sierra shed some light on how corn ethanol's CO_2 emissions vary considerably depending on how the mill processes the corn into fuel. If the mill depends on coal for its power, there is a 4 percent increase in greenhouse gas emissions over gasoline. If the mill uses natural gas, there is a reduction of 22 percent, and if biomass is the source of power, there is a 54 percent decrease in emissions.[102] Methane gas and wind energy could reduce the amount of fossil fuel in ethanol, but they are not yet making a significant contribution.

Fred Krupp reported that Alex Farrell and Daniel Sperling of the University of California assigned a number called "global warming impact" (GWI) to each fuel. GWI refers to grams of CO_2 per mega joule of fuel burned. The GWI score for gasoline was 92; for corn ethanol, 76; for Brazilian sugarcane-based ethanol, 36; and for cellulosic ethanol, 4. Corn ethanol was less than 15 percent more ecofriendly than gasoline. The U.S. Department of Energy concurred. Its research concluded that E-85 used in flex-fuel vehicles reduces CO_2 emissions by only 4 percent.[100]

Environmental lobbying groups like Friends of the Earth and Greenpeace have warned that biofuels are not as eco-friendly as they seem. That view is shared by the Royal Society, Britain's national science academy. It concluded that some biofuels may cause more climate change than gasoline when CO_2

---

102 Frances Cerra Whittelsey, Sierra, September/October 2007, 50–51

emissions from the manufacture of fertilizers and the processing of crops are accounted for. The Royal Society argues for a strict, worldwide certification system, similar to that used for other eco-friendly consumer goods, to inform consumers on how green a particular biofuel is.[103] In May 2009, the EPA took the important step of proposing a rule that would require "life cycle analysis" of biofuels' impact, including changes in land use. "If palm oil production requires razing rainforest in Borneo, for example, that would have to be accounted for."[104]

When the total emissions of growing, harvesting, and processing corn are factored in, it becomes clear that first-generation biofuels are not as environmentally friendly as we would like them to be.[105] A team of scientists working on behalf of the International Council for Science (ICS), a Paris-based federation of scientific associations, concluded that "so far the production of biofuels has aggravated rather than ameliorated global warming" because most analyses have underestimated the importance to global warming of nitrous oxide (N_2O) by a factor of three to five. "The amount of this gas released by farming biofuels crops, such as maize and rapeseed, probably negates by itself any advantage offered by reduced emissions of CO_2," according to ICS scientists. N_2O emissions are important because N_2O's ability to trap heat is almost three hundred times that of CO_2's over the course of a century. N_2O results from the interaction of soil bacteria with nitrogen-rich fertilizers that are used in modern agriculture. Corn, in particular, has been described as a plant that is not good at assimilating N_2O from fertilizers. **The California Air Resources Board also stated that ethanol's overall emissions are worse than gasoline's.**[92] Princeton University researcher Tim Searchinger has shown that producing corn ethanol has twice the warming impact of gasoline. Even substitutes like switchgrass can double emissions.[104]

Growing crops for fuel also has been blamed in part for deforestation, a process that is credited with a lot of greenhouse gas emissions—about 18 percent of the world's total emissions. Indonesia, the world's third-largest contributor of greenhouse gases, is experiencing a rapid slashing and burning of its rainforest for lucrative palm oil plantations. Brazil said deforestation of the

103 The Economist, January 19, 2008, A Special Report on Corporate Social Responsibility, 3–18

104 Sierra, "Biofuels," November/December, 2009, 52

105 George W. Huber and Bruce E. Dale, Scientific American, July 2009, 52–59

Amazon reached a record rate in the last five months of 2007. To reduce de-forestation, governments and international organizations must be proactive in stopping it. Economic pressures are the main cause of deforestation. High agricultural crop prices and high prices for biofuel are the main incentive to cut down forests to make way for agricultural crops, palm oil, sugar cane, and small grains. It is estimated that forest owners of Guyana would need to get at least $580 million a year to maintain their forests, the equivalent of what they could earn from exploiting their forests for logs and agriculture. Environmen-talists blamed the high grain prices for triggering an expansion of farming.

The financial cost of any potential ecological benefit of ethanol versus petrol should also be evaluated against the cost of other emission-sparing measures. The federal government subsidizes ethanol to the tune of 51 cents per gallon, with state governments adding another 10–40 cents per gallon in other tax incentives. It is estimated that the 51-cent-per-gallon subsidy alone cost taxpayers more than $4.5 billion in 2009. Corn growers also benefit from other various federal agricultural subsidies. **The Organization of Economic Cooperation and Development (OECD) calculated that each ton of avoid-ed CO_2, using corn ethanol as a substitute for gasoline, costs more than $500!** That is about twenty-five times more expensive than mitigating one ton of CO_2 through the European Union's Emission Trading Scheme, the largest market in CO_2 emissions. At the end of 2009, it cost around $20 to mitigate one ton of CO_2 through the European market. The OECD called for an end to all biofuel subsidies.

Former Vice President Al Gore, who supported subsidies for the produc-tion of ethanol when he was in office, now believes that policies in favor of ethanol production "have been implemented so far in ways that do far more harm than good."[16]

Another controversy that has crept into the biofuel debate is the impact on food supplies of growing crops for fuel.

Ethanol vs. Food

The global food crisis has shone a harsh spotlight on the consequences of government meddling in agriculture. It is said that poor people go hungry, in part, because America pays it farmers to divert crops from food to fuel. In 2007, the UN food envoy, Jean Ziegler, called using arable land to make fuel a "crime against humanity." Until alternative technologies are available, said Andrew Kimbrell, executive director of the Center for Food Safety, "crop-based biofuels will continue to deprive the hungry of desperately needed food."

In June 2008 the United Nations Food and Agricultural Organization (FAO) hosted a global agricultural summit in Rome. Jacques Diouf, director general of the FAO, told the conference that billions of dollars of annual subsidies "have had the effect of diverting 100 million tons of cereal from human consumption, mostly to satisfy a thirst for fuel for vehicles."[106]

The International Food Policy Research Institute agrees with the UN's assessment. It says producing fuel from crops—corn in the United States and rapeseed and soy in Europe—creates a shortage of food, thus putting upward pressure on the price of food with grave consequences for the billion people living in poverty. It estimates that one-quarter to one-third of the sharp increase in grain prices is attributable to the diversion of crops to biofuel.[107]

Even the agricultural community does not dispute that U.S. subsidies for corn-ethanol have caused food prices to increase, but calculations differ widely. The U.S. Department of Agriculture says biofuel policies have raised world food prices 3 percent. The International Food Policy Research Institute arrived at a figure as high as 30 percent, and a recent World Bank study suggested it could be as high as 75 percent. In 2009 Ron Gray, chairman of the Illinois Corn Marketing Board, admitted, "Ethanol continues to be a key driver in corn prices."[108]

Cornfield   Ethanol refinery

Ethanol subsidies have the effect of diverting a substantial portion of the U.S. corn crop to automobile fuel tanks, applying upward pressure on the price of a food staple. (Photos: The Author/IStock Photo # 3946666)

---

106 Marcus Walker, The Wall Street Journal, June 4, 2008, A12

107 Marianne Lavelle and Kent Garber, U.S. News & World Report, May 19, 2008, 36–42

108 Ron Gray, FarmWeek, February 11, 2009

Moral questions have been raised now that much of our corn crop – 51 percent in 2011 - is diverted to the production of ethanol. Thanks to subsidies funded by taxpayers, there is concern that all of us taxpayers are applying upward pressure on the price of a food staple, corn being ubiquitous in the food-supply chain. [109] Biofuel critics often make the point that all subsidies distort market forces.

An issue almost never mentioned when biofuels are discussed is the amount of water needed to grow those crops. Irrigation for agriculture consumes two-thirds of the world's fresh water. According to Fred Krupp, author of *Earth: The Sequel*, each ton of biomass requires about one thousand tons of water.[90] Furthermore, the process of transforming that biomass into fuel requires a lot of water. It is estimated that each gallon of ethanol processed from corn requires four gallons of water. **All told, the corn-ethanol portion of the fuel in our cars has been produced at a water cost twenty or more times greater than that of the gasoline fraction, when the entire production cycle is taken into consideration.**[110] At a time when water is becoming an increasingly scarce commodity, those statistics matter. As Andrew Liveris, CEO of Dow Chemical Co., pointed out in an August 23, 2008, report on the Business of Water, "Water is ultimately more important than oil because it is more imminently crucial to life and there is no substitute." Recently, residents of Urbana-Champaign, Illinois, opposed a local ethanol plant's petition to withdraw two million gallons a day from the local aquifer to produce one hundred million gallons of ethanol a year.[110] Their position was certainly defensible in light of the water-depleting realities of corn-ethanol fuel.

Clearly, the first-generation ethanol is not a long-term solution. The September/October 2008 issue of *Sierra* reported on a survey by the National Center for Public Policy Research. The survey results indicated that most Americans want Congress to reduce or eliminate its mandate that the United States produce 36 million gallons of biofuel annually by 2022, nearly half of which will likely come from corn.

A positive aspect of the biofuel industry is the number of jobs it has created. The average ethanol plant adds $110 million to the local economic

---

109 Michael Pollan, The Omnivore's Dilemma: A Natural History of Four Meals (New York: Penguin, 2006)

110 Michael E. Webber, Scientific American Earth 3.0, Volume 18, Number 4, December 2008, 34–41

base, creates more than six hundred new jobs and at least $1.2 million in local and state tax revenues. The report was issued by Harvesting Clean Energy, a project of the non-profit Climate Solutions. Brazil's biofuel industry, which supplies 50 percent of its transportation fuel, is estimated to employ about one million people.

The silver lining of the present ethanol industry is that it is expected to eventually lead to the development of a cellulosic ethanol industry. Proponents of cellulosic ethanol claim that it counters two of the criticisms of corn ethanol: It does not reduce the food supply or impact food crop prices, and it has defensible ecological credentials. In his January 2007 State of the Union message, President George W. Bush announced a 22 percent increase in funding for research by the Department of Energy, which would include funds for research in "cutting-edge methods of producing ethanol, not just form corn, but from wood chips, stalks, or switchgrass." He went on to say, "Our goal is to make this new kind of ethanol practical and competitive within six years."

Cellulosic Ethanol

Second-generation ethanol made from cellulosic stock has been nicknamed "grassoline." Cellulosic ethanol's substrate include agricultural residues, such as cornstalks, corn stover and wheat straw; fast-growing perennial grasses, such as miscanthus and switchgrass; high-biomass sorghum; energy-cane, a specially tailored sugarcane developed by Ceres; wood residues, such as sawdust; and woody materials; brush and trees. The idea is to take the cellulose of which the plants' cells are made and turn it into ethanol, hence the term "cellulosic ethanol."

Jim Wimberly, a biomass energy consultant, compared energy produced from corn-based ethanol and soy oil to energy produced from cellulosic crops. Conservatively, the energy yield of cellulosic crops dwarfs the energy yield of corn and beans. One acre producing 40 bushels of soybeans yields 6.3 million British Thermal Units (BTU) of biodiesel energy. One acre yielding 150 bushels of corn produces 29.6 million BTU from ethanol. One acre producing 12 dry tons of switchgrass yields 69.6 million BTU. Switchgrass and miscanthus are perennial crops that don't need replanting for up to twenty years but need about three years of growth before one can start yearly harvesting, with peak production reached after five years.

It is quite clear that U.S. fuel needs will be substantially satisfied by biofuels only if diversified cellulosic biomass is tapped. According to a study by the U.S. Department of Energy, the United States can produce at least 1.3 billion tons of cellulosic biomass every year—enough to produce biological fuels equal to one-third of the current U.S. consumption of fuel[16]—without decreasing the amount available for our food, animal feed, or exports. That would include utilizing products like sawdust, other construction debris, and wood collected from the clearing of underbrush, a measure that would greatly reduce the incidence of forest fires. The U.S. Department of Agriculture claims the country could produce enough cellulosic biomass to generate 100 billion gallons of ethanol a year without decreasing the size of the traditional food crops.[104]

Biomass-conversion technologies are poised to grow from the laboratories to the marketplace. The U.S. Department of Energy predicts commercial production of cellulosic ethanol in 2012. Cellulosic ethanol already is being extracted from corn cobs in a parallel process to the conversion of corn kernels to ethanol. A pilot project by POET, the Sioux Falls, Idaho, company that is the world's largest producer of ethanol, has already transformed its 125 million-gallon Iowa plant into a facility that also produces 25 million gallons of cellulosic ethanol from corn cobs and kernel fiber. Company scientists estimate that the combination will produce 27 percent more ethanol from each acre of corn. DuPont, in a joint venture with Danisco/Gen-Corp., a Danish-based technology company, plans to launch a 25-million-gallon-per-year Midwest corn cob-to-ethanol demonstration facility in 2012, followed by a second 15-million-gallon switchgrass plant in Tennessee by 2012. DuPont anticipates a potential 2-billion-gallon annual corncob-to-ethanol market, assuming a reliable biomass supply chain.[111]

DuPont is also working with the oil giant BP to develop advanced "biobutanol." Biobutanol, an alcohol that contains four carbon atoms in its molecule whereas ethanol has two, has limited water-absorption issues so it can be transported via pipelines and blended with gasoline at conventional refineries. Because biobutanol's energy content is close to that of gasoline, it offers greater fuel efficiency than ethanol when blended with gasoline. Dennis Magyar of DuPont claims that biobutanol could be blended at 16 percent without adverse effect to refineries or automotive systems. It can be produced from corn, wheat, and sugar cane at existing ethanol plants. A British demon-

---

111 Martin Ross, FarmWeek, "Logistics challenge to cob-based fuel," July 27, 2009, 8

stration plan, under construction in 2010, is expected to produce commercial quantities by 2013.[112]

Brazilian Ethanol

Brazil, which turned to biofuels in response to the 1970s oil shocks, is the poster country for the ethanol industry. **Brazilian ethanol infrastructure is the most developed of any large country. Already, ethanol accounts for approximately half of all transport fuel consumed in Brazil.** As early as 2007, 77 percent of their new cars could run on 100 percent ethanol.[113] Government policies favor ethanol because the industry employs over a million people. The use of ethanol eliminates the need to import crude oil and insulates the country from wild swings in the price of oil.[28] For the Brazilian consumer, the attraction is that ethanol sells for 1,799 reals versus 2,649 reals for petrol.

Brazilian ethanol is the product of the distillation of sugarcane. That process uses much less energy than the production of ethanol from corn, which requires the starch in corn to first be converted into sugar, an energy-intense process. Eliminating that step substantially reduces the cost of Brazilian ethanol and dramatically improves its ecological credentials. The UN Development Program (UNDP) maintains that sugarcane-based ethanol reduces greenhouse gas emissions by up to 70 percent versus a 13 percent reduction for corn ethanol.[114] Sugarcane ethanol is not only much friendlier to the environment than corn-based ethanol, but it displaces a lot more gasoline than corn does. Moreover, sugarcane ethanol does not carry the stigma of being responsible for higher food prices and hunger in hundreds of millions of people. All the sugarcane needed to satisfy the Brazilian ethanol needs is grown in only 2 percent of Brazil's agricultural land.

---

112 Martin Ross, Farm Week, "Biofuels not 'going away,'" July 27, 2009, 8

113 The Economist, "Ethanol. Fuel for Friendship," March 3, 2007, 44–46

114 Martin Ross, FarmWeek, December 3, 2007, 3

Sugarcane harvest   Brazilian gas station
Sugarcane-based ethanol yields 8.2 times as much energy as is used in its production and reduces greenhouse gas emissions by up to 70 percent. (Photos: Istock Photo #14012567/The Author)

Brazilian ethanol is not welcomed in the United States. The United States imposes a 54-cent per gallon import tariff on ethanol to shield American farmers and ethanol distillers from foreign competition.[114] The United States and EU have blocked a Brazilian proposal to classify biofuels as "environmental goods," which would qualify them for tariff reduction or elimination under World Trade Organization (WTO) proposals.[114] The UN Development Program (UNDP) in November 2007 called for the elimination of the United States and European tariffs on imported Brazilian ethanol. Charlotte Hebebrand, chief executive of the International Food and Agricultural Trade Policy Council, argued the RFS's ambitious mandate will drive ample demand for U.S. ethanol, eliminating the need for trade barriers. The fact that sugarcane-based ethanol yields 8.2 times as much energy as is used in its production versus just 1.5 times for corn ethanol also militates in favor of opening up our markets to Brazilian ethanol. The United States should start opening its markets to Latin American producers since the country will need about four times more ethanol than it currently produces to meet President Bush's 36-billion-gallon target in 2022. Joel Severinghaus, an Iowa Farm Bureau trade specialist, sees little threat from imports with tariff reduction or elimination, since it accounts for only 5–6 percent of total U.S. ethanol consumption. One of the greatest deterrents to large-scale U.S.-bound ethanol exports is the growing demand for ethanol in Brazil, where most new cars can run on 100 percent ethanol.

In 2008, Steve Ruh, chair of the National Corn Growers Association's Ethanol Committee, argued in favor of retaining the current import tariffs until

U.S. ethanol resources can more fully develop.[114] Renewable Fuels Association spokesperson Matt Hartwig makes a valid point when he calls the 54-cent tariff a "credit offset" that ensures that foreign ethanol producers don't benefit from the 51-cent-a-gallon federal ethanol tax credit intended to spur domestic biofuel expansion. The blender's tax credit applies to either domestic or imported ethanol. Even in the presence of import tariffs, about 450 million gallons of ethanol enter the United States yearly, most of it from Brazil. [115] Costa Rica also exports a lot of its ethanol production to the United States.

Importing ethanol from Brazil or Costa Rica does not satisfy the goal for energy independence but it is still preferable to relying on fuel from Brazil, Cost Rica, and Columbia than from Venezuela and the Middle East. The goal should be broader. It should emphasize energy security, clean energy, and renewable energy. Jeb Bush, the former president's brother, before stepping down as governor of Florida, urged the president to devise "a comprehensive ethanol strategy for our country and our hemisphere."[113]

Biodiesel

B iodiesel is the other biofuel that is being developed as a low-emission, homegrown, renewable fuel. Biodiesel is the result of the transformation of plant material and animal fat into diesel fuel or the refining of oil from seeds. Here in the United States, the conversion of soybean oil to biodiesel by transesterification accounts for 80 percent of biodiesel production.[116] There is also an effort to extract oil from distillers dried grains (DDGs), a by-product of the processing of corn for ethanol.[117] Soy oil has the advantage of having one of the lowest "cloud points"—about 32 degrees—which is the temperature at which most biodiesel fuels form crystals, affecting cold-weather performance.[116] In Europe, rapeseed and soybeans are the two main oil seeds. In Indonesia and Malaysia, palm seeds are the main source of fuel oil. Palm plantations yield the most fuel per acre, 610 gallons, more than double the amount extracted from coconut groves. By comparison, soybean fields produce 46 gallons per acre. Unfortunately, palm oil is often associated with deforestation, primarily in Malaysia and Indonesia. Partially as a result of this practice, Indonesia has

---

115 Martin Ross, FarmWeek, August 25, 2008

116 Martin Ross, FarmWeek, February 25, 2008, 6

117 Kay Shipman, FarmWeek, September 22, 2008, 3

become the third-largest source of greenhouse gas pollution.

Research is ongoing to develop new sources of vegetable oil for use as fuel.

For example, Pennycress, a winter annual in the mustard family, has an oil content of 36 percent. It can be planted following corn/soybean harvests and harvested prior to spring planting, according to Sudhir Seth, CEO of Biofuels Manufacturers of Illinois, a company that has a 45-million-gallon-per-year biodiesel operation. Seth extols the agronomic characteristics of pennycress. It has low water and nutrient needs and grows during the off season, thus not interfering with food crops.[118]

There is new interest in making biodiesel from fat. In April 2009, High Plains Bioenergy started operating a biorefinery next to a pork-processing plant in Guymon, Oklahoma. The refinery uses pork fat, a by-product of the butchering process, and converts it into biodiesel. The plant is expected to produce 30 million gallons of biodiesel a year. Dynamic Fuels, a joint venture between Tyson Foods and the energy company Syntroleum, is scheduled to open a plant in Geismar, Louisiana, that will use the fat from Tyson's chicken, beef, and pork operations to produce 75 million gallons of biodiesel annually.

The federal renewable fuel standard (RFS) called for an initial 500 million gallons of biodiesel and other "biomass-based diesel fuel" use in 2009 and one billion gallons by 2012. U.S. biodiesel production reached 450 million gallons in 2007. The biodiesel industry has set a goal of supplying 5 percent of the nation's diesel fuel by 2015. In 2006 America's trucks, tractors, and other diesel-powered engines consumed 60 billion gallons of diesel fuel.[119] All diesel engines can run on up to 5 percent biodiesel and 95 percent petroleum diesel mix, referred to as B-5, without warranty issues or modification but most require modifications to be operated with pure biodiesel, B-100. Tests have shown slightly better city fuel economy with B-5 and B-100 than with petroleum diesel.

The biodiesel industry, like the ethanol sector, benefits from government largesse, i.e., taxpayer money. The biodiesel industry receives a $1 per gallon federal biodiesel blender's tax credit and additional biofuel sales tax credits in some states. Illinois, for instance, eliminates sales tax on diesel fuel containing a minimum of 11 percent biodiesel. In Illinois, that translates into a 28.1-cent per gallon price reduction.

---

118 Martin Ross , FarmWeek, November 3, 2008

119 The Economist, "Alternative energy. Canola and soya to the rescue," May 6, 2006, 30–31

Biodiesel's Credentials

The benefits of displacing petroleum-based diesel with biodiesel are more compelling than the benefits of substituting ethanol for gasoline. Data released in 2011 from the University of Idaho and the U.S.D.A. reported by Martin Ross in FarmWeek, July 25, 2011, shows that for every unit of fossil fuel energy used to produce biodiesel, the return is 5.54 units of renewable energy. There is little or no concern that adding soy oil to diesel fuel increases food prices or creates a scarcity for human consumption. Soy oil accounts for only 20 percent of the soybean, the main portion (80 percent) being protein meal used mostly as animal feed. Actually, the increased demand for soy oil created by the biodiesel industry has added value to soybean crops, giving farmers an incentive to plant more soybeans, resulting in more plentiful supplies of soy protein for human and animal consumption. Still, there is ongoing research to develop other oil crops that would yield more oil than do soybeans. Other sources of biodiesel include sunflowers, mustard, canola, Camelina, and peanuts.

Soybean field – Soybean-based biodiesel is credited with a greenhouse gas reduction of 59.7 percent over petroleum diesel. (Photo: The Author)

Even though biodiesel production does not deprive the world of afford-able food to the extent that ethanol does, the reality is that the biofuel crop as a whole competes for land with crops for food. One should not forget that un-til such crops are grown hydroponically, they may be grown on land that could grow food. In the September 29, 2008, issue of *FarmWeek*, Daniel Grant quot-ed Bill Lapp, president of Advanced Economic Solutions, as saying, "Strong demand for soybeans, corn, and wheat likely will ensure an annual battle for acres around the world."[120] Lapp remarked that oilseed demand is growing at 4 percent annually while soybean yields are increasing at only 1 percent, and he expected that trend to continue. He projected that the world may need to plant an additional thirty-five million acres of soybeans alone to meet increas-ing demand.

National Biodiesel Board CEO Joe Jobe stresses efforts to improve soybean yields and oil contents. He believes that plant science research could improve the number of bushels harvested per acre by 15 percent and the amount of oil per bushel by 5 percent over the next seven years. Martin Ross, in a *FarmWeek* article, said considering that a normal U.S. soybean crop amounts to 3 billion bushels, such improvements alone could produce two billion gallons of new biodiesel fuel.

One issue with biodiesel production that is getting more attention is the correlation between increased demand for vegetable oil and the rate of defor-estation. Some argue that more efforts should be directed at the restoration of marginal land for farming to help non-forest areas yield more crops.

It so happens there are, within our shores, millions of acres that once pro-duced crops that have been taken out of production by our federal govern-ment with the main goal of supporting crop prices. We pay our farmers not to grow crops on those acres. Those acres could be returned to production but several special interest groups are lobbying to prevent such action.

Conservation Reserve Program

The Conservation Reserve Program (CRP) consists of 34.5 million acres of idled land. As a point of reference, in 2009 the amount of U.S. land planted with corn totaled 86.48 million acres; with soybeans, 77.45 million acres; and

---

120 Daniel Grant, FarmWeek, September 29, 2008

with wheat, 59.13 million acres. Farmers are being paid through the United States Department of Agriculture (USDA) to not grow crops on those CRP acres. Those 34.5 million acres are enrolled in ten– to–fifteen-year contracts. Farmers cannot return those acres into production during the life of the con-tract without incurring a fine. In Illinois, farmers receive an average of $26 per year from the USDA for each acre that they enroll in the program.

Those acres are also referred to as the set-aside acres. This program was initiated decades ago to take some land out of production to support crop prices when crops were too plentiful and prices depressed.

The role of the CRP needs to be redefined in view of the new realities. Cer-tainly, farmers usually don't enroll their most productive land, but now that grain prices are higher, marginal crop acres suddenly look like good crop acres. In Senate testimony in 2006, Keith Collins, USDA chief economist, estimated that 4.3 million to 7.2 million CRP acres could be used to grow corn and soy-beans "in a sustainable way." Iowa State University Extension Economist Rob-ert Wisner estimated that a total of 7.1 million CRP acres located in the Corn Belt would be suitable for corn and soybean production. Additionally, many of the remaining acres would be appropriate for growing switchgrass and other cellulosic ethanol crops.[120]

It is expected that many of the 3 million or so acres on which contracts are due to expire in the next two years will not be re-enrolled on account of the present attraction of crop prices, reducing the impact on corn prices of the rapid ethanol expansion. The American Farmland Trust and conserva-tion groups, such as the National Wildlife Federation, the Environmental Defense Fund, and the Sierra Club, have lobbied the agricultural secretary, urging him to reject requests to allow penalty-free release of CRP acres to agricultural production. The EU had a similar program but with global food prices soaring and arable land in short supply, the European Union in May 2008 suspended a requirement that farmers keep 10 percent of their land fallow, a program that was designed to cut overproduction and prevent the collapse of grain prices.[121] The United States should follow suit. So far, the USDA has resisted pressure from many sources to end this program even though grain supplies (carry-over stocks) are dangerously low and grain prices high.

---

121 John W. Miller, The Wall Street Journal, June 18, 2008, A9

Emerging Science

B iotechnology involves engineering biological molecules and microorganisms to produce new properties. Another goal of bioengineering is to replace dirty chemical processes with cleaner biological ones.

Research is ongoing on various ways to break down cellulose into fermentable sugars. Cellulose is made of carbon, oxygen, and hydrogen atoms.
Gasoline consists of carbon and hydrogen. The challenge to transform cellulose into gasoline is to displace the oxygen atom from the cellulose. Cellulose
is the molecular structure that lends stiffness to plants and is highly resistant
to decomposition. Cellulose is made up of thousands of glucose molecules
tightly bound together by hemicellulose. This stable molecule makes it very
difficult to break cellulose down into its glucose building blocks.[104]

The U.S. Department of Energy (DOE) is studying how bacteria and enzymes in the rumen of cows process cellulose from grass and hay into energy. At the University Of Illinois Institute Of Genomic Biology, scientist Bryan
White stated that ruminant enzymes have adapted to handle a tremendous
variety of plant material. But he added that at least two hundred enzymes
may be involved in the process. DOE is also looking into the process by which
termites break down cellulose as a source of energy. Steen Riisgaard, chief executive of Novozymes, a biotechnology company, imagines a future in which
bio-refineries are producing fuels and other chemicals from biomass such as
agricultural waste. He reckons that using industrial biotechnology to convert
agricultural waste into other chemicals including fuels could reduce the need
for oil by 20–25 percent.

Alga-culture is carving a place for itself in the biofuel world. It consists of
growing algae that are capable of producing lipids that can be processed into
biodiesels and carbohydrates that can be processed into ethanol. Some algae
cells contain as much as 60 percent oil.[30] Arizona Public Service is installing a
full-scale alga-culture to produce biodiesel. Sapphire Energy of San Diego, California, is another company involved in algae-oil production.[122] The company,
which counts Bill Gates as an investor, projects that within two years, it will
produce a million gallons of diesel and jet fuel a year.[30]

Scientists are working on a new generation of biofuels, making hydrocarbons instead of ethanol, molecules so similar to those of gasoline to be used

122 Melinda Wenner, Scientific American Earth 3.0, Volume 19, Number 1, 2009, 46–51

as "drop in" fuels. Synthetic Genomics of San Diego, California, a firm founded by Dr. Craig Venter, who ran the human genome project in the 1990s, is hard at work figuring out how to use bacteria and algae to produce biofuels.[122] The challenge is to find, among thousands of species of algae, which would be the most suitable organism to genetically manipulate into the ideal algae. The goal is to engineer single-celled algae to secrete "fuel-ready hydrocarbons" and excrete their products into the medium in which they are being raised, a process that he calls "biomanufacturing." The oil would then be collected without having to sacrifice the algae.[123] Solazyme, based in San Francisco, wants to feed its single-celled algae sugar, leaving the photosynthetic step to others. Since algae require a lot of CO_2 to grow, the plan is to grow the algae near sources of CO_2 such as power plants and oil refineries, to capture their CO_2 emissions, an added benefit.[123]

Codexis of Redwood City, California, makes specialized enzymes and genetically engineered bacteria that can turn sugar into straight-chain alkenes similar to those in diesel fuel and jet fuel. Amyris of Emeryville, California, employs genetically engineered yeasts to make its straight-chain alkanes.[123] Scientists are also working with fungi. A fungus found growing in trees in Argentina by botanist Gary Strobel of Montana State University is the only organism known to synthesize hydrocarbons. The challenge is to manipulate the fungus to produce higher yields of the hydrocarbons.[124]

Alga-culture is also receiving interest for another environmental benefit: Its ability to remove carbon dioxide from the atmosphere. California-based Origin Oil Inc. has pioneered a technology that separates algae-oil from its biomass without a dewatering operation. The company touts its unique algae-to-oil platform but also promotes its CO_2-absorption capability. On January 25, 2011, Origin Oil Inc. announced that it had received an order for the first commercial application of its technology. Australia-based MBD Energy plans to install the system at its Queensland's 1.45-gigawatt Tarong Power Station. MBD Energy will grow its oil-producing algae using its CO_2 emissions.[125]

---

123 The Economist, "The future of biofuels. The post alcohol world," October 30, 2010, 84–86

124 Science Illustrated, "Fungus Fuel on the Horizon," July/August, 2009, 19

125 Origin Oil (www.originoil.com)

Some scientists take a different approach. They are exploring ways to take oil out of the manufacturing processes by using biological ones. Novozymes is working on a biological process to make acrylic acid, substituting starch or bio-mass for fossil fuels. One stage uses enzymes; the other relies on engineered microbes. Around 40 percent of acrylic acid produced is used to make super-absorbent materials, such as that used to make diapers; most of the rest goes into paints and coatings. One company, DSM, based in the Netherlands, has been working with enzymes since the 1990s. It developed a biological proc-ess to produce the widely used antibiotic Cephalosporin in a much cleaner way than the chemical processes used to make the drug. Its latest focus has been to find a biological method of producing succinic acid, which is used in the manufacture of a wide range of products, including spandex, deicing salts, and acidity regulators in food. DSM's biological approach uses enzymes for fermentation and genetically engineered microbes in the next stage. Efforts to remove oil from chemical processes need to be part of the efforts to reduce oil consumption.

The Energy-intense American Diet

"And no matter what makes it onto your dinner plate tonight, guess what one of the other main ingredients will be? Oil. And I mean petroleum." Laura Stec and Eugene Cordero, Cool Cuisine, 2008 [126]

"America's food is drenched in fossil fuels." Michael Pollan, The Omnivore's Dilemma, 2006 [109]

It takes five hundred gallons of oil each year to produce food for one per-son. Producing food that never gets eaten is, in itself, a major drain on fuel supplies. It is estimated that three hundred million barrels of oil is needed to produce the food that is discarded each year by Americans.

Agribusiness consumes an enormous amount of fuel. Food carries the energy cost of tilling the land; manufacturing and applying fertilizers, her-bicides, and pesticides; planting the crops; cultivating the fields; harvesting the crops; drying the seeds and moving the crops to the elevators for stor-

---

126 Laura Stec and Eugene Cordero: Cool Cuisine 2008, 6

age. It is estimated that up to 16 calories of fossil fuel are required to produce a single calorie worth of grain.[89] Since most consumers don't live on the farms where the food was produced, food assumes the additional energy cost of trucking to the processing plants, being processed, packaged, and then shipped to grocers where some of it is refrigerated or kept frozen.

Producing animal protein is especially energy intensive. Only 5–25 percent of the nutrients consumed by animals raised for consumption are converted into edible protein. Red meat production is the least efficient process. **It takes about thirteen pounds of grain and thirty pounds of forage to produce one pound of beef.** It was estimated that almost seven barrels of oil—283 gallons of it—were burned to raise Grandview Rebel, Marina Willson's champion steer that weighed in at 1,250 pounds. Since only part of his body was destined to your dinner plate, **the pound of beef on your plate represents three-quarters of a gallon of oil.**[40] Consider that before ordering your next steak and think about how impressive he was before being slaughtered.

Weighing in at 1,250 pounds, Marina Willson's champion steer Grandview Rebel is ready for auction at a county fair in Maryland. Raising this steer has taken an agricultural investment equal to 283 gallons of oil - represented here by the drums. That includes everything from fertilizers on cornfields to the diesel that runs machinery on the farm. A pound of beef takes three-quarters of a gallon of oil to produce. (Photo: National Geographic, June, 2004)

Pigs and chicken are more efficient processors of plant material into animal protein. It takes 6 pounds of grain to produce a pound of pork and only 2.3 pounds of grain to produce a pound of poultry meat.[127]

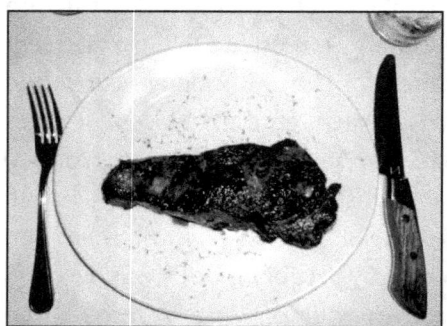 

Red meat vs. poultry meat - It takes thirteen pounds of grain and 30 pounds of forage to produce one pound of beef. It takes only 2.3 pounds of grain to produce one pound of poultry meat. (Photos: The Author)

Such statistics will matter more and more as the middle class swells around the world. Meat and dairy products currently make up one-third of humanity's protein intake, but demand is growing fast. In 2000, global meat consumption was 230 million tons per year. By 2050, it is expected to reach 465 million tons.[127] Carnivorism is increasing at an alarming rate in some of the most populous countries in the world. In 1985, Chinese ate an average of 44 pounds of meat. In 2009 they consumed 109 pounds. Of concern is the fact that Chinese annual per capita meat consumption has a lot of potential for growth.[109] Brazilians eat 197 pounds of meat per year. The U.S. annual per capita meat consumption was 273 pounds in 2007, according to the USDA.

The affluence of Americans and the growing middle class of developing countries allow more people access to produce and other foods grown in faraway places. Americans eat 2,000 pounds of food a year, of which about 260 pounds is imported.[128] According to Rich Pirog, quoted by Douglas Farr in *Sustainable Urbanism*, "The American plate of food travels an average of 1,494 miles."[5] Ethnobotanist Gary Paul Nabhan was quoted as saying, "Should I assume that I have a God-given right to access the entire earth's bounty?" John

---

127 Bijal Triverdi, "Dinner's Dirty Secret," *New Scientist*, September 13, 2008, 8

128 *Green Guide*, Spring 2008, 86

Cloud, a senior writer for *Time* magazine, framed the issue succinctly. "How much Middle Eastern oil did it take to get that California apple to me?" He quoted nutritionist Joan Dye Gussow, a Columbia University Teachers College professor emeritus, who has said that "shipping a strawberry from California to New York requires 435 calories of fossil fuel but provides the eater with only 5 calories of nutrition."[129]

The plastic bags in which we cart our food home from the grocery store contribute to the fuel intensity of our diets. We throw away 98 percent of the 380 billion plastic bags that are manufactured each year at a cost of 12 million barrels of oil.[126] Outlawing plastic bags in San Francisco alone reduces oil consumption by nearly 800,000 gallons a year, according to city officials.[130] Interestingly, plastic bags have been banned in Rwanda, Bhutan, Bangladesh, and South Africa. In Mumbai, India, Taiwan, and in Ireland, people must pay for plastic bags.[130]

Overeating

O vereating puts a strain on many of our scarce fuel resources and results in weight gain. The basis for categorizing people as overweight or obese is the body-mass index (BMI). People are considered overweight if their BMI is between 25 and 29.9. They are obese if their BMI is 30 or more.[131] It was estimated in 2006 that 66 percent of Americans were above their normal weight and 34 percent were clearly obese, more than double the percentage of obese Americans in 1980. Today, 72 million adults are obese. Collectively we are 4.6 billion pounds overweight, according to Thomas Frieden, director of the Centers for Disease Control and Prevention.[132] Its 4.6 billion pounds of fat cells that need to be fed and hydrated. They place an unnecessary burden on the food and beverage industries. It is 4.6 billion pounds weighing down cars and planes. Every additional one hundred pounds of weight carried by a car increases its fuel consumption by 2 percent. Aircraft fuel consumption is even more sensitive to the total weight of the aircraft. In July 2008, U.S. Airways announced

---

129 John Cloud, Time, March 12, 2007, 43–50

130 The Economist, "The War on Shopping Bags. Plastics of Evil," March 31, 2007, 38

131 Corey Binns, Popular Science, March, 2009, 52–53

132 Nanci Hellmich, "Obesity is a Key Link to Soaring Health Tab," USA Today, July 28, 2009

that it would remove the onboard flight entertainment center from its planes. By removing the five-hundred-pound devices, company executives estimated they saved $10 million per year in fuel costs. Think of the cost of flying all the excess fat that is on board! The average American being 23 pounds overweight, a 200-passenger payload amounts to an extra 4,600 pounds, resulting in an appreciable fuel draw down.

Overweight people are less likely to walk or ride bicycles, even to the nearby places they need to go. They are less likely to take public transportation because they have to walk at both ends of the line. Fred Krupp, president of the Environmental Defense Fund and coauthor of the book, *Earth the Sequel*, told TV interviewer Charlie Rose on June 6, 2008, **Americans presently use 1 billion gallons of gasoline more per year that they did in 1960 solely as a result of obesity.**

The trend in obesity in Americans twelve to nineteen years of age is alarming, having more than tripled since 1980 to about 18 percent. It doesn't bode well for our future adults. Former President Bill Clinton, keenly aware of the consequences of obesity in our society, launched the Alliance for a Healthier Generation. In his book, *Giving*, Clinton wrote, "Today, 12.5 million American children are obese and an additional 13 million are overweight."[133] One of First Lady Michelle Obama's missions is to reduce childhood obesity.

Food Waste

Reports point to rich countries throwing out 25–30 percent of the food that is purchased. Add to this the food that is discarded before it is sold and the scale of the problem is considerably larger.[134] **It is estimated that 96 billion pounds of food are thrown away each year by Americans, 320 pounds per person.**

Reliable data on the amount of food waste is scarce, so Kevin Hall and colleagues at the National Institute of Diabetes and Digestive and Kidney Diseases in Bethesda, Maryland, devised a new way of assessing the problem. They calculated the calorific consumption of the American population, and then compared those data with recorded levels of food production. They took into account imports and exports. **They found that the average American wastes 1,400 calories a day! That amounts of 40 percent of America's total food**

133 Bill Clinton, Giving (Alfred A. Knopf, New York, 2007)

134 The Economist, "A Hill of Beans," November 28, 2009, 94

supply. Producing those wasted calories accounts for more than one-quarter of the country's consumption of fresh water and uses about 300 million barrels of oil each year.[134] That is equivalent to fifteen days of U.S. oil consumption. Some consideration also must be given to the greenhouse gases emitted in the process of producing all that food, as well as to the gases that emanate from the discarded food rotting in landfills.[134] Reducing food waste needs to be a concern of the distributors, the retailers, and the consumers.

Food is not the only energy-intensive part of our diet. What we drink also carries a high cost. We consume about thirty billion single-serving bottles of water each year. It takes approximately 17 million barrels of oil just to make the plastic for the water bottles and production of the bottles consumes over 1.5 million barrels of oil each year.[126] Transportation of the empty bottles to bottling plants and transportation of the filled bottles to the distributors' warehouses and then to local stores burns fuel and clogs highways and streets. Then, the empty bottles are shipped to landfills or recycling centers. According to the Container Recycling Institute (CRI), only 23 percent of plastic bottles get recycled. A six-pack of aluminum cans carries the greatest cost. It takes almost three times as much energy to manufacture as does a two-liter plastic bottle, yet less than 40 percent of cans are recycled. In the United States alone, more than 50 billion aluminum cans are discarded each year. Recycling of aluminum offers some of the largest gains in the recycling industry, the production of aluminum from bauxite ore being one of the most energy-intensive processes in the global economy. Ninety-five percent of that energy can be saved by processing recycled aluminum instead of producing new aluminum from bauxite.[16]

A *U.S News and World Report* article eloquently summed up the insanity of drinking bottled water. "The containers are often filled in faraway lands, then shipped overseas, transported across the country in trucks and stored in refrigerators at your local convenience store. Compare that with the environmental impact of turning on your tap, filling your glass, and sipping away." [135] The irony is that 40 percent of bottled water comes from city water supplies. **Bottled water might well be the most needlessly wasteful product of modern times**.

135 V. H., Bye-Bye, Bottled Water," U.S. News & World Report, December 31, 2007/January 7, 2008, 62

Grocery store selection of bottled water – It takes about 17 million barrels of oil just to make the plastic for the 30 billion single-serving bottles of water consumed each year. Bottled water might well be the most needlessly wasteful product of modern times. (Photo: The Author)

Our diets deplete another of our important resources: water.

The Water-intense American Diet

"It seems we are already approaching an era of 'peak water.' The situation should already be considered a crisis but the public has not grasped the urgency." Michael E. Weber[110]

"Water is the oil of the 21st century," Andrew Liveris, CEO, Nestle [136]

What we eat and what we drink have a lot to do with the depletion of our water resources. Worldwide, agriculture uses 70 percent of all water consumed. In the United States, 41 percent of all water withdrawals are for grow-

---

136 The Economist, "Business of Water. Running Dry," August 23, 2008, 53–55

ing crops. Globally, industry is the second-largest consumer at 22 percent, and domestic use accounts for 8–10 percent of consumption.[137] Worldwide agriculture uses about 325,000 cubic kilometers of water each year, almost three times the 125,000 cubic kilometers withdrawn by industry, thermal power plants taking the lion's share.

Irrigated crops – In the United States, 41% of all water withdrawals are for growing crops. (Photos: Istock Photo # 2069470, 6034042)

Fresh water, like oil, is not evenly distributed. Nine countries account for 60 percent of all available supply—Brazil, Canada, Columbia, Congo, and Russia being particularly blessed. The United States has a fair amount, but the quantity being withdrawn exceeds the annual recharge.[137]

Water shortages are already a major concern in many parts of the world. There is a lot of water on earth but only a small fraction of the total is useful. A full 97.5 percent is salty. Of the 2.5 percent that is not salty, 70 percent is frozen either at the poles or in permafrost.[137] **According to the World Health Organization, about 2.4 billion people live in highly water-stressed areas,** a situation that will worsen with population growth and urbanization. The United Nations projects there will be more than 4 billion people living in nations defined as water-scarce or water-stressed by 2050.[137]

Some countries are already struggling with water scarcity. China and India, with one-third of the world population, have less than 10 percent of the available fresh water. China's Northern provinces, a region that grows 60 percent of the country's crops and is home to 40 percent of its people, is experiencing the worst drought in at least fifty years.[138] The lack of rain is endangering the country's best wheat-production area and straining the clean water supply to millions of people. Pervasive overuse and decades of wasteful practices have contributed to the region's water-supply shortages. The situation is dire enough for the Chinese government to launch thousands of rocket shells filled with capsules of silver iodide into clouds to produce rain. The authorities have also been trucking water to thousands of villages with dry wells. India is facing water shortages of China's magnitude. Almost half of India's 604 districts are affected by drought, precipitation having been the scantiest in decades. The rapid melting of Himalayan glaciers that India shares with China is expected to deprive its great rivers, the Indus and Ganges, of summertime water source.[137]

Heavy subsidies for water in India and in many parts of the world are a reason for wasteful habits. Indian farmers pay nothing for their water, and the electricity to pump water out of the ground is free or heavily subsidized. Indian subsidies are not confined to farmers. Many cities price their water well below cost, fostering abuse. Residents of Delhi draw 220 liters per person a day, more than residents of Paris, France.[139]

Water shortages are a factor in this country. Twenty-two million people are living in water-stressed areas. Las Vegas gets its water from Lake Mead through two channels drilled through rock. The uppermost taps the lake at 1,050 feet above sea level and the lower at 1,000 feet. In January 2011, the lake was only 40 percent full, its water level down to 1,086 feet above sea level. [140] California, Nevada, and Arizona are constantly under the threat of water shortages. Farmers are already suffering the effects. In 2009, 250,000 acres of Fresno County, California, the nation's most productive county, went fallow for lack of water. Statewide, about 500,000 acres remained unplanted.[141] Steven Chu, President Obama's energy secretary and a Nobel Prize-winning physicist, spoke of dire consequences, especially for California, the nation's leading agricultural producer, if the advance of global warming cannot be slowed. He warned that the West and Upper Midwest could face severe water shortages

138 Michael Wines, The New York Times, February 25, 2009, A5

139 The Economist, "India's Water Crisis. When the Rains Fail," September 12, 2009, 27–29

140 The Economist, "The Drying of the West," January 29, 2011, 32

141 William M. Welch, U.S.A Today, July 28, 2009, 3–A

to the extent that California's agricultural economy could be wiped out and major cities could be in jeopardy. A recent study by University of California–Berkeley researchers estimated California has some $2.5 trillion in real estate assets—including agriculture—endangered by warming. [142] Farmers in Kansas need to reconfigure how they will grow their crops because the state of Kansas recently lost a lawsuit to Missouri over interstate water use. Georgia is fighting to keep its water from Florida and Alabama to service the rapidly growing population of Atlanta in the face of its rivers running dry. City officials are concerned that Atlanta will face crippling water shortages unless the city gains access to the water of Lake Lanier.[143]

Since agriculture is responsible for 41 percent of all water consumption in this country, our diets greatly influence water withdrawals. **Our meat-rich diet requires around 5,000 liters of water a day to produce**—an enormous amount when compared to the 2 liters of water we drink per day. In contrast, the vegetarian diets of Asia use about 2,000 liters a day.[20]

Water consumption as it relates to our diets should raise concerns. The Ogallala Aquifer that underlies the U.S. Great Plains, the breadbasket of the country, is not rechargeable by precipitation. The Ogallala Aquifer is a vast underground reservoir of water that was trapped about three million years ago when sediments covered the area east of the Rocky Mountains, creating the Great Plains. It is being depleted at an annual volume equivalent to eighteen Colorado Rivers. It is not replenishable. Large-scale tapping of the aquifer started after World War II with the advent of diesel-powered pumps, transforming one of the least productive farming regions of North America into one of the most productive.[144] Water tables are also falling in China and India, two countries heavily dependent on unrechargeable aquifers. India is the world's largest user of unrenewable ground water, with some 20 million boreholes providing water for over 60 percent of its irrigated area. Satellite maps released by NASA show that northwestern India's aquifers fell by one foot a year between 2002 and 2008.[139]

Some farmers are responding by switching to crops that require less water and are adopting better irrigation practices. It is estimated that as much as 70

142 Jim Tankersley, Chicago Tribune, "Energy Chief's Dire Forecast," February 4, 2009

143 Jon Spayde, Experience Life, June 2010, 51–56

144 Jane Braxton Little, "Saving the Ogallala Aquifer," Scientific American Earth 3.0, Volume 19, Number 1, 2009, 32–39

percent of water used by farmers never gets to crops. Instead, it is lost through leaky irrigation systems or by running into rivers or draining into groundwater. Better irrigation practices could bring huge savings. Changing irrigation practices could improve water efficiency by 30 percent, according to Chandra Madramootoo of the Internal Commission on Irrigation and Drainage. [20]

Other measures are being employed to make better use of our water resources for agricultural purposes. Genetic engineering of crops to improve their drought resistance or reduce their need for water will play a role in reducing agricultural water requirements. Expansion of water-storage capacity to allow for more controlled application of water to crops would also help stretch water resources. Improved trade practices could make better use of available water. Substantial disparities exist between the amounts of water needed to grow the same crops in different parts of the world. Growing rice in the United States or China requires less than half the water it does in India or Brazil. It is the same situation for wheat. But when it comes to soybeans, Brazil requires about 40 percent less water than the United States, roughly 60 percent less than China, and only one-quarter as much water as needed in India.[20] Rainy England draws only 3 percent of its total water consumption to grow crops.[137] Individuals can do their part by eating less beef. It takes only one quarter as much water to produce the same amount of chicken.[137]

What we drink also has a significant impact on water needs. A large quantity of water is needed to produce beverages that have become staples in the developed world. **Growing the beans needed for our morning cup of coffee requires 1,120 liters of water per liter of coffee.** A cup of tea requires only about one-tenth the amount. It takes almost 1,000 liters of water to produce a liter of wine, about three times the volume of water needed for the same quantity of beer. A liter of apple juice requires about 950 liters of water, while a liter of orange juice comes at a cost of about 850 liters of water. Ironically, a liter of bottled water has 3 to 4 liters of embedded water. José Lopez, the Chief Operating Officer of Nestle, remarked that it takes four liters of water to make a liter of product in Nestlé's factories but 3,000 liters of water to grow the agricultural products that go into it. JP Morgan reckons that five food and beverage giant companies—Nestle, Unilever, Coca-Cola, Anheuser-Busch, and Danone—consume 575 billion liters of water a year. Of Nestlé's 481 factories worldwide, 49 are in extremely water-stressed regions. Nestle has responded by cutting its water consumption by 2.9 percent between 1997 and 2006 while almost doubling the volume of food it produced.

Lester R. Brown, founder and head of the Earth Policy Institute and author of *Mobilizing to Save Civilization*, warns we desperately need a new way of thinking when it comes to water consumption.[145] Water use and supply need to be brought into balance. Population growth and the expanding middle class are reasons enough to treat water as an important commodity. More people consume more water. Estimates call for water consumption to double every twenty years, which some call an unsustainable rate of growth. Since the earth is playing host to an additional 70 million people each year, it is expected that the world population will require an additional 1,500 cubic kilometers of water per year by 2030.[145]

We must think of water as an important resource and price it appropriately to foster conservation. Heavy subsidies for water in most parts of the world encourage squandering. Michael E. Weber, contributor to Scientific American Earth 3.0, stresses the importance of putting a realistic price on water to promote conservation. "Without that, we send a confusing signal that everyone can be blasé about wasting water."[110] We need to be mindful of the consequences of our daily dietary selection and the impact of our energy consumption on our "water footprint." In the words of Alexandra Cousteau, the granddaughter of undersea explorer Jacques Cousteau, "Water will be the principal defining crisis of this century. History will be made over how we manage our water resources." [146]

Reducing greenhouse gas emissions needs to be an integral part of the efforts to avert water shortages, and the ensuing food shortages. Already one billion people go to bed hungry each night, partly for lack of water to grow their food.[134] Agriculture as it exists today has been shaped by a climate system that has changed little in the eleven-thousand-year history of farming.[145] Global warming accelerates the hydrologic cycle, the rate at which water evaporates and falls again as rain or snow.[20] This higher rate tends to increase precipitation in wet regions and decrease it in arid ones. It brings longer droughts between more intense periods of rain.[20] Since few countries have adequate water storage and delivery systems to better utilize local precipitation when it comes as torrential rain, it complicates water-management practices. Ac-

145 Lester E. Brown, Scientific American, May 2009, 50–57

146 Karen Blankfeld Schultz, Scientific American Earth 3.0, December 9, 2008, 10

cording to a 2007 study, the global average withdrawal of fresh water was 9 percent of the amount that flowed through the world's hydrologic cycle. Latin America and Africa captured less than 6 percent.[20] Global warming also melts glaciers that act as natural regulators, storing water in winter and releasing it in summer.[20] As glaciers disappear, less water is available for crops during the growing season. The United States will not be spared. Research scientist Gregory J. McCabe of the U.S. Geological Survey claims that an increase in the average temperature of only 1.5 degrees Fahrenheit across the Southwest could compromise the Colorado River's ability to meet the water needs of Nevada and six other states.[110] Already the water level of Lake Mead is low, threatening the water supply of Las Vegas and the Hoover Dam's ability to generate the city's electricity.

The Greenhouse Gas-intense American Diet

H ere's how Al Gore sums up the ecological impact of the American diet: "In the United States, government research shows that with chemical fertilizers, herbicides, and heavy fuel use, U.S. agriculture contributes nearly 20 percent of U.S. CO_2 emissions."[16] Gore would have been more accurate had he said, "20 percent of greenhouse gas emissions," but the message remains. Our diets have a profound impact on the earth's environment.

Agriculture is credited with 6.2 percent of our carbon dioxide emissions, not an insignificant amount. **When considering other associated emissions, the ecological impact of our diets surpasses the impact of our driving.** A 2008 study chronicled by Bijal Trivedi in the *New Scientist* concluded that the annual "foodprint" of the average American household—taking into consideration methane and nitrous oxide as well as CO_2 emissions—is 8.1 tons of CO_2 equivalent (CO_2 eq).[127] That is almost double the 4.4 tons of CO_2 emitted by the average car in one year. Livestock alone account for 18 percent of global greenhouse gases: 9 percent of all CO_2 emissions, 35–40 percent of methane, and 65 percent of nitrous oxide, the latter two emissions having dire consequences for our planet's climate. Methane is 21 times as effective as CO_2 in trapping heat in the atmosphere and nitrous oxide is 296 times as potent as CO_2.

Scientists are trying to mitigate the greenhouse gas emissions attached to farm animals by applying advanced genetics to livestock and crops. Researchers at the University of Guelph, Ontario, are working on developing a geneti-cally modified pig that digests phosphorus more efficiently, reducing phos-phorus content in manure by 65–70 percent. [147] Scientists are also working on changing rumen microbes to reduce the amount of methane produced in the rumen of cows. A dairy cow typically emits four tons of CO_2 annually. [148] A Cornell University scientist found that giving cows recombinant bovine soma-totropin, a biotech hormone that boosts per-cow milk production, reduces the number of cows needed to produce the same amount of milk. Accord-ing to the study, giving the hormone to one million cows would produce the same amount of milk using 157,000 fewer cows, saving 491,000 metric tons of corn, 158,000 tons of soybeans, and achieving a reduction in carbon emissions equivalent to removing 400,000 cars from the roads.[147]

New Zealand has set a very ambitious goal of "carbon neutrality" by 2020. That could be a model for sustainable U.S. agriculture. New Zealand livestock, sixty million sheep and millions of cows, reportedly account for 30–40 percent of the country's greenhouse gas emissions. Agriculture is absolutely central to New Zealand's economy. To make its agriculture sustainable, New Zealand researchers are counting on more energy-efficient feedstock and vaccinations that reduce animal methane emissions.[147]

Our diet also indirectly contributes to deforestation, a major source of greenhouse gas emissions. Agricultural land and grazing acreage increase at the expense of rainforests as demand for food grows. The recent drop in beef consumption as a result of the 2009 recession is believed to be the main reason for the 70 percent drop in conversion of Brazilian rainforest to cattle ranches.[149]

It is important to realize that our diet has profound consequences on three important resources: oil, the atmosphere, and water. Consuming less food, making better food choices, drinking fewer processed beverages, and drinking tap water are sure ways of reducing one's oil consumption, carbon foodprint, and water usage. There is room for significant savings of money, energy, and greenhouse gas emissions in our diet. Substantial savings could be gained by reducing food waste and maintaining a normal weight.

147 Martin Ross, FarmWeek, August 4, 2008, 4

148 Martin Ross, FarmWeek, April 27, 2009, 1

149 Dashka Slatter, Sierra, July/August 2009, 16

Being more judicious about what we eat and how much we eat not only saves resources and reduces greenhouse gas emissions. It improves self-esteem, lengthens lives, and makes people more productive. Obesity was blamed for $45 billion in lost productivity in the workplace in 2008. Being more judicious about our diets would reduce health care expenses. Americans who are 30 percent or more overweight cost our health care system an estimated $147 billion in 2008, according to a study by government scientists. Obesity-related health problems account for 9.1 percent of all medical spending.[131] Obesity is often a precursor to diabetes. The United States spent $174 billion treating diabetes in 2007. New projections show that more than one-third of U.S. adults could suffer from the disease by 2050. Doctor John M.R. Kuhn stated in *Time*, July 7, 2008, "As a physician, I believe obesity is a far greater public health hazard than tobacco. It is associated with an increase in cancer, diabetes, heart disease, depression, gastro-intestinal disorders, heart failure, and the list goes on." Obesity-related problems result in unnecessary pharmaceutical, diagnostic, medical, surgical, and rehabilitation activities that consume human resources, fuel, and other natural resources.

Obesity-related medical costs matter. Many consider rising health-care costs to be the greatest challenge the nation will face in the future as it tries to balance its budget. The cost of providing health care for workers and retirees also will burden U.S. corporations, placing them at a disadvantage vis-à-vis increasingly efficient foreign competitors.

The poor choices individuals make regarding what they eat and what they drink places unnecessary burdens on their own budgets. Purchasing bottled water is a needless expense. You pay more for a bottle of water than an equivalent amount of gasoline. Savings on bottled water and soft drinks could help families meet their mortgage obligations, buy health-care insurance or health club memberships. Bottled water sales, excluding water-cooler sales, was a $217 billion market in the United States in 2007, according to *Beverage Digest*, or about $1,500 per household., The soda market is more than four times bigger than the water market in dollar terms. Soft drinks are also blamed for a significant portion of the obesity problem in children and adults. A typical 12 oz. soda contains the equivalent of ten teaspoons of sugar. Americans consume a whopping 42 pounds of high-fructose corn syrup each year, most of it in the form of sugary drinks.[126]

Another consequence of the American diet is the strain that it puts on the world food supply and prices. Overeating applied upward pressure on food prices here and abroad, making food staples less affordable to the one billion people living on $1 a day and affecting the diets of an additional 1.5 billion living on $2 a day. Overeating contributes to food shortages in poor countries, resulting in riots and the toppling of governments. It has its most significant impact on the emerging economies where food accounts for 30–40 percent of the consumer price index, as compared to 15 percent in the G-7 economies. [150] **Jacques Diouf, the UN's Food and Agricultural Organization (FAO) director general, condemned excess food consumption by the world's obese for some of the price inflation of food products.**

Organic Foods

According to Bijal Triverdi, a writer for the *New Scientist*, Nathan Pelletier, a researcher at Dalhousie University in Halifax, Nova Scotia, found that organically grown grain crops have a much smaller carbon footprint, consuming only 39 percent of the energy and producing only 77 percent of greenhouse gases of their non-organic counterparts.[127] The main reason for the savings is the elimination of nitrogen fertilizers from the cultivation process. Every ton of synthetic nitrogen fertilizer requires the burning of enough natural gas to release 4.6 tons of CO_2 into the atmosphere.[16] Fertilizers account for roughly 1 percent of the world's total energy consumption.[127] Organic farming also has been proved to increase the carbon content of soil.

Organic food section – Organically grown grain crops consume only 39% of the energy and produce only 77% of greenhouse gases of their non-organic counterparts. (Photo: The Author)

---

150 The Economist, "Inflation in Emerging Economies. An Old Enemy Rears Its Head," May 24, 2008, 91–93

The share of farmland used for organic production has been expanding in developed countries, according to the Organization of Economic Cooperation and Development (OECD) report on agriculture and the environment. In 2004, Switzerland had the greatest share of agricultural land area devoted to organic farming at 10 percent, followed by Austria at more than 9.5 percent. Finland and Italy devoted about 7 percent of their land to organic farming, followed by Denmark and Sweden at 6 percent each. The United States had only 0.25 percent of its land under organic cultivation. In 2007, Australia and Uruguay joined the club of countries with 10 percent of their land organically farmed. In 2007, about 76.6 million acres of land around the world carried organic certification to meet the $40 billion international demand for organic foods.

Seafood Diet

No one has done a rigorous comparison of industrial fishing with various aquaculture schemes with respect to energy consumption and emissions. But when eating fish as a source of protein, there are a few facts to consider. Fleets of fishing vessels scouring the seas are completely dependent on fossil fuels. They account for about 1.2 percent of global oil consumption and emit more than 130 thousand tons of CO_2 into the atmosphere every year. They typically provide us with cod, tuna, swordfish, and other deep-water fish. They come with greater ecological baggage than small fish like herring and anchovy, which travel in schools. It is estimated that those small fish can be captured at a fuel cost of about 12 gallons per ton of fish whereas tuna, swordfish, sole, flounder, and cod require up to forty times that amount of fuel.[127] One advantage of relying on wild fish as a source of animal protein is that it does not deplete scarce water resources.

Farm-raised fish vary a lot in their ecological impact. One of the most carbon-intensive stages of fish farming is producing fish-meal. Energy also goes into keeping the water at the right temperature, keeping the fish tanks clean for disease prevention and losses from diseases. Fish with the lowest carbon footprint are the farmed herbivorous species, such as tilapia, carp, bream, and catfish.

Farmers' Markets

Much has been said about the advantages of supporting the local farming community, especially with respect to energy consumption and carbon emissions. Growing food locally reduces the energy needed to bring food to the consumer, but in a much smaller way than one would think. According to a 2008 study published in *Environmental Science & Technology* by Christopher Weber, a researcher at Carnegie Mellon University in Pittsburgh, Pennsylvania, and reported by Triverdi, [127] transportation accounts for only 11 percent of the food's energy consumption and total greenhouse emissions. The majority of greenhouse gases come from the actual production and include CO_2 emissions, methane released from livestock and manure, and nitrous oxide emissions attributed to fertilizer and manure. An advantage not to be underestimated is the benefit of putting money into the local economy.

Pike Place Farmers' Market, Seattle, Washington – Buying locally grown food supports the local farming community and reduces the energy needed for transportation. (Photo: IStock Photo #5214687)

An interesting offshoot of growing food locally is the integration of agriculture with the urban environment. Most American cities have a lot of vacant land. A Brookings Institute study found that seventy major cities averaged 15 percent vacant land area. Chicago is estimated to have twenty thousand acres of vacant land. City Farm, currently farming two acres in Chicago, has plans to expand its operation. It sells heirloom tomatoes, salad greens, and other produce to twenty restaurants and it stocks farm stands. It collects food waste from the restaurants to use as compost.[151] Urban farming is attracting much interest in Detroit, Michigan, a city with forty thousand acres of vacant land.

Will Allen, who played basketball in the American Basketball Association and later professionally in Belgium, founded Growing Power in Milwaukee, Wisconsin, in 1993. He is an ardent promoter of urban gardening, especially in low-income neighborhoods where people might not otherwise have access to fresh and healthy foods. He teaches people how to grow food organically and close to home to cut down on carbon emissions and fuel consumption. He operates urban farms in Chicago as well as Milwaukee.

Agriculture has even started to expand skyward. Most green roofs until now have been created to manage storm water, reduce the urban heat island effect, and save energy. Today, green roofs are also used for garden space. Marc Boucher-Colbert in Portland, Oregon, is growing a variety of produce—lettuce, tomatoes, peppers, cucumbers, eggplants, and summer squash—on the roof of his grocery store. The Uncommon Ground restaurant in Chicago has an organic vegetable rooftop garden that supplies its chef with a variety of vegetables, among them tomatoes, carrots, and peas.[151]

Eli Zabar, owner of the Vinegar Factory, a food market on East Ninety-First Street in New York, has gone one step further. In 1995, he began building greenhouses atop the buildings in which he operated his market. Covering about a half acre, they produced tomatoes, greens, other vegetables, and berries, which Zabar offered in his market.[151] With luck, Zabar pioneered a trend that will gain momentum to reduce the amount of energy consumed to transport food and protect our food supply by diversifying food-production areas, an insurance against price spikes associated with drought, bacterial contamination, labor shortages, or other calamities. It may lead to hydroponic culture in urban high-rise buildings.

We need to take seriously the impact of our eating and drinking habits on our environment as well as on our health. Our diets affect oil consumption, water usage, the availability and affordability of food staples for many around the world, and our greenhouse gas emissions. The good news is that individuals have a lot of control over their eating habits. For the ecologically conscious American, shifting just one day a week from eating red meat and dairy prod-

---

151 Alex Wilson, Environmental Building News, February 2009, 1, 8–15

ucts to eating either chicken, fish or vegetables, fruits and soy products, is more important than buying local food.

Veganism

One sure way to spare some of our most valued resources—arable land, water and oil—while improving one's health is to become a vegetarian, or at least consume less animal protein. Vegetarians also have a lower CO_2 equivalent footprint. Gideon Eshel and Pamela Martin of the University of Chicago calculated that switching from the average American diet to a vegetarian diet could reduce annual emissions by almost 1.5 tons of CO_2 equivalent per person.[127]

Research by the Natural Marketing Institute suggests that only 2 percent of Americans self-identify as vegetarians but you should not be afraid of being marginalized if you adopt veganism.[152] You will be sharing your eating preferences with some leading members of our society. In the November 8–14, 2010, issue of *Bloomberg Businessweek*, Joel Stein lists as vegans former President Bill Clinton; Senator Dennis Kucinich; *Time Magazine* editor and billionaire philanthropist Mort Zuckerman; casino magnate Steve Wynn; pro-footballer Tony Gonzalez; ex-NBA star John Salley; and Bill Ford, executive chairman of the board of Ford Motor Company. Most adopted veganism for health reasons. Steve Wynn was so impressed with the health benefits of veganism that he purchased ten thousand copies of the documentary *Eating* in which Mike Anderson explains the benefits of his strict meat- and oil-free diet. He gave one to each of his employees. "If they're sick, we're picking up the tab," said Wynn. Twitter cofounder Biz Stone adopted veganism for moral reasons after he paid a visit in 2000 to Farm Sanctuary, an animal rescue organization. Few, if any, vegans have given up animal proteins to conserve oil, water, arable land, or to reduce their carbon footprint, but we should be appreciative of the ecological benefits of their dietary choices.

The need to conserve our resources should be a consideration when buying groceries and when eating out. It should be a consideration when deciding where to live, what size house to build, what car to buy, where to vacation. Conservation is key to crafting a sustainable life-style but we should not be lulled into expecting that conservation alone will allow us to meet the needs

152 Kristin Ohlson, Experience Life, The New Veganism, May 2009, 42–44

of the more than one hundred million new Americans who will join us in the next twenty years.

Estimates are that water needs will double in the next twenty years. The world will require 40 percent more food by 2030, 40 percent more energy. The world will use 45 percent more oil in 2030 than it did in 2006, assuming a growth in demand of only 1.6 percent a year. Americans will require an additional seven million barrels of oil each day two decades from now. We must plan to grow more food, generate more stationary energy, extract more water from the hydrologic cycle, and find more oil. Extracting more domestic oil is important because we already depend on imports to satisfy so much of our needs.

U.S. Oil Exploration

The United States first became a net importer of oil in 1948. Imported oil has led to supply anxieties, price spikes, lost jobs, trade deficits, compromised foreign policy decisions and an overall loss of geopolitical clout. It is time we give serious consideration to expanding our own supplies.

Fortunately, the United States is blessed with substantial reserves. Most of the United States' untapped reserves are located in the eastern portion of the Gulf of Mexico, in the Outer Continental Shelf (OCS) surrounding the contiguous forty-eight states, the Arctic National Wildlife Refuge (ANWR) and some areas of Alaska. That oil is untouched because exploration has been banned by federal law for almost thirty years. In 1981, Congress added a rider to a spending bill that barred energy leasing on 85 percent of the OCS surrounding the contiguous forty-eight states, virtually all coastal waters outside the western portion of the Gulf of Mexico and some areas off Alaska. [153] The federal moratoria responded to a blowout on Union Oil's Platform A, six miles offshore from Santa Barbara, California, that spilled an estimated 80,000 to 100,000 barrels of oil in 1969.[154]

The federal offshore drilling ban stemmed from an era in which technology to drill in waters far from shore was in its infancy and had a bad record for spills. For years until BP's Deepwater Horizon drilling rig accident in the Gulf of Mexico on April 20, 2010, the industry had been extracting oil in waters

153 Investor's Business Daily, A Redefined 'GOP': Get Our Petroleum, June 19, 2008, A10

154 Nansen G. Saleri, The Wall Street Journal, May 7, 2010

thousands of feet deep and distant from the coastline without accidents of any ecological impact. Currently, 27 percent of domestic supply comes from offshore sources, mostly from the Gulf of Mexico (1.6 million barrels), and 72 percent of oil production in the Gulf in 2007 came from deepwater drilling. Offshore oil accounts for one-third of the world's oil supply.[154] **According to the Department of the Interior, more than seven billion barrels of oil have been extracted in federal waters since 1985 with less than 0.0001 of a percent spilled.**

The stellar record of offshore exploration and the mounting toll of imports on the U.S. economy prompted a shift in attitude toward offshore exploration. Extracting oil from untouched reserves started attracting support from the general population when motorists started feeling the pain of escalating prices at the pump. A Rasmussen poll released June 17, 2008, revealed that 67 percent of Americans favored drilling for more oil.[155] Public support to open new areas for exploration allowed the Bush administration to overcome opposition to drilling. In September 2008, the ban on oil and gas exploration off the Atlantic and Pacific coasts was allowed to expire.

Offshore drilling continued to elicit contentious debates. The battleground between opponents and proponents of opening up offshore drilling shifted to state legislators, states having jurisdiction over drilling off their coasts. Legislation by the states is necessary to grant the option of opening up OCS resources off their shores. Some state governments along the Atlantic seaboard, notably Virginia and Florida, had warmed to the idea of permitting offshore exploration in the hopes of generating revenue and creating jobs.[153] [156] Offshore drilling is a boon for the coastal economy. Oil- and gas-related businesses contribute $70 billion each year to the economy of the state of Louisiana. In 2008, the oil and gas industries employed 1.8 million people.[157] Following the Gulf spill, Florida Governor Charlie Christ, retracted his support for offshore drilling. To the end of his tenure as governor of California, Arnold Schwarzenegger opposed expanding offshore drilling, even though in 2010 the majority of Californians favored drilling.

---

155 Terry Jones, Investor's Business Daily, "Surging Oil Primes Political Pump for New U.S. Drilling, June 19, 2008, 1

156 Stephen Power, Laura Mackler and Russell Gold, The Wall Street Journal, June 18, 2008

157 Robert Samuelson, Newsweek, May 1/May 18, 2009, 46

Public support for increased energy independence continues to be strong. In December 2009, a Rasmussen poll revealed that 68 percent of Americans favored offshore drilling in domestic waters.[158] On March 21, 2010, in an address at Andrews Air Force Base, President Obama proposed developing traditional sources of energy as well as pursuing new renewable sources. The president talked of offering future federal lease sales in certain deepwater areas in the eastern portion of the Gulf of Mexico and shallow areas in the Atlantic Ocean from Delaware to mid-Florida. The final decision governing which areas would be offered for lease will be part of the 2012-2017 lease plan, which is being developed.[159] Industry executives say the area being discussed for new drilling is far smaller than what was proposed by President Bush's administration. Mr. Obama specifically said there would be no lease sales in Alaska's Bristol Bay, the Pacific coast, northern Atlantic and southern Florida.[159]

Less than one month after President Obama's announcement on new exploration, an explosion on the Deepwater Horizon rig killed eleven workers and started an oil spill of several thousand barrels a day into the waters of the Gulf of Mexico, causing an environmental disaster of unprecedented magnitude that tarnished the extraordinary safety record of U.S. offshore drilling over the past forty years. The accident should be viewed in the context of that record and should not shift our focus away from our most important goal of achieving energy security. The Gulf produces 1.6 million barrels a day and is the main reason U.S. oil production has inched up in the last two years.[154]

We also need to keep in mind that immensely greater human and wildlife suffering and environmental degradation result from our unabated reliance on coal and other fossil fuels than will result from the Gulf spill. The impact of our life-style on the atmosphere affects the lives of hundreds of million people and animals around the globe. Yet our inordinate energy consumption keeps power plants busy burning coal and natural gas and feeds the need for additional plants. Africans and others around the globe suffer from our greenhouse gas emissions without deriving any benefit to compensate for the harm they suffer. We, at least, reap some benefits from oil exploration: high-paying jobs, improved trade balance, better national security, enhanced geopolitical status, and a federal income boost from oil leases, corporate taxes, and personal income taxes.

---

158 Matthew Philips, Newsweek, "Journey to the Center of the Earth," March 22, 2010, 52–55

159 Russell Gold, The Wall Street Journal, April 1, 2010, A-5

Lessons must be learned from BP's Deepwater Horizon accident as were learned from the Challenger space shuttle accident and the Exxon Valdez oil spill. The former led to better management of the risks of space exploration and the latter produced safer tankers. The scandalously close relationship between the regulators and the industry must end. The Minerals Management Service, the agency responsible for enforcing safety standards, must be reformed. The unacceptably inept response of BP to the accident underscores the need for the federal government to set up a strike force to respond to such emergencies. We have fire departments to prevent neighborhoods from burning. We have bomb squads to diffuse explosives. We maintain backup systems to access the space station. We need to have the ability to respond to emergencies at the level of sophistication dictated by circumstances under which the oil companies drill before they are permitted to explore. The agency responsible for supervising the drilling operations and the response team must work with the oil companies in the design of the drilling equipment and the establishment of protocols for exploration to reduce risks and facilitate intervention in the event of an accident. Taxpayers pay for fire protection. The oil industry needs to pay for that protection.

The risks of U.S. oil production are balanced by substantial benefits. How much oil is within U.S. borders is still a matter of conjecture, but it is a significant amount by all accounts. The U.S. government estimates that the deep waters of the Gulf of Mexico hold around 18 billion barrels of oil.[155] (The much-talked-about Lula field off the coast of Brazil holds an estimated 8 billion barrels.) There are even claims that the OCS contains as much as 86 billion barrels. Estimates of the accessible oil in ANWR are usually around 10 billion barrels. The Green River Basin stretching through Wyoming, Colorado, and Utah, and the Bakken Formation in North Dakota and Montana are major deposits. Survey results suggest hundreds of billions of barrels of recoverable oil.[155] The federal government estimates that in the areas under consideration for exploration by President Obama there is between 7.5 billion and 40 billion barrels of oil and gas equivalent. Industry analysts believe those figures are likely low.[159]

The American Petroleum Institute (API) estimates that lifting drilling restrictions in the OCS, ANWR in Alaska and the federal land in the Rockies would increase domestic production of crude oil by 36 percent by 2030 and natural gas by 10 percent.[160] This would amount to about 2 million additional

---

160 John Hart, FarmWeek, December 22, 2008, 11

barrels of oil per day and 5.3 billion extra cubic feet of natural gas per day. **The API further estimates that increased drilling would generate $4 trillion in royalties over the life of the operation and create 160,000 jobs by 2030.**[160] Revenue generated should be an important consideration in weighing the pros and cons of offshore exploration.

The political opposition to expansion of drilling in presently barred areas still remains strong. A similar debate is taking place in Norway, a country of large oil and gas reserves. Norway is the world's fifth biggest producer of natural gas and a substantial producer of oil. Norwegians are expressing concern that when the oil and gas they export are burned abroad, they generate a lot of emissions in addition to the emissions released in the process of extracting these fuels from below the North Sea. It is the subject of a far-reaching political debate. There are calls to limit new exploration for oil and gas to reduce hydrocarbon exports. Some think Norway needs to go to that extent to fight global warming. Norway was one of the first countries to adopt a carbon tax back in 1991 and its government has pledged to make the country carbon neutral by 2030, ahead of its previous target date of 2050.[161]

Passage of legislation to allow drilling in new areas would not reduce oil imports until years from now. The EIA estimates that at the earliest, the first new offshore oil would reach market in 2017. It would also come at a cost of enormous capital investments. Conservation supported by an effective gasoline tax, fuel efficiency mandated by ever-higher CAFE standards, the development of truly oil-sparing alternative fuels, and plans to reduce industrial and residential oil consumption are all measures that need to be promoted. Together they would greatly reduce our need for oil, align our total energy consumption closer to that of our competitors, and reduce our country's carbon emissions.

Canadian Oil Supply

What about relying on Canada for our oil supply? Canada already supplies 19 percent of our oil imports. It is a most dependable supplier. The flow of oil from our northern neighbor is not vulnerable to storms or political embargoes. Canada is one of a few countries, along with Norway and England that does not misuse its oil riches. Canada welcomes foreign oil companies

---

161 The Economist, "Norway and the Environment. Binge and Purge, January 24, 2009, 28–30

and shares our values and respect for laws. Unfortunately, most of Canada's oil reserves consist of tar sands. Tar-sand deposits consist of a residue created when conventional oil escaped from its original location deep in the earth's crust and was degraded into tar by ground water and bacteria.[40] Canadian oil sands contain enough recoverable oil to rank Canada as the country with the second-largest oil reserves in the world after Saudi Arabia. The Alberta government estimates that the province's three main oil sands deposits contain 173 billion barrels of economically recoverable oil at today's prices but puts the total size of the deposits at 1.7 trillion barrels. Most of that tarry bitumen is located in the northeast portion of the province, around the town of Fort MacKay in the boreal forest that covers about 2 million square miles of Northern Canada.[162]

The main problem is that, increasingly, more of the oil that we import from Canada comes from oil sands now that conventional oil wells are less productive. Presently, it accounts for about 50 percent. The process of transforming bitumen into oil is so energy-intense that it emits as much as three times more carbon dioxide than is produced by the extraction of oil from conventional oil fields. The accelerated rate of extraction of oil from tar sands is the main reason why Canada's greenhouse gas emissions have risen 25 percent since 1999, making it one of the worst performing of the nations that signed the Kyoto protocol.[163]

The Canadian government is concerned about its carbon emissions but is not prepared to curtail its oil sands operation, which is expected to yield about two million barrels a day by 2020, an increase of roughly two-thirds over current production. It is promoting and funding carbon capture and storage (CCS) technology, but experts say CCS projects are much too expensive for consideration. Cost estimates for capturing CO_2 from the natural-gas-fired-boilers used to cook tar sands run between U.S. $216 and U.S. $240 per metric ton, according to an independent commission. Considering that one-tenth of a metric ton of CO_2 is emitted for each barrel of oil produced from the oil sands, CCS would add more than $20 to the cost of each barrel. [164]

---

162 Robert Kunzig, National Geographic, "The Canadian Oil Boom. Scraping Bottom, March 2009, 39–60

163 William Underhill, Newsweek, "Canada Plays Dirty," December 14, 2009, 10

164 Edward Welsch, The Wall Street Journal, "Canada's Oil Sands Bring High Cost, January 13, 2010, B4B

The impact on the environment of burning gasoline refined from tar sands is starting to matter. The other limitation inherent to Canadian oil imports is that it continues to be a drain on U.S. wealth.

■ Chapter Three: What You Must Do For Your Country:

* Create a favorable political climate for fuel-tax increases
* Demand higher fuel-efficiency standards
* Drive one of the most fuel-efficient cars available
* Reduce the number of miles you drive. Drive slower
* Use public transportation
* Quit drinking bottled water
* Decrease your consumption of red meat
* Don't waste food
* Maintain a normal weight
* Support the exploitation of our own oil and gas reserves

Chapter 4: Stationary Energy

A merica's extraordinary appetite for energy is not limited to oil. America's total energy consumption per capita is about twice that of the other main industrialized countries, France, Germany, Japan, and the UK. While the amount of energy use continued to grow in the United States up to the onset of the 2008-2009 recession, it was declining in Europe. In 2007, before the economic downturn, it decreased by 5.6 percent in Germany while that country's economy grew by 2.6 percent. The economic downturn that gripped the United States in the second half of 2008 coupled with perhaps unrelated energy conservation measures resulted in a decrease in energy consumption of 5 percent from April 2008 to April 2009, one of the few benefits of the recession. It is nevertheless expected to rise by more than 40 percent by 2030, according to the Energy Information Administration

The electricity-generation industry is by far the most voracious consumer of energy in the United States and in the world. More energy is spent generating electricity than is expended by our entire transportation system—40 percent compared to 28.5 percent. Heating our homes and our commercial and industrial buildings accounts for another significant portion of our energy consumption.

Coal and natural gas provide almost 80 percent of our stationary energy.

Coal

C oal is the earth's single-largest fossil-fuel reservoir of hydrocarbon. The energy contained in the world's coal reserves is greater than the energy of the known reserves of either oil or natural gas. It is plentiful throughout the world but few countries match our reserves. We have about 27 percent of the world's recoverable coal. It has been stated that "The coal in the ground in Illinois alone has more energy than all of the oil in Saudi Arabia."

The popularity of coal as a source of energy is not surprising. Coal is ubiquitous and has a high energy density. Most populous countries have substantial reserves. The extraction does not require any sophisticated technology, nor does the process of transforming it into electricity. Each year, the world burns

6.2 billion tons of coal, providing 41 percent of the world's electricity. Americans are even more dependent on it, drawing 49 percent of their electricity from the 1.1 billion tons that are burned in the United States. Australia is also infamous for its reliance on coal. Coal generates about 83 percent of its electricity and its coal exports to China help feed that country's coal-fired power plants, which supply more than 70 percent of China's electricity. China burns more than twice as much coal as the United States and projections are for that gap to widen dramatically by 2030.[18] China opens, on average, one coal-fired plant every week.[18]

Presently, the United States has more than six hundred coal-fired power plants. In 2009, more coal-fired power plants came on line than in any year in nearly two decades, as projects started several years ago were completed. Nearly two dozen plants are scheduled to start up in the next three years and twenty-two are under construction.[165] Some of the plants under construction will replace older ones scheduled for closure.[165]

The power-generating industry faces many challenges. The availability of water to operate thermal power plants, concerns about climate change, regulations on mercury and other contaminants, and moderation in electricity consumption are playing havoc with the industry's long-term plans. Federal legislation to cap greenhouse gas emissions looms large over plant development, coal being the most carbon-intensive way to generate electricity. Many utility companies are canceling or postponing plans to build coal plants. NV Energy shelved a $5 billion, 1,500-megawatt plant in eastern Nevada. Instead, it will turn to solar energy and other renewable sources. There are also state legislative roadblocks. As of May 1, 2009, ninety-seven coal-fired power plants had been rejected since 2001, nine having been denied approval in the first five months of 2009 alone.

Power plants are the second-largest users of fresh water. Power plants, whether running on coal, natural gas, uranium, or oil, consume enormous amounts of water. A typical 500-megawatt coal-fired power plant that recirculates its water uses around six thousand gallons of water per minute. Natural gas-powered plants consume almost as much. Southern Company, an electric utility based in Atlanta, Georgia, temporarily shut down some of its power plants in the summer of 2007 because of drought. Early in 2008, Duke Energy's

---

165 Mark Peters, The Wall Street Journal, March 31, 2010

McGuire Nuclear Station's water supply was less than one foot above its minimum level of operation.

About 40 percent of the freshwater usage in America is used to cool power plants, almost as much as consumed by agriculture. "We cannot build more power plants without realizing that they impinge on our freshwater supplies," warned Michael E. Webber, author, Scientific American Earth.[110] The amount of water needed to cool the plants impacts the available supply to everyone else.[110] Power plants are facing popular and legislative opposition on the basis of their water demand. Coal plants and nuclear-fired plants require 20,000 to 60,000 gallons of water for each megawatt of electricity generated, nuclear plants being the most demanding.[110] Wind turbines and solar systems require no water to produce electricity.

Coal has always had the image of a dirty fuel, primarily because of its particulate emissions (soot) and its toxic pollutants, mercury and sulfur dioxide, which were implicated in acid rain. It has been associated with asthma, other respiratory illnesses, and heart problems and it is blamed for many deaths. In China alone, the extraction of coal causes on average 4,000 deaths annually and air pollution attributed to the burning of coal was believed to result in 750,000 premature deaths in 2006 alone, according to the World Bank.[18]

Coal has been the focus of congressional legislation in the past. In 1970 Congress enacted the Clean Air Act, which mandated that the federal government and states regulate emissions from stationary sources and mobile sources (vehicles). That legislation gave birth to the Environmental Protection Agency for the purpose of enforcing the new law. In 1986 the Department of Energy initiated the Clean Coal Technology Program to regulate emissions of sulfur dioxide and nitrogen oxide in response to the growing problems of acid rain.

In this age of new awareness of the implications of dumping CO_2 into the atmosphere, coal's reputation has been further tarnished. Coal-fired plants are responsible for perhaps 8 billion of the 28 billion to 30 billion tons of created CO_2 released every year worldwide. **In 2007, U.S. coal power generation released 2.56 billion tons or 42 percent of the country's CO_2 emission, a full 80 percent of the power-generation industry's total emissions.** The eight plants completed last year will emit an estimated 170 tons of CO_2 each day.[165] In Wise County, Virginia, a plant being built by Dominion, over activists' opposition, will emit 5.3 million tons of CO_2 a year into the atmosphere, roughly the equivalent emission of 1 million cars. It is reasonable to expect, as the United States moves toward joining the international community to rein in greenhouse gas emissions, that coal-fired power plants will be the focus of efforts to reduce greenhouse gases. A coal-fired power plant produces roughly twice as much CO_2 per unit of electricity generated as does a plant that runs on natural gas, the second-worst electricity-generating fuel. The oldest plants are the dirtiest. Plants built before 1980 emit nearly three-quarters of the industry's carbon but they constitute less than half of all coal-fired plants.[166]

Coal mining   Coal-fired power plant

In 2007, U.S. coal power generation released 2.56 billions tons or 42 percent of the country's CO_2 emissions. (Photos: IStock Photo #2688461, 2846059)

Some moderation in coal usage in the United States has been observed in the last few years. U.S. coal production had risen steadily since 1970, from 610 million tons to a peak of 1.16 billion tons in 2006. But output has leveled off and even decreased in the last two years. In 2007, production dipped slightly to 1.14 billion tons, only 20 million tons over the 1998 output.[167] Power companies are keenly aware of the impact of burning coal on the environment, and they face looming, costly regulations. Hence, they are taking steps to improve the efficiency of their coal-fired plants and investing in other cleaner energy sources. Jim Rogers, the CEO of Duke Energy, which operates twenty coal-fired plants emitting a combined 100 million tons of CO_2 each year, said in an

166 David Biello, Scientific American Earth 3.0, Volume 18, Number 5, 2008, 34–41

167 Max Rust, Phil Geib, and Michael Hawthorne, Chicago Tribune, February 3, 2009

interview in April 2009 that he has plans to decarbonize his company by 2050. But Rogers, whose North Carolina plant alone burns 19,000 tons of coal every day is in no rush to start the process; he has retained powerful lobbyists to oppose legislation and regulation to reduce carbon emissions. During the same interview, Jim Hansen, NASA's climate specialist, opined that to avoid climate disasters the world needs to impose a moratorium on new coal-fired plants now and phase out existing plants in the next twenty years. Some governors are already on board. The governors of Kansas and Florida, among others, are blocking new plants.

Carbon Sequestration

"The key to having our coal and burning it, too, is carbon capture and storage."
Dashka Slater, Sierra, July/August 2009

"Extracting carbon dioxide from power plant exhausts and storing it underground may be the only hope to avoid a climate change catastrophe from burning fossil fuels." David Biello, Scientific American, Earth 3.0, Summer 2009

Carbon sequestration is one strategy that is being considered to offset some of the climate effects of burning fossil fuels. Its main application is to store in safe places the waste CO_2 captured before it leaves the smokestacks. Unfortunately, the technology to capture and store carbon is still mostly at the demonstration stage but many researchers are experimenting with the process here and abroad. [168]

The process of carbon capture and storage (CCS) consists of three stages. First, CO_2 must be separated from the rest of the emissions. Second, the CO_2 needs to be compressed into a liquid form. Third, it must be stored underground in an escape-proof area.

Presently, there are three types of technology to capture CO_2 at power plants. One involves burning coal in a pure oxygen environment to produce flue gases that consist mostly of CO_2 simplifying the process of isolating it. The second uses various chemicals added to the smokestacks to separate CO_2 from the rest of the exhaust gases. The third is gasification, in which coal is

168 The Economist, "Carbon Capture and Storage. Trouble in Store," March 7th, 2009, 74–75

first converted into synthetic natural gas before being burned, allowing efficient CO_2 capture. All methods of capturing Co2 are expensive, adding about $0.04 per kilowatt-hour.

The next stage consists of compressing the CO_2 gas into a liquid, reducing it to one-six-hundredth of its original volume for ease of transportation. It can then be sold to potential users, such as makers of carbonated beverages or fire extinguishers. The 180-megawatt Warrior Run power plant in Maryland captures 96 percent of its CO_2 emissions for use in fire extinguishers. CO_2 is also sold to oil companies for injection into their wells to force out more oil. Injecting CO_2 into the ground is a practice already in use in North America to assist in the extraction of oil. The United States has more than a hundred oil fields using CO_2 injections to force more oil out of the ground. The Great Plains Synfuels plant in North Dakota has shipped as much as 2 million metric tons of liquid CO_2 a year to Weyburn Oil Field in Saskatchewan since 2000 to enhance the oil-recovery operation. Surplus CO_2 would be shipped, mostly by pipeline, to a suitable underground repository. The United States already has about 3,600 miles of CO_2 pipelines.[168]

Storage technology is not terribly complicated. It consists of boring wells deep into the ground into areas under impermeable layers. The liquid CO_2 is then forced into the ground into microscopic holes where it eventually dissolves into the brine that shares the pore space or over longer time spans, forms carbonate minerals with the surrounding rock. The Department of Energy estimates that the United States has the world's largest storage capacity at about 3,911 billion metric tons of CO_2, according to a 2008 atlas, more than enough for the 3.2 billion metric tons of CO_2 emitted each year by the approximately 1,700 largest industrial sources in the country.[169] Russia has the second-largest storage capacity, 2.1 billion metric tons, and Canada the third at 1.3 billion.

Small amounts of CO_2 have already been injected in safe repositories. BP and its partners have been pumping a million metric tons of liquid CO_2 a year into a deep saline aquifer in Algeria since 2004. Statoil Hydro of Norway, the world's largest CCS operator has been storing CO_2 stripped from its natural gas operation since 1996. It has stored more than 12 million metric tons of CO_2 under the North Sea.[168] Its incentive has been a Norwegian government tax on

169 Daniel Biello, Scientific American, "Storing Carbon in Fossil Fuels. Where It Comes From: Deep Underground," April 8, 2009

carbon of roughly $50 a metric ton. Olav Kårstad, an adviser for the company, stated, "It costs a fraction of the tax." [169] Statoil also injects about 1 million tons of CO_2 a year under the Saharan desert at its Salah natural gas plant in Algeria.[170]

CCS features prominently in all the plans to use coal in an environmentally acceptable way. Despite all the enthusiasm about CCS, however, there is not a single big power plant using CCS anywhere in the world.[168] Duke Energy CEO Jim Rogers estimates that it would cost $4 billion to build a CCS plant. There is only one small plant in America capable of capturing and storing CO_2, the Basin Electric Power Cooperative in North Dakota. The main challenge rests with the first stage: separating CO_2 from the rest of the emissions.

While the United States is looking for solutions, Europe has committed the most government funding for projects on CCS– $10.5 billion vs. $5.1 billion in the United States. The Italian pilot project at Enel's coal-fired plant near the city of Brindisi, is one of EU-sponsored initiatives. Solvents developed at the plant will be used at Enel's Porto Tolle plant with the goal to capture 1 million metric tons of CO_2 a year, or 90 percent of the 2,000 megawatts plant's carbon emissions.[170]

FutureGen, the highly publicized 275-megawatt power plant was the United States' first attempt at zero emission. It was to be built in Mattoon, Illinois, but lost its funding commitment from the Bush administration at the end of 2007. FutureGen's approach was to cook coal in a low-oxygen environment, creating a fuel gas made of hydrogen and carbon monoxide. The carbon would then be converted to carbon dioxide, compressed, and pumped underground while the hydrogen would be burned to generate electricity. The Bush administration spent an estimated $2.5 billion on advanced coal technology— a substantial amount, but far less than the $15 billion to $30 billion needed over the next ten years, according to estimates by CCS proponents.[171]

The Obama administration has picked up where the Bush administration left off. "FutureGen 2.0" calls for retrofitting an idled power plant in Meredosia, Illinois. It would be equipped with cutting-edge "oxy-combustion" technology using superheated oxygen. The process burns coal with less CO_2 emission, simplifying the process of capturing the remaining emissions. The isolated CO_2

170 Alessandra Migliaccio and Jeremy Van Loon, Bloomberg Businessweek, April 4-April 10, 2011, 59–60

171 Michael D. Lemonick, Scientific American, Earth 3.0, December 2008, 60–67

would then be piped to Decatur, Illinois, to take advantage of Archer Daniels Midland sequestration capabilities.[172] Pending federal approvals, ground will be broken in the fall of 2012.

States are also funding some research. Illinois at the end of 2008 appropriated $18 million to a Taylorsville plant that "would capture half its CO_2 emissions and either pump the gases deep underground or pipe them to oil fields in the Gulf of Mexico."[172] Illinois geologists and Archer Daniels Midland Company of Decatur, Illinois, started on a project to store CO_2 deep in the ground with the goal of developing a storage model for carbon sequestration. The Illinois project consists of taking the CO_2 emissions from ADM's ethanol plant, removing the moisture, and injecting the CO_2 into the ground at a depth of 7,000 to 8,000 feet. By injecting carbon dioxide into the ground through an injection well at a pressure of 1,500 pounds per square inch, its volume will be reduced to one-fourth of 1 percent of its original volume. Drilling of the well started at the beginning of 2009. The project is one of seven projects funded by the U.S. Department of Energy.[171]

The technology that uses chemicals to reduce CO_2 emissions is being tested in Pleasant Prairie, Wisconsin. Wisconsin Electric and the Electric Power Research Institute are testing a process that uses an ammonia-based chemical to bind CO_2 in a smokestack so it can be sequestered. Unfortunately, the reaction removes only a little more than 1 percent of the plant's emissions.[173]

Much is at stake in finding "environmentally correct" ways to utilize coal. Coal has applications even beyond being burned to produce electricity. Coal-liquefaction is a process that transforms coal into synthetic oil. This technology is used today in South Africa where three coal liquefaction plants produce about 150,000 barrels of oil a day. One ton of coal generates about two barrels of synthetic oil.

The United States and the rest of the world are a long way from using coal in an environmentally acceptable manner, considering the issues associated with mining in addition to greenhouse gas emissions, but any progress in mitigating the effects of burning coal would benefit the United States and the planet. The most effective incentive to clean up the process of burning coal is to make the power-generating industry pay for its CO_2 emissions. That was the incentive that prompted Statoil Hydro to implement CCS in the 1990s. The

172 Martin Ross, Farm Week, November 3, 2008, 4

173 Matthew L. Wald, Scientific American Earth 3.0, Volume 18, Number 5, 2008, 26–33

United States' failure to set an effective mechanism for pricing CO_2 pollution to make the process economically feasible has caused inaction in this country.

Geoengineering

While some are struggling with how to prevent CO_2 emissions from reaching the atmosphere, others are focusing their efforts on removing CO_2 from the atmosphere or mitigating the effects of atmospheric CO_2 on the climate.

Geoengineering is the science of remediating the created causes of climate change. Technologies being explored include hazing the stratosphere to prevent sunlight from reaching the Earth's surface and sucking excess carbon out of the atmosphere using chemical processes or plants.

Some scientists have proposed making the atmosphere more reflective by releasing chemicals into the stratosphere to form small sulfate particles, like those spewed by volcanoes, to produce a screen. Sulfur dioxide and sulfuric acids are two chemicals that are capable of forming small particles of sulfate when released as a vapor at high altitude. Drones, or newly designed aircraft, have been proposed as vehicles that could eject the chemicals at altitudes of sixty-five thousand to eighty thousand feet. Investments of one billion to two billion dollars a year could be sufficient to cool the earth by one to two degrees, a small fraction of the cost of avoiding greenhouse gas emissions or preventing their escape into the atmosphere.

Such technologies have many detractors who claim they distract from the efforts of reducing emissions; they fear their deployment might produce unintended consequences. Hazing would damage the ozone layer, allowing more ultraviolet radiation to reach the earth's surface. The hydrologic cycle would be affected. Every computer model of chemically induced stratospheric haze shows some decrease in rainfall, especially in China.[174]

Removing Co_2 from the atmosphere is less controversial. It is a function that has been carried out by plants since the beginning of time. Many scientists are focused on ways to enhance the process of photosynthesis. The novel approach consists of forcing air through scrubbers that chemically extract the CO_2 from the atmosphere, concentrate it, and sequester it underground.[175] This energy-intense process is not finding much support.

---

174 The Economist, November 6th, 2010, 99–102

175 The Economist, "Carbon Capture. Scrubbing Alaska," March 7, 2009, 22–23

Considering all the issues relative to the presence of increasing amounts of CO_2 in the atmosphere, the focus should be on deriving more of our energy from carbon-benign sources and finding ways to reduce energy consumption.

Natural Gas

N atural gas has been touted as one of America's solutions to reducing the country's oversized carbon footprint. It is much less offensive to the atmosphere than coal. Figure 6 compares the emission levels of several pollutants for natural gas, oil and coal. Natural gas wins for most pollutants.

Fossil Fuel Emission Levels

Pollutant	Natural Gas	Oil	Coal
Carbon dioxide	117,000	164,000	208,000
Carbon monoxide	40	33	208
Nitrogen oxides	92	448	457
Sulfur dioxide	1	1,122	2591
Particulates	7	84	2744
Mercury	0.000	0.007	0.016

Figure 7: Fossil Fuel Emission Levels in Pounds per Billion BTU of Energy Output; Source: Energy Information Agency, 1998, NaturalGas.org

In 2007, the United States met 24 percent of its total energy demand from natural gas. Natural gas supplied about 64.9 million residential customers and 5.5 million commercial and industrial customers. Natural gas also was used to power 120,000 vehicles, mostly trucks and buses and a small number of cars. In 2007 domestic sources produced more than 88 percent of United States consumption.[176]

The United States has a lot of gas in the ground, but as Tony Meggs, BP's recently retired group vice president for research and technology, said in 2009, "The issue is not whether it's there as much as whether you can get it out at any reasonable cost."[177] The United States' reserve of natural gas is estimated at 6

---

176 Daniel Yergin, The Wall Street Journal, January 23, 2007

177 Thomas K. Grose, U.S. News & World Report, "Can Natural Gas Break Our Oil Habit?" April 2009,

trillion cubic meters, a substantial amount but less than one-tenth of the combined reserves of Russia and Iran. The following bar graph lists the countries that hold the largest natural gas reserves. Their reserves are listed in trillion cubic meters (1 cubic meter = 9 cubic feet).

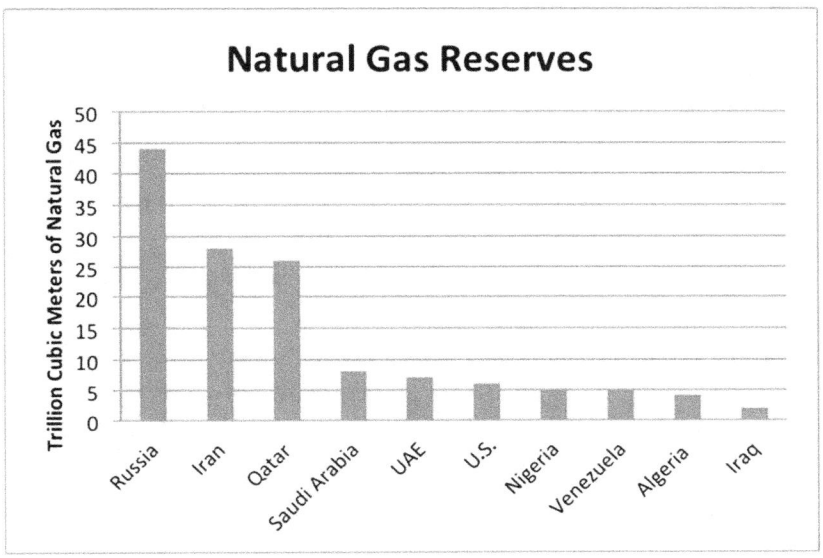

Figure 7: Natural Gas Reserves; Source: The Economist, Pocket World in Figures, 2011 edition

The three countries with the largest reserves, Russia, Iran, and Qatar, have more than 55 percent of the world's proven reserves.[177] Those same countries benefit from large reserves of another strategic commodity: oil. We should be concerned that those three countries are in the process of forming a cartel that will be headquartered in Doha, Qatar. Russia already draws enormous clout from its natural gas exports. It is currently the main supplier of this hydrocarbon to many European countries. Lithuania depends on Russian natural gas for 100 percent of its supplies; the Czech Republic, for 80 percent; Greece, for 78 percent; Hungary, for 75 percent; Poland, for 70 percent; Turkey, for 62 percent; and Germany, for 42 percent. Americans must realize that the more natural gas they import, the more strategic power they confer to Russia and other countries with large reserves. Energy policies will be a key factor in the new world order.

25–27

Domestic supplies currently meet most of our needs. But the fact that our reserves are dwarfed by the reserves of countries that also own another strategic source of America's energy—oil—adds to the imperative of being self-sufficient for natural gas by using electricity more efficiently and accessing more of our own reserves.

Recent advances in extraction technology hold promise. Mitchell Energy, a small firm, pioneered a technical breakthrough to access vast new reserves. The technique, referred to as "fracking", consists of horizontal drilling and hydraulic fracturing. The new drilling technique allows the drill bit to penetrate the earth vertically, and then turn sideways and continue drilling horizontally for hundreds or even thousands of meters. Hydraulic fracturing involves blasting a mix of water, sand, and a cocktail of chemicals into the rock formulation that contains the natural gas, shattering the rock and allowing the gas to seep to the well for extraction.[178]

These techniques are allowing access to vast reserves of shale gas at an attractive cost. New shale prospects are spread across North America. The Barnett Shale in Texas and the Marcellus Shale that stretches from Tennessee to New York are the two standout reserves. The Marcellus Shale may contain 490 trillion cubic feet of gas, enough to heat U.S. homes and power electric plants for twenty years, according to Terry Engelder, professor of geosciences at Pennsylvania State University. In 2009 the Barnett Shale and other reservoirs previously considered unexploitable were supplying 14 percent of our gas consumption. As a result, the United States overtook Russia as the world's biggest producer of natural gas, extracting 593.4 billion cubic meters of gas, almost 66 billion cubic meters more than Russia.[179]

The economic impact of exploiting these previously inaccessible reserves are impressive. Thousands of jobs have been created. In 2009, just in Pennsylvania, 44,000 jobs and $389 million in taxes came from gas drilling according to a report by Jim Efstathiou, Jr. published in the March 7-March 13, 2011 issue of *Bloomberg Businessweek*. Owners of land sitting atop shale gas reserves stand to benefit handsomely. Signing bonuses can range from $2,000 to $5,000 per acre and royalties paid on the value of the gas extracted can reach 20 percent.

Increasing domestic production of natural gas is also important from a trade balance perspective. There is talk in the industry that the United States

178 The Economist, "Natural gas. An Unconventional Glut", March 13th, 2010, 72–74

179 The Economist, Pocket World in Figures, 2011 Edition, 55

will become a net exporter of natural gas. Ports for receiving liquefied natural gas (LNG) imports, mostly from Russia, that are under construction or in the planning stage on the west coasts of Canada and the U.S. are now being thought of as future export terminals.[178] In the summer of 2010, Cheniere Energy Partners applied to the Department of Energy to add liquefaction capabilities to its facility at Sabine Pass, Louisiana. The shift in the gas market has even caused Gazprom to postpone development of its Shtokman gas field in the Barents Sea. [178] Natural gas also has been promoted as a solution to our dependence on foreign oil. T. Boone Pickens, a high profile Texas oil tycoon, has been leading the most public campaign in support of natural gas. He advocates substituting natural gas for gasoline to power our cars and trucks. This idea has not gained much support in the United States but access to vast new reserves gives impetus to the idea. Converting the country's 8 million semi-trailer trucks to natural gas could halve the U.S. import of Middle Eastern oil, according to Randy Eresman, head of Encana, a Canadian gas company. Europeans and South Americans are already fueling up with natural gas.

The technical advances developed in the United States also have geopolitical ramifications. Shale being ubiquitous, new techniques offer opportunities to access vast reserves of gas throughout the world, further shifting the balance of power underpinned by oil and gas production. China, India, and Australia have vast reserves of "unconventional" gas and so does Europe, until now uncomfortably dependent on Russian supplies. The International Energy Agency estimates the total global unconventional reserves to be about 921 trillion cubic meters, more than five times the size of proven conventional reserves.[178] Other innovations are being contemplated. Liquefying natural gas at its point of extraction in remote offshore locations and shipping it directly to its destination would simplify the whole process. There is even talk of exploiting the methane that is trapped in permafrost, further increasing the scope of new production.[180]

Natural gas also has the potential to play a major role in the U.S.'s effort to drastically reduce its greenhouse gas emissions. According to the Energy Information Administration, natural gas-fired electricity generation is expected to increase dramatically over the next twenty years. Already, most of the new electricity generation in the United States comes from natural gas. Gasifying the country's power generation could easily be accelerated since coal-fired

---

180 The Economist, "Unconventional Gas. This Changes Everything", March 13th, 2010, 16–17

plants can be made to burn natural gas. The country's gas-fired capacity is more than double its actual production capacity. A price of $30 a ton on carbon would quickly displace a lot of coal, according to industry analysts. Ironically, proponents of a carbon tax might see less opposition to the political process. Oil companies are rapidly increasing their stake in natural gas, and car manufacturers stand to benefit from the lower emissions credited to plug-in electric cars if power generators draw more of their electricity from the more carbon-benign natural gas. Both industries have historically opposed any limitation on carbon emissions.

Some environmentalists are cool to the benefits of new sources of natural gas. They point to the danger of overreliance on unconventional gas at the expense of renewable sources of electricity. In spite of its new-found abundance, natural gas exists in finite quantity. It is a fossil fuel that emits considerable amounts of carbon dioxide and its extraction is still a messy process. Lawmakers in Congress want to study the ecological impact of the hydraulic fracturing and the Environmental Protection Agency has raised concerns about potential risks of new extraction methods. The results of the Agency's study of the effects of fracking on drinking water is expected in 2014. While there has been no documentation of fracking fluids contaminating drinking water, the Delaware River Basin Commission, which manages the watershed that supplies drinking water to 15 million people in New York, Pennsylvania, New Jersey and Delaware has put gas drilling on hold while it drafts rules.

Shale exploration is also likely to draw more opposition in densely populated Europe. The French government ordered moratoriums on shale exploration early in 2011 in response to environmental pressure from José Bové, a French activist. On March 11, Prime Minister Francois Fillon extended the ban until June when reports on the environmental and economic effects are due. The French company, Total, and other companies, that were awarded permits a year ago, were set to start drilling outside Paris and near Bordeaux. Bové, a Green party deputy, is taking his battle to the European Parliament.

Considering that the United States' per capita energy consumption is about twice that of many industrialized countries blunting the country's competitive edge and considering the ecological impact of energy generation, more emphasis needs to be placed on measures to reduce energy consumption.

Energy Conservation

Individuals have many energy-saving opportunities that do not require much sacrifice. Twenty-two percent of all electricity used in the United States is for lighting. Don't leave lights on in your garage, your closets, your bathrooms, and other spaces when no one is in those rooms. Install the most energy-efficient light fixtures available. In 2005 the U.S. Energy Information Administration (EIA), determined that 31 percent of total residential energy consumption was from appliances and electronics, an 84 percent surge from 1978. Unplug electronic devices when not in use to avoid drawing standby energy. According to the EIA report referenced above, a full 20 percent of residential energy consumption was from water heating. Install the most energy-efficient water-heating system available; lower the thermostat of your water-heater; switch to cold-water detergents and use hot water efficiently. Forty-nine percent of residential energy use is for the purpose of space heating and cooling. Challenge your family to cut energy consumption. Review your utility bills and compare your previous month's usage to the same month the previous year. Involve the whole family. Set goals and offer rewards if goals are met. Educate family members about the issues relative to excessive energy consumption. Understanding the issues is crucial to energy conservation.

Many opportunities exist for conserving electricity outside the home. How often do you drive past playgrounds late in the evening and see floodlights illuminating soccer fields, baseball fields, or other large areas when it has been raining all evening? How often do you see parking lots illuminated when there is plenty of daylight to assure people's security because no one adjusted the timer as daylight hours changed? How often do you see highways illuminated all day long? How often have you observed elevators operating at airports and retail outlets when no one is using them? In most countries of Europe and Asia, elevators operate only when triggered by pedestrians. Our state, civic, and business leaders must set examples of responsible use of energy and other resources to support individuals' commitments. Reduction in electricity consumption is important because every saved kilowatt-hour of electricity avoids the need to generate 2.2 kilowatt-hours since, on average, 2.2 kWh of electricity are lost in transmission for every kWh used.

Many opportunities for savings exist in businesses and industries. According to the Pacific Gas and Electric Food Service Technology Center, commercial food-service equipment, primarily in restaurant kitchens, consumes over $10 billion of energy per year in the United States with as much as 80 percent of that energy wasted by poor management and inefficient equipment.[181] Because chefs usually don't pay the bills, they are unmotivated to save energy. Some of America's largest corporations realize the economic benefits of trimming their energy consumption and embrace the responsibility to be eco-friendly. Linda Fisher, chief sustainability officer at DuPont, argued that the starting point is to find out the size of a company's current carbon footprint. "We find with energy and greenhouse gases, if you start to measure, people reduce usage." DuPont has gone from environmental villain to darling of the green movement by slashing energy usage and greenhouse gas emissions to 72 percent below 1990 levels while increasing business more than 30 percent. DuPont claims it has saved $3 billion over the past fifteen years with its conservation steps.[181]

Energy Efficiency: Negawatts

Due to intrinsic inefficiencies, 33 units of energy consumed at the point of use require 100 units of primary energy.

Most studies conclude that energy efficiency is the most sustainable way and the most cost-effective way to curb energy consumption and carbon emissions. A report published in 2009 by McKinsey & Company concluded that widespread deployment of energy-efficiency measures could decrease energy consumption by 23 percent of projected demand by 2020. It calculated that energy-sparing measures could result in $1.2 trillion in savings, far exceeding the $520 billion investment required to implement them. [182]

Since 1970 energy efficiency has met about three-fourths of the demand for new energy-related services. According to John Laitner, director of economic analysis of the American Council for an Energy Efficient Economy, "The energy-related challenges of the 21st century require a dramatic shift—from an emphasis on energy use to an emphasis on energy efficiency."[183] Energy efficiency implies building more efficient appliances, such as refrigerators, water heaters, and washer-dryers. It implies building energy-efficient motors and

---

181 Bret Schulte, U.S. News & World Report, October 9, 2006, 24

182 Popular Mechanics, "We Have to drill our Way Out of the Energy Dilemma, July 2010, 78

183 Industry Week, "Growing the Energy Efficiency Market," July 2008, 22

fuel-efficient cars, trucks, and aircraft. Simply by buying more efficient refrigerators over the years, Americans have saved more than 200 terawatt hours annually, according to Art Rosenfeld of the California Energy Commission.[184] **Steven Chu, Energy Secretary, remarked that the energy saved from the roughly 150 million refrigerators in use today in the United States relative to 1974 standards is more than all the wind and solar energy that is now being generated in the country.**[185]

In America, all buildings account for 36 percent of total energy use, and 30 percent of greenhouse gas emissions.[186] Owners of America's 4.8 million commercial buildings expend $107.9 billion on energy costs every year and owners of industrial buildings spend $94.4 billion. According to the EPA, an estimated 30 percent of that cost could be saved by implementing efficiency measures, saving tens of billions of dollars and reducing greenhouse gases by an amount equivalent to removing 30 million vehicles from our roads. IBM estimates that about half the electricity generated for building is wasted.[68]

In 2005, 41 percent of total energy use in homes was for space heating and 8 percent for air conditioning, according to the U.S. Energy Information Administration. Few efficiency measures match the benefits and return on investment of weatherizing and constructing high-energy buildings. The EPA sponsors a program promoting building efficiency. In 2008, more than 3,300 commercial and industrial buildings earned the EPA's Energy Star rating, saving more than $1.1 billion in energy costs and avoiding more than 7 million metric tons of greenhouse gases. There are now more than 6,200 Energy Star-qualified buildings and plants in the United States. The cities with the greatest number of Energy Star-rated buildings in 2008 were, in decreasing ranking: Los Angeles; San Francisco; Houston; Washington, D.C.; Dallas-Fort Worth; Chicago; and Denver.[187]

The Energy Star rating is also designed to promote the energy efficiency of new homes. To earn the Energy Star label, a house must score at least 15 percent better than what the "model" guidelines stipulate. This standard is widely viewed as being too low. Worse, the guidelines do not take into consideration

184 The Economist, "Energy Efficiency. The Elusive Negawatt," May 10, 2008, 78–80

185 Kevin Conley, Popular Science, July 2009, 54–58

186 The Economist, "The Rise of the Green Building," December 4, 2004, 17–23

187 The Daily Green (www.dailygreen.com), March 4, 2009

size. The EPA intends to roll out new standards "to reward appropriate small-ness and penalize wasteful largeness."[188]

Another standard of building efficiency and environmental impact is the Leadership in Energy and Environmental Design (LEED). It was developed by the U.S. Green Building Council (USGBC) in 1993. The program aims to minimize site disturbance, construction-material waste, energy consump-tion, water usage, and car dependence. It addresses the indoor environmental quality of commercial and industrial buildings as well as of homes. The design standards reward small home sizes and address the environmental impact of constructing, maintaining, and operating buildings. A building that achieves a platinum rating is estimated to have reduced its environmental impact by 70 percent and a gold-rated building by 50 percent compared with an equivalent conventional building.[186]

The residential building programs reflect the fact that homes are respon-sible for 21 percent of all energy used. The USGBC developed the LEED system as a means to evaluate a building's energy efficiency, resource efficiency, and environmental impact. Its LEED program has been in effect for commercial buildings since 1998. It was implemented for residential construction in 2005, revised in 2007, and evolved into guidelines for entire neighborhood develop-ments, the LEED-ND, in 2008.[189] LEED certification is the most recognized ac-colade for green construction. It has grown from ninety-three projects in 2001 to over five thousand projects in 2007.[190] At the beginning of 2010, there were twenty-four thousand new projects in the pipeline and 430 million square feet of LEED-certified office space, according to the USGBC.[68] USGBC efforts to expand green building standards are being rewarded. Over two hundred mu-nicipalities and thirty-four state governments had adopted LEED into some form of legislation, ordinance, or policy at the end of 2009.[191]

The greatest impact of the LEED program could come from the new set of standards that grades entire neighborhoods, LEED-ND. The new standards are the result of a partnership of the U.S. Green Building Council, the Con-

188 Jeffrey Ball, The Wall Street Journal, June 26, 2009, A10

189 Green Building Rating System for New Construction & Major Renovations, Version 2.2, October 2005

190 Daniel Brook, Scientific American, Earth 3.0, Volume 18, Number 4, December 2008, 54–59

191 Nadav Malin: Environmental Building News, April 2010, 3-4 Green Building Rating System for New Construction & Major Renovations, Version 2.2, October 2005

gress for the New Urbanism, The National Resources Defense Council, builders, developers, and the environmental community.[192] The standards reward
densities, access to public transportation, and degree of integration into the
larger region.[190] It goes well beyond trying to save the world one building at a
time. Douglas Kelbaugh, professor of architecture at the University of Michigan, praises LEED's acknowledgement that density matters. "The average urban home consumes half as much energy as the average suburban home and
significantly less energy than a suburban green home," he said. His point is that
even green sprawl isn't green.[190]

The LEED system is not without shortcomings. The paperwork needed for
compliance is cumbersome and supervision of the project can be expensive.
Critics contend that the money could best be spent on energy-saving measures or alternative energy-generation devices. Kelbaugh is a staunch supporter
of high-performance buildings but feels that the LEED program is not always
the best guideline to follow. He actually designs to what he says is a master
standard, the American Institute of Architects' 2030 Challenge. Its goal is to
produce buildings that have half the carbon footprint of comparable buildings by 2010, and carbon-neutral buildings by 2030.[190] Some people argue that
energy-efficiency requirements need to be tightened. The highest-rated LEED-
certified building today wouldn't meet the minimum standards required in
Germany.[68]

"Passive House" design is a concept that has recently been introduced in
the United States.[193] It is entirely performance-based, focusing only on energy
use without regard to indoor air quality, water conservation, building materi-
al-sparing measures, or access to public transportation. "Passive House" construction aims at getting the energy loads so small that buildings can achieve
net-zero energy status using only a small photovoltaic array. It accomplishes
that through hyperinsulation, minimum air leakage, passive solar gain, and
highly efficient windows.

The "Passive House" movement is making great strides in Europe. More
than fifteen thousand buildings, including single-family homes, apartment
buildings and commercial buildings have been built to the standard, mostly in
Germany, Austria, and Scandinavian countries. It is estimated that 17 percent
of new homes in Austria are being built to the standard. Katrin Klingenberg

192 Blake Murrillo, CE News, September 2007, 22–25

193 Alex Wilson, Environmental Building News, April 2010, 10–15

founded the Passive House Institute U.S. (PHIUS) to promote the standards in the United States.[193]

The push to build more energy-efficient homes and commercial buildings is laudable but more emphasis must be placed on improving the efficiency of existing homes and buildings. Some 115 million homes exist in the United States and fewer than one million are added each year, even in good times. In 2009 and in 2010 , fewer than 500,000 homes were built each year. **The federal government estimates that homes that already exist will use about 90 percent of the energy that will be consumed by the country's housing stock in 2030, pointing to the importance of retrofitting our existing stock of buildings.**[194] Remy Logan, associate partner at Richard Meir Architects, a New York firm, is confident that in the next twenty-five years, three-quarters of all U.S. buildings will be new or substantially renovated.[68]

To maximize return on investment, capital expenditures in energy efficiency need to be appropriated according to the amount of energy consumption of various sectors. In 2004, investments in appliances and electronics amounted to a disproportionate portion of investments (48 percent) considering that these devices consumed only 8 percent of the total energy expenditures.[195] Homes consume 21 percent of all energy used in the United States, according to federal figures. Yet studies show that houses commonly waste 30 percent of the energy they use.[194] Retrofit your home first, and then upgrade appliances and lighting fixtures. Return on your investments will exceed the return on many other investments you could make and you will have the satisfaction of doing something good for the country and the earth.

Owners of commercial buildings are making large investments in energy efficiency. One Penn Plaza, a fifty-seven-story New York skyscraper, is preparing to install a natural gas-powered generator that will produce some 6.2 megawatts of electricity. Vornado Realty Trust, which owns the skyscraper and many other New York City buildings, is among a growing number of commercial landlords installing the energy-efficient cogeneration plants. They can also make good use of the excess heat generated by the power plant to heat the buildings. The cogeneration plants are said to produce electricity at a cost of about eight cents a kilowatt hour, roughly half the cost of buying electricity from ConEd. Generating power onsite has the added advantage of eliminating

---

194 Jeffrey Ball, The Wall Street Journal, Packing Heat: The Firepower of the Lowly Caulk Gun, A11

195 Industry Week, "Growing the Energy Efficiency Market," July 2008, 22

transmission losses. Only 40 percent of each volt generated by ConEd reaches the customer, according to some accounts, the other 60 percent being dissipated into the grid. In addition, cogeneration is fired by natural gas, a cleaner fuel than the coal that feeds most utility power plants. The new owners of Chicago's Sears Tower, now known as Willis Tower, are planning a $350 million energy-efficiency upgrade.[196]

One Bryant Park, a 2.1-million-square-foot high-rise office building under construction in New York City, is being touted as the nation's greenest. It is likely to achieve LEED platinum certification based on its wide range of green features, including onsite wastewater treatment, optimized day lighting, rainwater harvesting, and an advanced thermal energy storage (TES) system. Its TES system consists of forty-four 1,600-gallon tanks where ice is made each night and used during the daytime to allow cooling loads to be shifted to nighttime when electricity cost is lower. Each tank provides 162-ton hours* or 570 kWh of cooling capacity, enough to provide cooling for 10,000—12,000 square feet of office space.[193]

A golden opportunity exists for China to improve its overall energy efficiency. In the next twenty years, China's housing boom will add housing and office space equivalent to America's entire stock.[197] The landmark seventy-one-story Pearl River tower under construction in Guangzhou, billed as the world's most energy-efficient skyscraper, is an example of the trend in China's commercial property market. Such developments reflect the country's desire to leapfrog the United States by building state-of-the-art green buildings.[198] **America needs strong incentives to improve its energy efficiency to remain competitive in a rapidly changing world.**

Energy efficiency is one of the most powerful tools available to strengthen America's economy. Energy efficiency has helped Americans use only half as much energy to produce the same amount of economic output in 2007 as

---

*A ton-hour is a quantity of cooling equivalent to 12,000 BTU or 3.5 kWh. The term goes back to the days when cooling was provided by blocks of ice. One ton is the amount of cooling that is achieved by two thousand pounds of ice as it melts over a twenty-four-hour period. When mechanical air-conditioning systems are sized, one ton of cooling is equivalent to the cooling effect of one ton of ice over a twenty-four-hour period.[193]

196 Alex Applebaum, New York Times, February 25, 2009, B7

197 The Economist, "America, China and Climate Change," November 21st 2009, 31–32

198 Jonathan Cheng, The Wall Street Journal, "The Big Chinese Companies Talk to the Skyline, January 13, 2010, C6

was necessary in 1970. In 1970, it took about twenty-six barrels of oil-equivalent energy to produce $10,000 of GDP. In 2007, it took about 13.4 barrels. Energy efficiency measures would also provide an economic stimulus. According to an *Industry Week* report, "Investments in technology that is more energy efficient technology could ultimately result by 2030 in an efficiency market worth more than $700 billion—and total additional investments over the period 2008–2030 of nearly $7 trillion."[195]

Energy-efficiency measures save more than they cost, while renewable energy alternatives cost more than they save, according to a McKinsey & Company study. By almost all accounts, measures to reduce demand are a lot cheaper than building capacity, and they emit little or no carbon. A report published in 2009 by McKinsey & Company determined that the United States could cut its output of greenhouse gas emissions by more than 11 percent using conservative steps that would "pay for themselves and earn a profit." These "negative cost opportunities" would require little or no technology innovation. The study concluded that a further 17 percent reduction would be achieved with efficiency improvements that had only a moderate cost.

Public Policies

The drive for energy efficiency is hampered by the fact that electricity and fuel are priced too cheaply to justify the investments in energy efficiency. It is no coincidence that Denmark has both high power prices and a highly energy-efficient economy.[199] Among American states, for every cent per kilowatt hour by which prices exceed the national average, energy consumption drops by about 7 percent of the average. George David of United Technologies is of the opinion that higher fuel and power prices are the only motor needed to improve energy efficiency. That would also drive energy conservation.[199]

Incentives are also needed on the demand side. Most efficiency investments pay for themselves within a few years, but all require some capital expenditure. Since home builders are not the ones who will reap the benefits of lower energy bills, they must be compelled to build high-efficiency buildings and install Energy Star appliances and efficient heating and cooling systems. Similarly, homeowners—and especially renters—should be given incentives to

---

199 The Economist, "Energy Efficiency. The Elusive Negawatt, May 10, 2008, 78–80

invest in CFL bulbs and other energy-saving improvements in order to over-come the barrier of initial capital outlays.[199]

The other tool at our disposal is to support legislation and incentives that favor clean energy: a carbon tax, cap and trade, renewable energy stand-ards, etc. Legislators need public support to introduce and pass new legisla-tion. Contact your representatives to express your support for legislation that would transition our economy to one that is less carbon intensive. There are plenty of ways you can be good citizens without picketing.

The lack of leadership at the federal level in the areas of energy efficiency and carbon-emissions reduction has prompted states and civic leaders to take on the challenge. Some cities mandate energy audits of houses offered for sale as an incentive for builders and sellers to improve the efficiency of their homes. Since January 1, 2008, Santa Fe, New Mexico, has had an ordinance that requires builders of new homes to provide a Home Energy Rating Systems (HERS) Index score in order to receive a certificate of occupancy. Although it doesn't mandate minimum levels, it allows buyers to compare energy-ef-ficiency ratings when shopping for a new home. New York City passed a law requiring owners of large buildings to conduct energy-efficiency surveys, but stopped short of compelling the owners to renovate their properties.

The city of Austin, Texas, long at the forefront of green urbanism, has gone further. As of June 1, 2009, the city has had an ordinance requiring the customers of Austin Energy, which supplies most of the city's residential and commercial users, to perform energy audits. The Energy Conservation Audit and Disclosure (ECAD) ordinance requires owners of houses more than ten years old to have an energy audit performed before resale and to disclose the results to prospective buyers. The part of the ordinance that covers multi-family buildings constructed before June 1, 1999, requires those buildings to be energy-audited prior to June 1, 2011. If the building uses more than 150 percent of average energy use per square foot for similar buildings, the owner must make improvements within eighteen months to bring energy use down to 110 percent of average.[200]

Other cities are making an effort to improve their energy efficiency and reduce their dependence on fossil fuels. Mayor Sam Adams of Portland, Or-egon, has called on the local utility company to phase out coal. His goal is to save enough energy to cause the closing of the city's main power supplier, the

---

200 Allyson Wendt, Environmental Building News, Volume 19, Number 2, August 2009, 6–7

coal-fired 585-megawatt Boardman Plant, which supplies 15 percent of Portland's power. Michael Armstrong, Portland's senior sustainability manager, is charged with the task of reducing energy consumption and promoting alternative energy. Armstrong's Bureau of Planning and Sustainability is running a pilot program to weatherize five hundred homes. Upgrades to insulation, windows, and other features are partially paid for by the federal stimulus program. The cost is added to the homeowners' utility bill but spread over fifteen years. The energy savings usually offsets the extra charges. The ultimate goal is to retrofit one hundred thousand homes.[201]

Antonio Villaraigosa, mayor of Los Angeles, the birthplace of sprawl and smog, announced in his second inauguration address that by 2020, Angelenos would "permanently break our addiction to coal."[201] That is a tall order for a city that gets 42 percent of its electricity from coal. David Freeman, head of L.A's Department of Water and Power, has overseen the distribution of 1.4 million compact fluorescent bulbs and converted 140,000 street lights and all of the city's traffic lights to low-power, light-emitting diodes.

Los Angeles civic leaders realize it will take more than that to wean L.A. off coal. The city is investing in renewable energy. The new Pine Tree Wind Farm, eighty wind turbines with a combined rated power output of 120 megawatts, is the largest city-owned wind farm in the country. The city extracts methane from sewage and has a 400-megawatt geothermal project. The city also is promoting solar initiatives.[201] While Villaraigosa wants L.A. to set itself as an example of sustainability for other cities to follow, Seattle, which gets only 1 percent of its power from coal, remains the poster city for eco-responsibility.[201]

In September 2009, Chicago's Mayor Richard Daley and the city's environmental chief, Sadhu Johnston, unveiled an ambitious plan to reduce carbon emissions to one-quarter below 1990 levels by 2020, with the ultimate goal of an 80 percent reduction by 2050. The Chicago Climate Action Plan includes energy-efficient retrofits of up to four hundred thousand homes and ninety-two hundred high-rises and factories.[202]

Mayor Daley launched the green-roof movement when he had the roof of City Hall covered with vegetation in 2000, establishing Chicago as the undisputed leader in green roofs. In 2010, the city boasted five hundred green roofs covering seven million square feet. That is the most for any North American

201 Paul Tullis, Sierra, January/February 2010, 22–29

202 Josh Boak, Scientific American, Earth 3.0, Volume 18 #5, 2008, 46–51

city, but it still represents less than one-tenth of 1 percent of the city's buildings. In contrast, an estimated 15–20 percent of Germany's flat roofs are covered by vegetation; the total surface area measures billions of square feet. The city of Toronto, Canada, passed a law in 2009 requiring that all new buildings with at least two thousand square meters of floor area have roofs partially covered with vegetation.[203] Green roofs' credentials include rainwater absorption, reduction in heat-island effect, improved building energy-efficiency, and an increase in the roof's lifespan. In addition, green roofs provide wildlife refuges and enhance esthetics. They come at an additional initial cost of $15 to $50 a square foot. Green roofs are part of President Obama's plan to improve the energy-efficiency of federal buildings.

Other greening measures are being promoted in the context of improving cities' environmental credentials. Reducing the surface area of paved yards in favor of grassy surfaces minimizes the heat-island effect and helps manage storm waters. Civic leaders and homeowners should also support planting trees in public and private spaces.

Some cities have set the lofty goal of becoming carbon-neutral. Vancouver, Canada; Rizhao, China; Arendal, Norway; and Vaxjo, Sweden are attempting the feat of balancing the amount of their greenhouse gas emissions with the amount eliminated, according to the United Nations' Environment Program. All four municipalities see economic opportunities in a green economy.[18] Masdar City, near Abu Dhabi, is being built from scratch with the goal of being the world's first city to be environmentally sustainable with zero carbon emissions.

One of the challenges of reducing energy consumption and phasing out fossil-fuel power generation is the reluctance of utility companies to participate in schemes to reduce demand for the product they sell—electricity—or eliminate their cheapest source of energy—coal, which would reduce their profits. Legislators need to find ways for utilities to profit by implementing energy-saving measures. California decoupled electricity profits from sales volume decades ago. In the past thirty years, California's total per capita electricity consumption has remained flat even though its per capita economic output has almost doubled. Per capita electricity use increased by more than 60 percent in the rest of the nation over the same period with similar economic-output gain. The total savings for California from energy efficiency since 1993 has been valued at roughly $1 trillion.[16] In 2007,

203 Blair Kamin, Chicago Tribune, "Green Roofs Still Only Budding," April 21, 2010, Section 1–4

California adopted a scheme called "decoupling plus," a technical term that reflects the way energy producers get paid. Under this scheme, utilities are rewarded on the basis of the amount of electricity and gas their customers save instead of how much they consume. Through government regulations, utilities make higher profits when energy conservation targets are met. Five other states have decoupled profits from sales volume and nine more states may follow.[204] **The American Council for an Energy Efficient Economy says a tough national standard could eliminate the need for 450 power plants by 2030.**[204] Other countries also have schemes to improve energy efficiency. Japan imposes a fine on its thirteen thousand factories with the highest energy use if they don't improve their energy efficiency by 15 percent a year.[199]

America's goal to improve its competitive position in the world would be well served by reducing its total energy consumption. It also would help the country burnish its ecological credentials. Energy use and greenhouse gas emissions are closely related, since most of our energy comes from fossil fuels. Fossil fuels power our cars, heat our buildings, grow our food, and produce our electricity.

Concerns that CO_2 emissions from burning fossil fuels are degrading our planet's ecosystem have mobilized the international community in efforts to reduce energy consumption, develop alternative sources of energy, and find ways to mitigate CO_2 emissions. The United States needs to be engaged in, if not leading, these efforts.

Carbon Dioxide

I t is universally accepted that greenhouse gases play a major role in setting a planet's temperature. Too much greenhouse gas in the atmosphere surrounding Venus causes Venus to be too hot to support life. Too little greenhouse gas in Mars's environment makes it too cold to spawn life. About 1 percent of the earth's atmosphere is composed of greenhouse gases, primarily water vapor, CO_2, nitrous oxide, methane, and ozone. Together these gases reflect enough heat back to earth to maintain the average temperature of the atmosphere at around 60° F. Predictable weather patterns have set the stage for the distribution of human population throughout our planet, determine

---

204 Michael Grunwald, Time, January 12, 2009

what types of fauna and flora thrive in various areas, and what human activities are most appropriate.

Because of its abundance, carbon dioxide (CO_2) is the main greenhouse gas responsible for regulating our planet's temperature. CO_2 is relatively transparent to visible light from the sun, allowing the sun's rays to warm the planet. The earth absorbs heat from the sun and radiates part of it back into space in the form of infrared radiation. Because CO_2 is relatively opaque to infrared radiation, it prevents some of the heat from escaping the earth's atmosphere.

The main reason why CO_2 is at the center of the discourse about climate is the striking correlation between the concentration of CO_2 and the average temperature of the earth over the last millennia. Data is available on the concentration of CO_2 in the atmosphere going back 650,000 years. Measurements were obtained by analyzing the concentration of CO_2 in air bubbles trapped in ice, the age of which could be determined. Scientists also can assess the temperature of the atmosphere of the corresponding years by calculating the ratio of different isotopes of oxygen of the air trapped in the ice. Before the industrial revolution, the atmosphere held around 280 parts per million (ppm) of CO_2. At no time in the last 650,000 years has CO_2 concentration in the atmosphere exceeded 300 ppm. Furthermore, analysis of the data has revealed that spikes in CO_2 levels coincided with spikes in temperature.

Charles D. Keeling, an atmospheric chemist, pioneered collection of current information on the concentration of atmospheric CO_2. He first began monitoring air at the top of Mauna Loa on the island of Hawaii and at the South Pole in 1958. At that time, the atmosphere contained 316 ppm. The CO_2 readings, known as the Keeling Curve, have been climbing. Based on samples from forty countries, global concentration of CO_2 reached the level of 381.2 ppm in 2006 and 387 ppm in 2009, according to the World Meteorologic Organization. The Global Carbon Project reports that since 2000, carbon dioxide emissions worldwide have been increasing at three times the rate observed during the previous decade. The Intergovernmental Panel on Climate Change (IPCC) reckons that if emissions continue to grow at their current rate, by 2100 the concentration of CO_2 in the air will have risen to 800 ppm.

Monitoring of CO_2 levels in the atmosphere is about to take a new dimension, thanks to a satellite data collection. On January 23, 2009, the Japanese space agency, JAXA, launched "Ibuki," the first satellite dedicated to monitoring CO_2 and methane. It will gather data from 56,000 points around the globe, orbiting earth every one hundred minutes. It is capable of detecting CO_2 changes as small as one part per million.

On February 24, 2008, the American space agency NASA launched the Orbiting Carbon Observatory (OCO), a $278 million satellite dedicated to the study of atmospheric CO_2 levels. Unfortunately, the rocket that launched OCO from the Vandenberg Air Force Base in California failed to reach its orbit and crashed near Antarctica. One of the goals of the satellite, which took eight years to develop, was to help understand where CO_2 enters the atmosphere and where it gets absorbed, information necessary to shed light on the contributions of forest fires and other global phenomena on CO_2 emissions. On March 4, 2011, OCO's sucessor, the Glory, suffered a similar fate. NASA's Taurus XL launch vehicle carrying the Glory Spacecraft failed to reach orbit. The Glory was designed to distinguish the relative influence of natural and human-caused atmospheric aerosols on the global climate. Satellite data collection may not be as accurate as readings taken on the ground, but the coverage will more than compensate for that deficiency.

Researchers estimate the carbon cycle turns over about 330 billion tons of CO_2 each year, about 30 billion tons of which is attributable to human activities. Analysis of carbon isotopes, among other things, show that carbon dioxide from industry accounts for a major portion of that amount.[205] Decaying dead wood and other vegetation, forest fires, volcanic eruptions, and wildlife also contribute a lot of CO_2 and other greenhouse gases.

Plants act as a counterbalance to the emissions by a process called photosynthesis. Photosynthesis is a process by which the chlorophyll molecules of plants, when activated by sunlight, split H_2O molecules and combine the resulting free hydrogen with CO_2 extracted from the air. The process produces carbohydrates that plants turn into sugars, or, by another chemical process produces new plant matter. The oxygen electrons are released into the atmosphere through the plants' stomata. ($6 CO_2 + 6 H_2O = C_6H_{12}O_6 + 6 O_2$)

Planktonic algae on the surface of the ocean absorb enough carbon for the oceans to act as the main sink for CO_2. Some of these algae drop to the floor of the ocean, permanently storing the carbon. Some algae form the basis of most sea animals' food chains. When these animals die, the remains that are not eaten sink to the sea floor where they are buried indefinitely. Researchers have tried with mixed success to seed the ocean with iron as a way of mak-

---

205 The Economist, "The Climate of science change. The clouds of unkowing," March 20, 2010, 83–86

ing the sea take more CO_2 out of the atmosphere, since this metal stimulates the growth of planktonic algae. A newly discovered "microbial carbon pump" is believed to account for a significant portion of the oceans' ability to extract CO_2 from the atmosphere. Jiao Nianzhi, a Chinese researcher, recently advanced the theory that a group of photoheterotrophic bacteria that constitute approximately 7 percent of the oceans' microbes, have a "predominant role in pumping carbon into a pool of compounds that cannot be turned back into carbon dioxide by living creatures, thereby building up a large reservoir that keeps carbon out of the atmosphere." It is estimated that the oceans absorb about half the 330 billion tons of CO_2 turned over in the carbon cycle every year.

Land-based plants absorb much of the remaining CO_2 and act as a conduit of carbon into the soil. The soil is an important store of carbon, containing about twice as much carbon as is currently in suspension in the atmosphere and more than three times as much carbon as is sequestered in trees and other plants.[16] It is estimated that between 7.5 percent and 10 percent of atmospheric CO_2 passes through the soil each year.[16] The rest returns to earth as chemical precipitation and a small amount remains in the atmosphere.

When governments started thinking seriously about climate change in the 1980s they turned to the United Nations (UN), which established the Intergovernmental Panel on Climate Change (IPCC) in 1989. It was designed to coordinate scientific efforts to determine what was happening to the climate.[205] It culminated in a declaration by the UN's IPCC in February 2007 that there is a "very high confidence" that human activities since 1750 have played a significant role in climate changes by overloading the atmosphere with CO_2, hence retaining solar heat that would otherwise radiate away. The conclusion was based on the research of nearly a thousand scientists from seventy-four countries. The study also made the case that global warming was already affecting the planet's ecosystem. A report issued in June 2009 by the U.S. Global Change Research Program (USGRP), which coordinates climate change for thirteen federal agencies, estimates that global average temperatures have risen approximately 1.5°F since the start of the industrial revolution in the middle of the eighteenth century, when people started to burn fossil fuel to power industrial machinery, and could rise another 2°F to 11°F before the end of the century based on different models of greenhouse gas emissions levels, mitigation efforts, and economic scenarios.[206] The question in the scientific community is not whether we will see change relative to global warming, but how much we will see.

Many still question the hypothesis that anthropogenic CO_2 emissions (30 of the 330 billion tons of CO_2 of the carbon cycle) play a role in climate change. The debate is complicated by the fact that atmospheric CO_2 levels and global temperatures don't move in tandem on a monthly or yearly timeframe but trend on a much longer timeframe, perhaps a decade. A case in point is that three independent research groups concluded that 2008 was the coolest year for our plant since 2000. Yet the global temperature was still the ninth- or tenth-warmest since the most reliable recordkeeping began in 1850, according to the United Nations' World Meteorological Organization, NASA's Institute of Space Studies, and the U.S. National Climatic Data Center. Taken together, their results added to a year that was slightly less than 1° F warmer than the twentieth-century mean but continued the warming trend of the planet that started decades ago. The fact that twenty-one of the hottest years on record have occurred in the last twenty-five years supports the theory that the planet is getting warmer. Data indicated that the world warmed by about 0.7°C in the twentieth century. Every year in this century has been warmer than all but one, 1998.[207]

Looking beyond year-to-year variations of climate change, there is growing evidence that the effects of rising temperatures are accelerating. When President Taft created Glacier National Park in 1910, it had an estimated 150 glaciers. In 2004, that number was down to thirty and most of those remaining had shrunk in area by two-thirds.[208] Alaska's low-lying ice fields are disappearing at two or three times the rate of a decade ago. Since 2003, for instance, more than two trillion tons of land ice in Greenland, Antarctica, and Alaska has melted, according to NASA geophysicists. Since 2000, Greenland has lost 355.5 square miles of ice, losing three times as much ice last year as the year before. The 965 square miles of tropical glaciers in the four countries of the tropical Andes—Bolivia, Columbia, Ecuador, and Peru—shrank by 22 percent between the 1960s and 1997. One of the main glaciers in the Cordillera Blanca

---

206 Alex Wilson and Andrea Ward, Environmental Building News, September 2009, 1, 8–15

207 The Economist, November 27, 2010, Adapting to Climate Change. Facing the Consequences, 85–86

208 Daniel Glick and Peter Essick, National Geographic, September 2004

range north of Lima shrank by more than 40 percent between 1995 and 2006. A glaciologist at the government's Natural Resources Institute reckons that it will be gone by 2015.[208]

The loss of glaciers is not just the loss of tourist attractions. Glaciers act as stores of water. They accumulate moisture during the winter months and release it in the spring and summer for the benefit of agriculture during the growing season—and for the benefit of people during the hot, dry months.

The loss of ice also becomes one of many negative feedback loops that accelerate global warming. Ice's white surface decreases the overall heat-absorbing capacity of the earth. Ice reflects 80 percent of the incoming solar radiation back into space, while blue water absorbs 80 percent of the radiation. The most concerning aspect of polar thaw is the release of CO_2 and methane gas trapped under the ice. Igor Semiletov of the University of Alaska-Fairbanks reported new seeps of methane gas bubbling from the previously frozen seafloor lodes along the Siberian coast. "We have enough data to worry," he said. Katey Walter, another researcher from the University of Alaska-Fairbanks, has been collecting samples of gas that has risen from thawing permafrost at the bottom of lakes in and around the Arctic for seven years. She claims that a complete Arctic thaw could release 50 billion tons of methane. Some scientists suspect that the reason global methane concentrations shot up in 2007 is the progressive thawing of some Arctic lakes. They are of the opinion that methane is responsible for one-third of the current warming trend, according to Sarah Simpson,[209] a writer for *Scientific American* magazine.

Scientists have long known that when permafrost, which averages eighty feet thick and is packed with dead plant and animal matter, melts, it releases carbon. Microbes that have been inhibited by low temperatures consume the animal and plant matter, releasing the methane. The amount of carbon released appears to have been woefully underestimated. According to Edward Schuler of the University of Florida, "It's about three times as much as was thought, about 1.6 trillion metric tons." That is about twice the amount currently in the atmosphere. If global warming continues to thaw the frozen soils of the far North, large quantities of CO_2 and methane would be released into the atmosphere. Schuler's measurements of how quickly carbon emissions can come out of permafrost were also a surprise: 1 billion to 2 billion tons per year.

---

209 Sarah Simpson, Scientific American, Earth 3.0, Volume 19, Number 2, Summer 2009, 30–37

As a point of reference, cars and light trucks on the U.S. roads emit about 300 million tons per year.[210]

Other changes accelerate the global warming trend. Warmer air holds in suspension more water vapor than does cooler air. As the planet's atmosphere warms, it holds more water vapor, a greenhouse gas, trapping more heat.[205] Global warming lengthens summers, increasing the number of forest fires, which are credited with large amounts of greenhouse gas emission.

The anthropogenic role of CO_2 on climate change is widely accepted but there are still pockets of opposition to the evidence within the scientific community, primarily in Australia, Europe, Japan, and the United States. *Wall Street Journal* reporter Kimberley A. Strassel wrote that the Polish Academy of Sciences has published a document challenging the notion of anthropogenic global warming. She also reported that Dr. Kiminori Itoh, a Japanese environmental physical chemist who contributed to a UN climate report, dubbed created warming "the worst scientific scandal in history." Norway's Ivar Giaever, a Nobel Prize-winner in physics, decries it as the "new religion." Strassel goes on to report that a group of fifty-four noted physicists, led by Princeton's Will Happer, is demanding the American Physical Society revise its position that the science is settled.[211]

The international scientific community, which is mostly supportive of the conclusions that human-related activities contribute to climate changes, has taken on the responsibility of reducing the world's greenhouse gas emissions.

International Movement to Curb CO2 Emissions

The international community's concerns about climate change gave birth to the UN Framework Convention on Climate Change (UNFCCC). It held its first convention in Rio de Janeiro, Brazil, in 1992. The main accomplishment of the first meeting was a commitment from its signatories, the United States being one of them, to inventory their greenhouse gas emissions. It was followed by the December 1997 meeting of the world's nations in Kyoto, Japan, which resulted in the Kyoto Protocol. It established guidelines restricting production of greenhouse gases, primarily Co_2. The goal of the Kyoto Protocol was to re-

---

210 Sharon Begley, Newsweek, August 3, 2009, 30

211 Kimberly A. Strossel, The Wall Street Journal, June 26, 2009

duce emissions to 5.2 percent below 1990 levels by 2012.[212] Most nations signed it. The notable exceptions were the United States, China, Australia, and India.

The emission-reduction goal agreed upon will not be reached by 2012. The U.S. government estimates that worldwide emissions of CO_2 have gone up 38 percent since 1992. U.S. emissions have risen from 6 billion metric tons of carbon in 1992 to 7.85 billion metric tons in 2005 and an estimated 8.0 billion tons in 2007, according to Gregg Marland of Oak Ridge National Laboratory. (The EPA estimated the total U.S. emissions in carbon-dioxide equivalent to be 7.15 billion tons in 2007.) The fact that large polluters, such as the United States, China, India, and Australia, refused to sign the Kyoto Protocol doomed the international community's efforts. The inability of some of the 181 nations that endorsed the Kyoto Protocol to live up to their commitments also is contributing to its failure. Japan, for one, has seen its overall emissions rise by 5.8 percent, according to the UNFCCC. Its CO_2 emissions from electricity-generation rose 15.1 percent from 1990 to 2007. Canada's CO_2 emissions have risen 25 percent since 1999, placing our northern neighbor in fifty-ninth place in the Capital Climate Change Performance Index for 2009, only one position better than Saudi Arabia. Other countries have been more successful. Great Britain has reduced its emissions by 15 percent since 1990, well inside its target under the Kyoto Protocol. Between 1990 and 2008 EU countries reduced their total carbon emissions by 6 percent but those gains were almost exactly canceled by the extra emissions associated with goods imported into the EU from China, according to a study conducted at the Center of International Climate and Environment Research, in Oslo, Norway. Add in other imports of such "embodied" carbon emissions from other countries, and Europe's overall emissions actually increased by 6 percent over that period.[213] Those statistics speak volumes about the need for all countries, especially the worst polluters, the United States, China, India, Indonesia, and Australia to implement measures to reduce their greenhouse gas emissions.

The UNFCCC sponsored a meeting in Bali, Indonesia, in December 2007 to lay the groundwork for the December 2009 talks in Copenhagen. The delegation sent by the Bush administration was less than cooperative. The European delegates threatened to pull out of those talks unless the American delegation agreed to keep some semblance of concrete targets in the outline for Copen-

---

212 Chris Mooney, Scientific American, Volume 19, Number 1 2009, 25–31

213 The Economist Technology Quarterly, Following the Footprints, June 4, 2011, 14-18

hagen meeting talks. One of the U.S. delegates, Paula Dobriansky, was booed by her fellow delegates. The resentment for the U.S. position was such that the delegate from Papua, New Guinea, Kevin Conrad, bluntly said, "If for some reason you are not willing to lead, leave it to the rest of us. Please get out of the way."[214] In the end, the only real achievement at Bali was a decision to set up a pilot project to investigate how to stop deforestation. "Aside from that, the conference produced nothing but a vapid statement of good intentions, from which America ensured that all substance was removed." The U.S. stance was unfortunate, since China and India strongly signaled that if the United States rejoined the world in addressing those issues, they were ready to do their part.

China's interest would be well served if it engaged in measures to curb climate-changing practices. China and India are among the countries that stand to suffer the most from global warming. China gets much of its fresh water for agriculture and drinking from glaciers on the Tibetan plateau and the Himalayas, which feed the Ganges, the Yangtze, and Yellow Rivers. The Himalayas have been warming three times as fast as the world average causing their glaciers to shrink at an accelerated pace. China is already experiencing its worst drought in fifty years, with three hundred million people facing water shortages and fifty million acres of crops being compromised.

The purpose of the Copenhagen meeting was to establish a protocol to replace Kyoto's, which is due to expire in 2012. Ideally, the 192 countries represented were to agree on a timetable to reduce their greenhouse gas emissions by certain amounts. The Obama administration played a leading role at the UNFCCC's meeting, which was hosted by the Climate and Energy Minister of Denmark, Connie Hedegaard, in spite of the fact that Congress had not finalized any agreement on emission-reduction means. It had been widely believed that if the United States had failed to engage, the deliberations would have produced little commitment from other nations. In fact, little progress was made. A notable accomplishment was a pledge of $10 billion a year, for three years, from developed countries to help developing countries reduce emissions and deal with the effects of climate change. Some of the money will go toward implementing a "REDD-plus" deal on deforestation, an issue on which real progress was made. [215]

---

214 Thomas Fuller and Andrew C. Revkin, New York Times, December 16, 2007

215 The Economist, "Climate Change After Copenhagen. China's Thing About Numbers," January 2, 2010, 43–44

China was especially critical of America's history of emissions. In a policy statement, China demanded that developed countries "take responsibility for their historical cumulative emissions and current high per capita emissions to substantially reduce their emissions."[216] China makes a valid point and probably echoes the feeling of many around the world. The United States' cumulative CO_2 emissions from fossil fuels between 1900 and 2005 have been estimated at 318,432 million metric tons. That compares with 92,950 million metric tons for China, 73,208 million metric tons for Germany, 55,034 million metric tons for the United Kingdom, and 25,895 metric tons for India.[217]

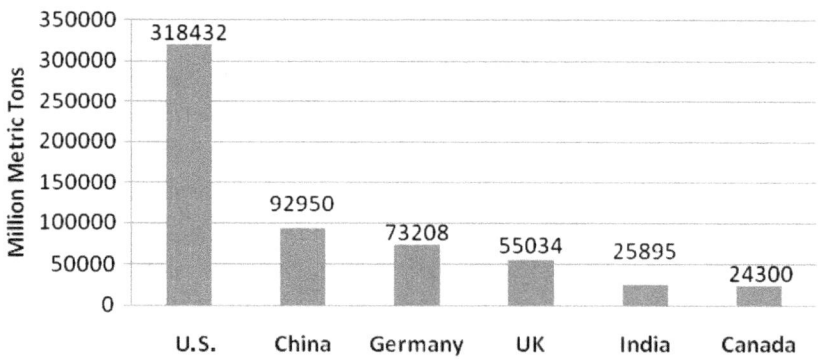

Figure 8: Cumulative CO_2 Emissions (1900–2005) from Fossil Fuels in Million Metric Tons; Source: James Hansen, Newsweek, December 14, 2009

The next gathering of the international community opened on November 29, 2009 in Cancun, Mexico. Progress was achieved mostly in mitigating the effects of global warming. It translated into an official UN process that included a transfer from rich countries to developing countries, of $100 billion a year starting in 2020, as climate assistance.[218] The notion that greenhouse gas emissions are affecting the climate is gaining enough support to prod the conscience of polluters. Polluting nations are starting to realize that assisting

---

216 Sharon Begley, Newsweek, September 7, 2009, 14

217 James Hansen, Newsweek, December 14, 2009, 54–55

218 The Economist, "The Cancun Climate-Change Conference. A Sort of Progress," December 18, 2010, 16

poor countries cope with the effects of global warming is a matter of justice, not just humanity.[219]

The Implementation of Climate-sparing Measures

"You cannot leave saving the atmosphere to poor people."[220] *Agus Purnomo of Indonesia's Climate-Change Control.*

The European Union already has a plan in place to reduce its emissions. In 2007 the twenty-seven members of the EU pledged to reduce their greenhouse-gas emissions by at least 20 percent from their 1990 level by 2020.[221]

Implementation of the European plan has not been easy. Some countries fret that heavy industry might flee to less restrictive countries like Asia. Countries that are dependent on coal for energy are concerned about the cost of it all. The EU had to make many concessions to newcomers to the EU, mostly ex-communist countries that rely heavily on coal for power and to heavy industries that face global competition. At the EU summit in Brussels in the waning days of his presidency of the European Union, Nicolas Sarkozy succeeded in persuading his colleagues to accept the binding rules to reduce carbon emissions by 20 percent from 1990 levels by the year 2020 but the EU leaders used financial sweeteners for the most affected countries to implement the plan. All agree that it will be expensive and painful. Almost eight of ten Europeans polled by the Euro-barometer last year said they would need to change their energy consumption behavior in the next decade.

Europe's plan is referred to as the Emission-Trading Scheme, or ETS. Under the ETS, companies get a fixed number of permits to pollute. As the companies grow, they must either implement measures that will keep their emissions at the same level or buy more permits in the open market in the form of credits sold by companies that have been able to reduce their emissions.[221] EU leaders promised to deepen the cuts by at least 30 percent if the rich countries joined in, seizing the environmental high ground.[221] The EU reiterated its 30 percent pledge at the Copenhagen meeting, saying it would enact further

---

219 The Economist, "How to Live with Climate Change," November 27, 2010, 15

220 The Economist, A Special Report on Indonesia, September 12th, 2009, 3–16

221 The Economist, "Climate Control," March 17, 2007, 59

emission curbs "if it judged the commitment of others to be suitably inspiring." After Copenhagen, that seems highly unlikely.[222]

The European Union's Emission Trading Scheme (ETS) is the largest market in carbon dioxide emissions. Clean Development Mechanism (CDM) is the currency that represents the credits traded between countries and industries that need to offset their emissions. The UN certifies the projects that are traded on the Cologne Exchange. In 2005, rich-world consumers spent $2.7 billion to offset 374 million tons of CO_2 equivalents, about half of Texas's annual emissions. In 2007, the program had expanded to $13 billion, according to the World Bank. The price of mitigating one ton of CO_2 was about $20 at the end of 2009. There was downward pressure on the value of the credits because the recession caused a reduction in the amount of CO_2 emissions to a level below the amount of pre-agreed carbon allowances.[223] Most of the traded credits involved reducing emissions of trifluoromethane, a by-product of refrigerant that is cheap to get rid of. Energy-efficiency projects and fuel-switching accounted for 50 percent of the new projects in 2007, while biomass, wind projects, and hydropower made up another 24 percent. China was the recipient of 60 percent of CDM money, getting credit for building gas-fired power plants instead of dirtier coal-fired ones. The question is whether China would build gas-fired plants instead of coal-fired plants anyway.

The ETS is under fire for being too small. Countries that stand to benefit from the UN-sponsored program are applying mounting pressure to mitigate more tons of CO_2 emissions per year. Passage of cap-and-trade legislation in the United States, lowered emission targets in the EU, and a stronger successor to the Kyoto protocol would greatly increase the size of the market.[223]

Australia, one of the few nations with a worse per capita greenhouse gas emission than the United States is joining the international community's effort to reign in carbon emissions. On July 10, 2011 Julia Gillard, Australia's prime minister unveiled a plan for a carbon tax. The plan, subject to parliamentary approval later this year, aims to cut Australia's emissions by 80 percent of their 2000 levels by 2050. It calls for the imposition of a tax of $25 per ton of carbon emissions from five hundred of Australia's biggest polluters. Three years later, the fixed tax will be replaced by market-based emissions-trading scheme.

---

222 The Economist, "Europe and Climate Change. Two Into Three Won't Go," May 29, 2010, 53

223 The Economist, "Carbon Markets after Copenhagen. Don't Hold Your Breath," February 6, 2010, 80–82

The Canadian province of British Columbia introduced a carbon tax in 2008. The tax was initially set at $10 per ton of CO_2 emissions, rising by increments of $5 per year to $30 in 2012. Because the tax started low and its rises were set in advance, businesses had time to plan cuts in their emissions. Since 2008, per capita fuel consumption has dropped by 4.5 percent more than elsewhere in Canada. Other benefits ensued. Unemployment in the province is slightly below the national average and growth slightly above. Furthermore, Gordon Campbell, the premier who introduced the tax, won reelection the next year.[224] U.S. politicians should be emboldened.

An aspect of offsets that Americans, especially, and Europeans must consider is the need to compensate developing countries for the harm that developed countries' historical emissions are causing them. Between 1900 and 2005, the United States' cumulative CO_2 emissions have been estimated at 318,432 million metric tons versus 25,895 million metric tons for India, as a point of comparison. Yet, India and many other developing countries are suffering disproportionally from climate changes and their emissions are still only a small fraction of the developed countries per capita emissions. (India emits one ton of greenhouse gases per capita compared to 20 tons per capita in the United States.)

Reducing Emissions from Deforestation and Degradation (REDD)

Climate change concerns have drawn attention to the role of forests to sustain not just wildlife but the planet itself. The international community's plan to mitigate the effects of anthropogenic CO_2 emissions on climate has only recently focused on the preservation of forest even though avoided deforestation keeps enormous amounts of CO_2 from being released into the atmosphere. Roughly half the dry weight of a tree is made up of stored carbon, most of which is released when the tree is burned or allowed to decay. **Deforestation is estimated to be responsible for 18 percent of total world emissions, more than all emissions from the world's cars, trucks, trains, and planes.**[225] In 2006, deforestation was blamed for more CO_2 emissions than the entire emissions of the European Union—5.43 billion tons versus 5.07 billion tons. Deforestation produced just slightly less CO_2 than the United States at

224 The Economist, "Greenery in Canada: We have a winner; July 23, 2011, 35-36

225 The Economist, "Paying to Save Trees. Last Gasp in the Forests, September 26th, 2009, 93–95

6.73 billion tons. Forests also have a value for their ability to extract CO_2 from the atmosphere. By one estimate, the Amazon rain forest alone is sequestering 1.3 billion tons of carbon each year.

In spite of their ecological importance, forests were not considered in the 1997 Kyoto Protocol in deference to the sovereign nations' right to control the use of their land. [226] The European Union Emission Trading System (EU ETS) has until now also banned forests from consideration. The realization that preventing deforestation may offer the "cheapest large-scale carbon sequestration option available," and one that is effective and easily verifiable, has moved forests to center stage of efforts to mitigate anthropogenic emissions. According to the Informal Working Group on Interim Financing for REDD, an investment of $17 billion to $30 billion between now and 2015 could save seven million acres of forest or seven gigatons of carbon emissions a year. That suggests a cost range of $2 to $4 per ton of avoided emissions. This estimate may not be valid in all cases. Indonesia's National Council on Climate Change estimates the cost of forgoing a palm-oil plantation at $30 a ton.

REDD traces its origins to the Coalition of Rainforest Nations, which was formed after the Kyoto Protocol excluded deforestation and degradation of forest as part of its global climate agreement. In 2005, a Coalition of Rainforest Nations initiated a request to consider reducing emissions from deforestation in developing countries. At the 2007 Bali UNFCCC meeting, an agreement was reached on "the urgent need to take further meaningful action to reduce emissions from deforestation and forest degradation." REDD gained further support at the Copenhagen meeting held in December 2009.[226]

REDD has benefitted from the support of international organizations, including the World Bank. The Norwegian government was an early proponent and a major financial supporter. At the 2007 Bali conference, the Norwegians pledged $500 million toward the creation and implementation of REDD activities in Tanzania. On December 16, 2009, the United States, Australia, France, Japan, Britain, and Norway pledged $3.5 billion as a down payment on a much larger scheme to "slow, halt, and eventually reverse" deforestation in developing countries. The money was a first installment of the $25 billion needed between now and 2015 to reduce deforestation by one-quarter.[226]

Ongoing negotiations on how to use forests to stabilize the climate are taking place in Bonn, Germany, but individuals and institutions are already

226 The Economist, "Climate Change and Forests. Touch Wood," December 19, 2009, 112

investing in programs to save existing trees. This voluntary market was already worth $705 million in 2008, more than double its dollar value the previous year, according to Ecosystem Marketplace, a consulting firm.[227] The efforts to raise the funds have been led by Prince Charles' Rainforest Project.[226] The heir to the British throne is a longtime advocate of forests.[228]

Issues still abound: How much money will be raised from government and how much will come from carbon trading? Who gets the money (national governments, regional authorities, or local people)? An example of its application is taking place in the municipality of Novo Aripuana in the state of Amazonas in the southeastern corner of Brazil, where area forest covering 1.2 million acres is being preserved. Local families have been issued a debit card to which 50 reals ($28) a month is being credited. Regular inspections will ensure that the trees are still standing.[225]

REDD received a big boost at the United Nations' Climate Change Conference held in Cancun in December 2010. One of the reasons for the added interest is technological advances in determining forests' sizes and assessing forests' carbon contents using high-resolution satellite images and computing capability. The Planetary Skin Institute's Automated Land-Change Evolution, Reporting and Tracking System (ALERTS) is one of the tools being developed. ALERTS is central to the implementation of REDD+, a system to reward countries for lowering rates of deforestation.[229]

Western governments are starting to act responsibly to protect forests. A 2008 amendment to America's Lacey Act has made it an offense to import illegal timber. The EU also passed a law criminalizing the import of illegal timber.

The sustainability of forests also depends on consumer sensitivity to the issues and good corporate governance. Since global demand for tropical food, biofuels, and timber is mounting, there is pressure for Western standards to be adopted up the supply chain. Nestle' stopped buying palm oil from its main Indonesian supplier, Sinar Mas, a conglomerate with a record of disregard for the rainforest, and said it would break its relationship with any producer linked to illegal deforestation. Wal-Mart has promised to trace its products "from the manger to the refrigerator."

---

227 The Economist, "Conserving Forests. REDDy and waiting," June 13, 2009, 64

228 The Prince of Wales, Newsweek, December 14, 2007 , 56–62

229 The Economist, December 18, 2010, Monitoring Forests. Seeing the World for the Trees, p 153–154

Consumers must do their part. When buying wood products, they should insist on Forest Stewardship Council-stamped products. A Home Depot survey conducted in the summer of 2010 suggested, however, that barely one-third of customers would pay the 2 percent premium for a certified product.

The World's Forests

According to the Food and Agriculture Organization (FAO) the total forested area of the Earth is roughly ten billion acres, covering about 31 percent of the earth's surface. The countries enjoying the largest areas covered by forest are Russia, Brazil, Canada, the United States, China, and Australia.

Not all forests are equal. Rain forests represent only about 20 percent of the earth's forested areas but they have about half of all the trees. There are also differences in the carbon density of forests, depending on their location. The tropical forests on either side of the equator have a carbon content estimated at forty-nine tons of carbon per acre while temperate-zone forests store about twenty-six tons of carbon per acre. Brazil and Indonesia have more than half the remaining tropical forests.

The earth has been losing forests for centuries. **It is estimated that the world has only half the forests that it had three hundred years ago.** The UN's Food and Agriculture Organization estimates that the world is still losing forests at a furious clip. FAO records show that around 29 million acres of forest have been lost each year in the past decade, an area the size of England. The countries losing forests at the fastest rate between 1990 and 2007 were Indonesia at 27.3 percent, Zimbabwe at 23.9 percent, Cambodia at 22.7 percent, Venezuela at 9.4 percent, and Brazil at 9.3 percent.[228] Brazil, because of its size, is responsible for about 48 percent of all deforestation in the world. It lost more than 7 million acres per year between 2000 and 2006. The state of Amazonas alone is projected to lose one-third of its forest by 2050 at the current rate of deforestation, "releasing a colossal 3.5 billion tons of carbon dioxide into the atmosphere."[225] The country experiencing the second greatest loss is Indonesia, which is losing in excess of 4 million acres per year.

The loss of forestland is partially mitigated by new growth and organized tree-planting programs covering about 16 million acres.[16] Europe and North America have long been restoring their forest cover but China is doing so more effectively than any other nation. China is credited for having planted two and a half times more trees in each of the last several years than has the rest of the world combined, 11.7 million acres in 2008 alone. At the impetus of Wangari Maathai, 2004 Noble Peace Prize laureate, the United Nations Environment Program launched the ambitious initiative "Plant for the Planet: Billion Tree Campaign" with the goal of planting seven billion trees. It has already suc-ceeded in planting more than three billion trees.[16]

Forests can also be lost to pests and diseases. About 30 million acres of the boreal forests of Canada have already succumbed to the mountain pine beetles and 7 million acres of U.S. forestland has already been affected. The reason given for those losses is "the lengthening of summer and the reduction in the number of cold snaps that kill off beetle larvae."[16]

American Response

"We need to account for the true costs of emitting greenhouse gas. We cannot continue dumping 70 million tons of CO_2 into our atmosphere every day as if it is a free open sewer." John Doerr, Scientific American.[230]

"Given the well-known environmental harms that result from our life-style, our failure to change amounts to a de facto plan to burden our children and grandchildren with the enormous cost of adapting to a changed global climate." Charles J. Kibert, Sustainable Construction, 2008.[231]

The American movement to curb CO_2 emissions has historically encoun-tered much opposition. In 1997, the U.S. Senate passed a resolution by a vote of 95-0 opposing any measure that would force the United States to cap greenhouse gases. President George W. Bush, shortly after his inauguration in 2001, announced he would not take any action to regulate CO_2 emissions, ush-ering in eight years of maneuvering to protect emitters from caps and financial hardship relative to their emissions. Even when the evidence of a link between manmade CO_2 emissions and climate changes was all but universally accepted, the Bush administration was to the end of its tenure unwilling to join the in-ternational community in developing a new protocol for the one the United States spurned, which is scheduled to expire in 2012.

---

230 John Doerr, Scientific American, Volume 12, Number 1, 2009, 16–17

231 Charles J. Kibert, Sustainable Construction, 2nd Edition, 2008

The president was not alone in his opposition to caps on emissions. Congresspeople and senators representing states that would be most affected by limits on emissions also opposed the legislation. They mostly represented states with large coal reserves, states that burn an inordinate amount of coal for power generation, states with large oil reserves, and heavily industrialized states. Not surprisingly, the National Petrochemical and Refiners Association, U.S. steel companies, and the National Association of Manufacturers have been lobbying against any measure to reduce emissions.

The U.S. Chamber of Commerce has also come out against caps. William I. Kovacs, vice president of the U.S. Chamber of Commerce, argues that such measures would put the United States in an "unfair disadvantage economically."[232] Kovacs goes on to say that the technologies needed to achieve mandated targets do not yet exist or are in embryonic stages of development. Yet he states, "Without incentives to make current energy sources capable of burning more cleanly, to capture and store greenhouse gas emissions, or to replace fossil fuels, the world will have no means of achieving meaningful greenhouse gas reductions." That seems like a pretty good argument in favor of incentives, not against incentives.[232] On more than one occasion, China and India have expressed their intentions to do their part to cut emissions if the United States shows the way, so reducing our emissions could have wide-ranging benefits for the planet. Kovac's concern should be that China will embarrass the United States by showing the way to the United States.

Even farmers who stand to eventually suffer disproportionately from climate change are lobbying against caps on emissions. After months of evaluating the impacts of congressional proposals, the National Corn Growers Association joined the Farm Bureau in opposing legislature to reduce emissions because they would experience higher energy and input (fertilizer) costs. Tim Lenz, president of the Illinois Corn Growers Association, stated, "Once it came out that it was not going to be beneficial to our growers in the long run, we felt that we could no longer stay neutral and that we had to oppose it."[233] Would you not expect farmers to be good stewards of the planet's ecosystem?

Recently some of our legislators have shown leadership in tackling emissions but their efforts have yet to bear fruit. The champions of imposing limits on greenhouse emissions in the Senate have been John McCain, Joe Lieberman,

---

232 William I. Kovacs, U.S. News & World Report, April 2009, 11

233 Martin Ross, FarmWeek, January 25, 2010

and Barbara Boxer. The original McCain and Lieberman bill was soundly defeated in 2003 and again in 2005 when it lost by a vote of sixty to thirty-eight.
A sweeping global warming bill introduced by senators Mark R. Warner and
Joseph Lieberman and backed by Senator Boxer that called for economy-wide
reductions in greenhouse gas emissions was defeated in the Senate as recently
as June 2008. The bill required that the United States reduce its greenhouse
emissions roughly 65 percent by 2050, a period during which emissions would
otherwise likely rise about 30 percent. Under the bill, the government would
print yearly a number of "permits" to emit a set number of tons of CO_2 equiva-
lents, some of the permits to be allocated free and some to be auctioned. The
proceeds of the auctions would net the government hundreds of billions of
dollars. Companies polluting in excess of their free permits would have to buy
more permits from companies that didn't use their allocated permits. The
bill's proponents argued that the measure would finance the shift to clean,
alternative fuels by generating billions of dollars in revenue to finance research
on green energy and investments in the infrastructure. Lacking support from
the Bush administration, the bill was defeated following intense lobbying by
heavy polluters, but it garnered a lot more support than previous attempts
had.[234] [235] [236] The bill's detractors argued that it would put the United States
at a competitive disadvantage with countries like China that don't yet impose emission caps. That's a weak argument. The EU is obviously not afraid
of American or Chinese competition since it is implementing a cap-and-trade
system and has been imposing a heavy tax on gasoline for years.

The fact that the United States spurned the Kyoto Protocol and that our
Washington legislators have been successful in blocking any climate legislation has not prevented states and cities from acting to reduce their emissions.
State governments are already considering ways to harmonize regional trading
systems with each other and with the EU's Emission Trading Scheme under an
effort called the International Carbon Action Partnership.

California has been leading the charge. As early as July 2002, California
Governor Gray Davis signed legislation to curb greenhouse gas emissions from
automobiles. Assembly Bill 32 followed in September 2006, mandating that

---

234 Siobhan Hughes and Stephen Power, The Wall Street Journal, June 6, 2008

235 Robert B. Reich, The Wall Street Journal, June 4, 2008

236 The Wall Street Journal, "Obama's Carbon Busters," December 12, 2008, A18

carbon emissions be cut to 1990 levels by 2020 and to 80 percent below 1990 levels by 2050. Arnold Schwarzenegger, who was California's governor from October 7, 2003 to January 2011, was a staunch supporter of measures to reduce emissions. On December 11, 2008, California adopted the most sweeping plan to cut greenhouse gas emissions. The Air Resources Board unanimously approved a plan that includes thirty-one new rules affecting all facets of life, including restrictions on where people may build their homes and what materials they can use. It includes a cap-and-trade program set to begin in 2012.[237] On June 20, 2009, after a four-year process, California was granted a greenhouse gas waiver, allowing the state to enact strict carbon-emission limits on vehicles, a request that had been denied two years earlier.[238]

California is not resting on its accomplishments. On November 16, 2010, Governor Schwarzenegger launched R20, a public-private partnership of regional players that seek measurable reduction in greenhouse gas emissions within five years.[239] Smartly, Californians are still in favor of protecting the earth's environment. Proposition 23, a November 2010 ballot initiative that would have suspended the "Global Warming Solutions Act of 2006," also known as AB32, was soundly defeated, garnering less than 25 percent of the votes. It is refreshing that Californians think their environment and that of the world is such an important asset. They probably also make the connection between clean energy and job creation.[239]

Other states have also been showing leadership in emissions reduction. In 2003, New York Governor George Pataki launched the Regional Greenhouse Gas Initiative, a confederation of northeastern and mid-Atlantic states that have created their own cap-and-trade program with the goal of reducing emissions 10 percent below the current level by 2019. Ten states were part of the group at the end of 2007. A milestone was reached in October 2008 when coal-fired power plants in those ten states started trading carbon on the open market, making it the nation's first cap-and-trade system for carbon dioxide. Five western states embraced a similar goal in February 2007. A group of three states and three Canadian provinces, members of the coalition called the Western Climate Initiative (WCI), agreed in 2010 to launch "the world's

---

237 The Daily Green, July 1, 2009 (www.dailygreen.com)

238 Angela Wu and Will Oremus: Newsweek, August 16, 2010, 8

239 Eric Pooley, Bloomberg Businessnews, November 29–December 5, 2010, 65

most comprehensive pollution market, one that incorporates transportation and nearly all other businesses." At least ten other states are mulling a similar commitment—either through the WCI or the Midwest group. The success of all those initiatives would result in half the U.S. population living in a cap-and-trade economy.[238] Regrettably, in May 2011, Chris Christie, the governor of New Jersey withdrew his state from the Regional Greenhouse Gas Initiative.

Civic leaders are doing their part. Mayor Greg Nichols of Seattle, reacting to the failure of the United States to endorse the international Kyoto Global Warming Accords, began a nationwide movement to bring U.S. cities into compliance. More than 430 mayors representing more than 61 million people have signed on.

State and local programs have already yielded tangible benefits. A report released by Environment Illinois, entitled "America on the Move," found that seventeen states and the District of Columbia have seen a decline in carbon emissions since 2005 as a result of state and local government initiatives in efficiency programs and investment in clean energy. It concluded that by 2020, state initiatives could reduce carbon emissions by 536 million metric tons, more carbon dioxide than is currently emitted by all but eight of the world's nations.

Influential people outside government are also weighing in. Robert Reich, former Secretary of Labor and author of *Super Capitalism: The Transformation of Business Democracy and Everyday Life*, points out, "The atmosphere belongs to all of us. It seems only reasonable that corporations should have to pay to use it. The citizens of Alaska and the province of Alberta, Canada, get yearly dividends from the oil companies that take away their natural resources. Why shouldn't the same principle apply to industries that use the biggest common resource of all?" Former Vice President Al Gore's campaign to raise public awareness of global climate changes and their relation to burning fossil fuels reached a crescendo with the publication of his book, *An Inconvenient Truth*, in 2007 and the awarding of the Nobel Peace Prize. Gore's campaign has done much to enlighten people of the consequences of burning fossil fuels.

Americans have expressed a strong desire to be good stewards of the planet's environment. Paul Ranker in the May/June 2008 edition of *Sierra* reported the result of a poll conducted by Opinion Research Corporation showing that "nearly nine out of ten citizens support a five-year plan to phase out carbon-based energy." They are not alone in their concern for the planet's ecosystem.

A McKinley survey conducted in September 2007 addressing issues that will be most important in the next five years revealed that out of sixteen issues, Americans listed healthcare benefits as number one and the environment as number two. The Englishmen and Brazilians listed the environment as number one. The Germans and the Chinese listed the environment as their number two concern.[103] The United States must assume a leadership role in curbing worldwide emissions, a central issue internationally.

The debate even found its way to our legal system. The EPA under President Bush decided in 2003 that the Clean Air Act did not cover CO_2 emissions but Massachusetts and several other states joined in a legal challenge, arguing that carbon dioxide is a pollutant. The states lost in a lower court but in June 2006 the U.S. Court agreed to hear the case. On April 2, 2007 the Supreme Court overruled the EPA and declared greenhouse gases, including CO_2, pollutants subject to control under the Clean Air Act.[240]

Following two years of testimony, the EPA on March 20, 2009, issued to the White House an "endangerment finding" that proposed to regulate carbon dioxide (CO_2) and five other greenhouse gases: methane (CH4), nitrous oxide (N_2O), hydrofluorocarbons (HFC) perfluorocarbons (PFC) and sulfur hexafluoride (SF6). (HFC and PFC are used as refrigerants, SF6 has medical applications). That ruling was an essential step toward giving the EPA the authority to regulate emissions of greenhouse gases across a broad section of the economy. On April 17, 2009, the EPA issued a provisional ruling that greenhouse gases are a threat to public health. A final decision had to await the result of sixty days of public hearings. The positive ruling granted the Obama administration legal authority to cap emissions from stationary emitters, such as power plants, and regulate tailpipe emissions.[241] [242] The EPA estimates about thirteen thousand facilities would be covered under the proposal. Those facilities account for between 85 percent and 90 percent of greenhouse gases emitted by stationary sources.[243] The EPA can use the Clean Air Act to enforce the measures allowing emissions to be regulated under existing laws.

240 Michael Northrop and David Sassoon, Environmental Finance, October 2008, 18–19

241 The Economist, "A Green Fig Leaf," April 25, 2009, 36

242 Jim Tankersley, Chicago Tribune, "EPA: Emissions Pose a Health Risk," April 18, 2009

243 Ian Telley, The Wall Street Journal, March 24, 2009

The "endangerment finding" by the EPA was a clarion call for our legislators to act. They did not want to lose the opportunity to politicize the process of reducing CO_2 emissions by ceding control to the EPA.[241] Emitters also preferred to see politicians set the rules.

Cap and Trade

"The easiest, most obvious and most efficient way to employ the power of the market in solving the climate crisis is to put a price on carbon." Al Gore, *Our Choice*, 2009 [16]

B roken down to its simplest form, cap and trade is a system in which each polluting company is allowed a certain amount of pollution, a given number of tons of CO_2 that is referred to as the cap. If company "A" exceeds its cap, it must buy credits in an open market, adding to its cost of operation. If company "B" lowers its emissions, it has surplus credits to sell in the open market, making them available to company "A"—that is the trade part of the cap-and-trade scheme. The price of the credits is determined by supply and demand. The goal is to reward companies that take steps to lower their emissions and penalize companies that don't. By making polluting industries pay a fee, it blunts their competitive advantage vis-à-vis the industries that don't pollute. For example, the cost, on average, of producing one megawatt hour of electricity from coal, accounting for both capital and operating expenses, is $59, according to Milo Sjardin, an analyst at Bloomberg New Energy Finance. Electricity from onshore wind costs an average of $91 per megawatt hour. Analysts have estimated that if carbon costs $30 per ton in the open market, the prices of coal-fired electricity would increase by $21 per megawatt hour, greatly reducing its competitiveness with wind energy.[244]

The Obama administration sent strong signals early on that it was serious about reducing America's carbon emissions. The appointment of Steven Chu, a Nobel laureate for physics, as energy secretary, the appointment of John Holden, who holds a PhD from Stanford and who has won countless awards for his work on climate change and alternative energy, as director of the White House Office of Science and Technology Policy, and the appropria-

244 Jim Snyder and Kim Chipman: Bloomberg BusinessWeek, August 2–August 8, 2010, 32–33

tion of money for clean energy out of the economic stimulus package are signs of the new administration's resolve to decrease America's carbon footprint. President Obama left no doubt of his intention to push for carbon-emission reductions when he addressed the United Nations September 22, 2009. During his speech, the president said, "If we fail to meet the threat from climate change now, we risk consigning future generations to an irreversible catastrophe." He went on to say, "The developed nations that caused much of the damage to our climate over the last century have the responsibility to lead."

Obama's ambitious agenda to reduce emission is supported by large sums of money. The budget for the Department of Energy (DOE) was increased from $24.2 billion in 2008 to $27 billion for 2009 and was the recipient of $38.7 billion from the stimulus package. A large portion went for expansion of research laboratories. Energy R&D received $7.8 billion, 18 percent more than the previous year. Chu calls it the "second industrial revolution."[245] Much of the money was in the form of research grants to universities and research laboratories, tapping the expertise of academia and industry, as well as government research centers. Major investments in superconducting transmission lines and breakthroughs in energy storage and carbon sequestrations will be needed to achieve the president's goal of reducing emissions by 80 percent by 2050. Some compare the enormity of the challenge to the Apollo Program that put a man on the moon.[245]

Obama's commitment to greenhouse-gas-emissions reductions created a favorable climate for proponents of legislation to accomplish such a goal. On June 26, 2009, the House of Representatives approved legislation, introduced by U.S. Representatives Henry Waxman and Edward Markey, known as the American Clean Energy and Security Act by a margin of 219 to 212.[246] The House set targets to reduce greenhouse gas emissions to 17 percent of 2005 levels by 2050 and created the framework for a national cap-and-trade system.

Unfortunately, the bill set emission-reduction targets far lower than science demands.[247] In addition, the bill gave away 85 percent of the carbon permits, worth hundreds of billions of dollars, leaving only 15 percent to be auctioned, which created several problems. Little revenue would be generated

---

245 The Economist, "Energy research. Energizer money," March 28, 2009

246 Greg Hitt and Stephen Powers, The Wall Street Journal, June 27–28, 2009,

247 The Daily Green (www.dailygreen.com), June 29,

and favoritism would play a part in the allocation of permits. This grand hand-out to polluters is meant to last until around 2030 (probably later, if industry lobbyists retain their clout) by which time all permits will be auctioned. The bill also allows carbon-trading offsets so generous that they undermine the efforts to reduce emissions. Worse, big polluters want the option of acquiring permits by funding projects that mitigate emissions in other countries where they may be cheaper than in the United States—inexpensive enough to re-move any real incentive to invest in emission-reduction measures. The Envi-ronmental Protection Agency estimates the price of emitting a ton of carbon dioxide under the Waxman-Markey bill passed by the House of Representa-tives June 26, 2009, would be 89 percent higher if it did not allow polluters to buy offsets overseas.[248] American Electric Power Company, one of the biggest CO_2 emitters in the country, estimates that it would have to spend roughly five times as much to retool its power plants to reduce its emissions by an amount equal to what it could offset by purchasing credits, essentially defeat-ing the purpose of the law. The National Commission on Energy Policy esti-mates that the offsets allowed annually under the U.S. system would amount to about 1.5 billion metric tons of CO_2, five times as much as all the offsets used by countries that ratified the Kyoto Protocol. Because the bill was so depend-ent on offsets, it was estimated that conventional coal-powered generation in the United States would only decrease from 1,992 terawatt hours in 2005 to 1,950 terawatt hours in 2020.

There is also the issue of "bogus" credits, credits being assigned to CO_2 emission-sparing practices that were already in place, such as no-till farming or some forest protection measures. As the Government Accountability Office concluded in a recent study, it is nearly impossible to ensure that international offset projects reduce greenhouse gases more than would have happened without subsidies. The agency concluded that Europe's use of offsets had an uncertain effect on carbon emissions.

The Senate version of climate legislation was being championed by Sena-tors John Kerry, Joe Lieberman, and Lindsey Graham. It was also shaping up as a watered-down version of the administration's initial idea, likely to be applied only to electrical utilities. The industrial, transport, and agricultural-related emissions would be addressed later. One year after passage of the House ver-sion, hopes for Senate passage of the bill were dashed when Senate Majority

248 Stephen Power, The Wall Street Journal, June 27–28, 2009

Leader Harry Reid unveiled on July 27, 2010, the "Clean Energy Jobs and Oil Company Accountability Act." The two most important clean energy provisions were omitted: a cap on carbon emissions from utility companies and a national Renewable Electricity Standard. The latter provision would have required the power industry to generate a minimum of 15 percent of its electricity from renewable sources by 2021.[249]

President Obama appeared to distance himself from the political process. That was inconsistent with the many strong statements he made to the American people and to the world about the need for the United States to reduce its greenhouse gas emissions and with his personal commitment to that goal.

The president could still have the last word. He made it clear early in his presidency that if Congress failed to act, he would use his authority to control greenhouse gases. The Supreme Court declaration that greenhouse gases are pollutants subject to control under the Clean Air Act confers him the authority to ask the EPA to regulate carbon emissions. The severity of those regulations would be at the government's discretion. The EPA's authority took effect in January 2011. It is now the only tool the government has to combat climate change. Lisa Jackson, the agency's administrator, has moved cautiously, making clear that she will target only the largest polluters. Not unexpectedly, the regulatory process is eliciting as much opposition as did the legislative process. Business groups led by the U.S. Chamber of Commerce are initiating lawsuits contesting the EPA's authority to regulate greenhouse gases under the Clean Air Act in spite of the Supreme Court ruling. Elected officials representing states that have stakes in the mining or burning of coal are joining in the effort to stop or postpone the EPA's plan. Texas Governor Rick Perry has filed a lawsuit against the agency for singling out power plants and refineries. Senator John Barrasso who, in 2010, helped kill the senate version of the energy and climate bill, has introduced a bill that would bar the EPA from regulating carbon pollution. The Wyoming Senator's position is in sharp contrast to his stated position shortly after he joined the Senate in 2007. He told his constituents that the country's biggest need was an energy policy to deal with CO_2 emissions. Senator James Inhofe of Oklahoma has also unveiled a bill to undercut the EPA's authority to regulate CO_2 emissions. Similar bills have been introduced in the House of Representatives. The seating in January 2011 of

---

249   Eric Pooley: Bloomberg BusinessWeek, "American Sits Out of the Race," August 2–August 8, 2010, 32

at least forty-seven new lawmakers who deny that scientific data prove human activity is warming to the planet will swell the ranks of those opposing
measures to make the United States more environmentally aligned with the
rest of the world. The newly elected senators and house members say they
will seek to rollback EPA rules.[250] Representative Darrell Issa, incoming chair
of the House Oversight and Government Reform Committee, plans to investigate how EPA's clean-air rules may affect the economy.[250] The newly elected
lawmakers say they also may try to block billions of dollars in federal funds
earmarked for wind, solar, and other alternative energy sources.[250] Elected officials and business leaders choose to ignore long-term benefits for the country
and the world in favor of short-term gains for their small constituencies or
their corporations.

Cost to Consumers

The anticipated rise in electricity cost and its impact on the economy are
other stumbling blocks to passage of carbon legislation. The authors of *Leveling the Carbon Playing Field* argue that the damage would be small.[251] Most
manufacturers do not use much energy. Energy makes up less than 1 percent
of the cost of making cars, furniture, or computers. Many energy-intensive
industries, such as power generation, have no foreign competition. They could
pass on extra costs to their customers. A few industries, such as cement, metal,
paper, and chemical, are global and use enough energy to suffer from foreign
competition. These industries accounted for only 5 percent of America's output. A study sponsored by Resources for the Future in America, a think tank,
concluded that America's industrial output would fall by less than 1 percent
if subjected to a carbon tax of $10 a ton (the European price was around $30
per ton in 2009). Another study, this one by the Pew Center on Global Climate
Change, assessed the effects of a $15 carbon price. It concluded that output
would fall by 2 percent or less in 80 percent of cases.

The cost to the consumer of implementing the House version of the bill
varied depending on the source. The nonpartisan Congressional Budget Office

---

250 Bloomberg Businessweek, "Climate Skeptics Storm the Capital," November 29–December 5, 2010,
33–34

251 Trevor Houser, Rob Bradley, Britt Childs, Jacob Werksman and Robert Heilmayr: Leveling the
Carbon Playing Field, 2008

(CBO) had estimated that the legislation would have had a modest impact, with a net annual economy-wide cost in 2020 of $22 billion, or about $175 per household.[252] Official EPA estimates put the average annual increased energy cost per household at $98 to $140. The cost of provisions contained in the Senate version known as the Kerry-Lieberman Climate Bill was pegged at $80 to $150 per household annually. It should be viewed as an investment in our future and a small price to pay to improve the environment for billions of people and gain the respect of the world.

The other part of the equation that is never mentioned when discussing the "increased cost per household" for electricity is the fact that **there are countless ways that people can decrease their energy use to mitigate the effects of higher unit cost.** Isn't that the purpose of higher electricity cost? Californians use 50 percent less power than the rest of the country in part because their electricity rates are higher. So much power is wasted.

Imperatives of Carbon Legislation

L egislation to set a price on carbon emissions to fairly account for the environmental cost of processes that emit greenhouse gases will benefit the environment, the clout of the United States in the world, and eventually the U.S. economy.

Raising the cost of activities that damage the atmosphere, more specifically the cost of energy generated by fossil fuels, is the best way to support investments in renewable energy and energy-efficient technologies and engage the country in the green revolution, which many view as the next big engine of economic growth. The International Energy Agency estimates that $33 trillion will be invested in the next twenty years to transition the world to low-carbon energy generation. Already, the global green economy is believed to be worth close to $4 trillion. Some analysts using rather elastic definitions estimate that there are already 800,000 "green jobs" in Britain in an industry worth 106 billion pounds ($175 billion). Germany estimates that green-tech could create one million new German jobs by 2020. The government's promise to put one million electric cars on the road by 2020 is one of many of Germany's initiatives.

In an article titled "America Sits Out the Race," Eric Pooley expressed concern that without a comprehensive climate and energy policy, the country risks

252 Stephen Powers and Greg Hitt, The Wall Street Journal, June 26, 2009

losing the jobs of the future. "Banks and venture capitalists increasingly are putting their energy money into China, where the market is large and secure, thanks to government mandates."[249] In the second quarter of 2010, China's investments in clean energy climbed 72 percent to $11.5 billion while U.S. investments amounted to $4.9 billion. During the year of uncertainty about the Senate's position on cap and trade, "the deployment rate of renewable energy projects in America withered," said Andy Karsner, former assistant secretary for energy efficiency and renewable energy.[249] The opposition to public policies that would foster our country's transition to a carbon-benign economy is short-sighted from an economic point of view. The lack of incentive in favor of renewable energy is keeping hundreds of billions of dollars on the sidelines. Deploying those funds would create countless jobs.

The benefits to the environment of carbon legislation are broadly recognized. If nothing changes in the way we generate power, the IEA estimates that worldwide greenhouse gas emissions will rise 60 percent by 2030, with coal-rich China leading the way and coal-rich America, India, and Russia close behind. If we continue to spill CO_2 into the atmosphere at about three times the rate at which it can be reabsorbed, it is projected that the CO_2 concentration in the earth's atmosphere will reach 880 ppm by 2100.

Passage of climate legislation is needed from a geopolitical standpoint. Tom Freidman, the author of *Hot, Flat, and Crowded*, believes that shifting from fossil fuels to a low-carbon economy is not just an opportunity for the United States but also a test. "It is a test of whether we are able and willing to lead."[253] At the climate talks in Copenhagen in December 2009, it was clear from the deliberations that if the United States failed to lead, progress in limiting greenhouse gas emissions would greatly suffer. The president pledged his support. Failure to enact legislation to reduce emissions undermines the power of the president in the international arena, a long-term loss for all Americans. Legislators should take that into consideration before opposing climate legislation for the sake of their own popularity.

We also need to show consideration for our allies and traditional trading partners by competing on a level playing field. All twenty-seven countries of the EU have signed the Kyoto Protocol and have enacted measures to live by their commitments. Leaders of those nations have expressed their frustrations with other countries' lack of commitment to environmental respect. France's

253   Thomas L. Friedman: Hot, Flat and Crowded, (New York, 10011, Farrar, Straus & Giroux), 2008

President Nicolas Sarkozy wants the EU to build in a "carbon tariff." Sarkozy says he will push for a Europe-wide carbon tax on imports from countries that "do not respect any environmental or social rule." It would be the epitome of shortsightedness if America failed to cap its emissions only to see its products subjected to an import tax that would blunt the United States' competitiveness and fill the coffers of foreign countries because we lacked the foresight and resolve to act responsibly as a nation.

President Sarkozy's idea of a European "carbon tariff" is surreptitiously being implemented, thanks to the quiet spreading of the carbon-footprint labeling movement. According to The Economist Technology Quarterly Report in the June 4, 2011 issue, French retailers, backed by the French environmental ministry are leading a movement to add carbon-footprint labels to a range of products from clothing to furniture. The practice consists of posting on product labels information on the quantity of carbon-dioxide emissions attributed to the product. The main purpose is to allow shoppers to choose the most environmentally benign products. Adding a carbon label to a product involves tracing the products components back up their respective supply chains and through their manufacturing processes. Some labels include information on "use-phase" emissions using statistical assumptions about consumers' behavior. The objective is the introduction of compulsory carbon-labeling rules possibly as soon as 2012. The labeling requirements will apply to imported goods as well as those made in France. Other European countries will be watching the French experiment closely, not least because their own exporters may soon have to adhere to the French rules. Inevitably, this will call for a European standard for carbon labeling.

American legislators who oppose the implementation of measures that promote energy efficiency and environmentally sound practices are ignoring a global movement that risks marginalizing American-made products. The "black footprint" logo has already been added to product labels in Japan, South Korea, Thailand, Canada, Switzerland and Sweden.

■ Chapter Four: What You Must Do For Your Country

❋ Make your home more energy efficient
❋ Support ordinances that will mandate higher energy efficiency for new

homes and commercial buildings

* Lobby for incentives to make existing buildings more energy efficient
* Lobby your senators and representatives to defend the EPA's authority to limit carbon emissions
* Support cap-and-trade legislation
* Buy the most energy-efficient appliances and light bulbs
* Install programmable thermostats; maintain indoor temperatures as close to the outdoor temperature as possible, especially when sleeping or absent from your home
* Accept higher energy cost as your contribution to a more livable planet for future generations
* View higher energy cost as an incentive for Americans to start saving energy

Chapter 5: Renewable Energy

The world is moving away from fossil fuels. The green economy is growing at a rate of 30 percent a year worldwide. Europe, China, and the Middle East all have plans to transition to more carbon-benign economies. Brazil already generates between 80 percent and 90 percent of its power from renewable sources, making energy one of Brazil's most important industrial sectors. The economy, the geopolitical interests, and the image of the United States would be well served by embracing renewable energy.

The United States is blessed with almost limitless renewable energy. Its wind assets are among the best in the world. Its solar energy could satisfy most of its electricity needs. A lot of its hydroelectric power potential remains untapped. Its West Coast sits atop enormous geothermal resources. The nuclear technology of some of its companies is world-class. The United States needs to start exploiting more thoroughly its prized natural resources and its scientific and technical assets.

A key component of plans to tap renewable energy is the expansion and the upgrade of the country's power transmission and distribution systems since much of our renewable energy sources are far from our large urban centers. It is also important from the standpoint of reducing energy losses and energy consumption. The "smart grid" has two main components: the transmission infrastructure and the end users' capabilities.

Smart Grid

"Just as the United States benefited from the national vision of an interstate highway system and, later, the 'information superhighway' that became the Internet, the development of a unified, national smart grid would create millions of new jobs and sharply reduce its CO_2 emissions." Al Gore, Our Choice, 2009 [16]

Modernizing America's electricity distribution network and refining customer utilization are critically important from the standpoint of the country's competitiveness with the rest of the world and the country's need to reduce its greenhouse-gas emissions. The so-called smart grid would reduce transmission losses, reduce energy consumption, and avoid system failures. Outages alone cost the American economy $150 billion a year.[254] It also is a necessary component of the drive to tap renewable energy resources, since the most productive wind and solar energy resources are mostly located in remote areas far away from the dense population centers.

It is well known that our transmission and distribution systems are wasteful, vulnerable, and too fragmented. **Huge amounts of power are lost to technological problems. For every kilowatt used, 2.2 kWh are lost on average as that energy is sent over transmission lines.**[255] New high-capacity power lines are needed. The Galvin Electricity Initiative, a nonprofit organization founded in 2004 by Bob Galvin, former CEO of Motorola, to lead a campaign to transform the way we generate, deliver, and use electricity studied the impacts of the outmoded power system on productivity and competitiveness.[256] It concluded, "At least a trillion dollars in gross domestic product is already being lost each year as a result, and that cost is growing rapidly as the digital economy expands."

Transmissions lines – For every kWh used, 2.2 kWh are lost, on average, as the energy is sent over transmission lines. (Photo: The Author)

The United States needs a new transmission backbone, connecting distant power-generating centers with large urban centers. The high-voltage transmis-

254 The Economist, "Smart Grids. Wiser Wires," October 10, 2009, 71–73

255 Peter Miller, National Geographic March 2009, 62–81

256 Galvin Initiative, www.galvinpower.org/

sion systems of the four main North American regions comprise around two hundred thousand miles of power lines. The main weakness of the system is that those transmission lines are controlled by five hundred different owners carrying power from thousands of power plants, complicating planning on a grand scale. Another problem is that the four regional systems are linked by transmission lines that don't provide nearly enough capacity to move power back and forth. There are also bottlenecks between areas of the same regional system that hobble the entire system.[257]

Transporting electricity in the form of alternative current (AC), as we do in America and the rest of the world, is very wasteful. High-voltage direct current (HVDC) can be transported long distance by wire without incurring any significant loss. For that reason, HVDC is considered the best choice for the transmission of electricity from remote solar and wind locations. It also has the advantage that cables can be laid underwater and underground at a lower cost than tower transmissions and with less public opposition. Europe already has an embryo of an HVDC grid. It links the Scandinavian countries, the Netherlands, and Northern Germany. America needs to invest in its infrastructure if it is going to be competitive in this changing world.

A major stumbling block to upgrading the transmission system is the multitude of jurisdictions that the lines must cross. The federal government needs more authority over states, local jurisdictions, and other interest groups to cut a path for those transmission lines. Implementing a truly efficient national grid requires a national strategy, not a state-by-state strategy. Some planners opine that a regulatory lever already exists: the 2005 Energy Act, which gave the Department of Energy "backup authority" to approve new power lines over state objections.[257]

President Obama has plans to modernize the nation's power network. Eleven billion of the $787 billion American Recovery and Reinvestment Act was set aside to help finance the upgrade. Utility companies and venture capital firms are also pouring billions of dollars into the grid. About seventy utilities are planning rollouts of smart grids at a cost of $64 billion through 2016.[258] The cornerstones of the federal plan are the installation of three thousand miles of

---

257 Daniel Glick, Newsweek, "Special Advertising Section. Sharp's Solar Solutions," August 3, 2009, 14–23

258 Paul Davidson, USA Today, January 30, 2009, 10B

transmission lines and the installation of forty million smart meters in homes, emphasizing the importance of conservation.[258]

An important component of a "smart grid" is the ability of the end user to adjust its power usage according to the availability and price of electricity at a given time, the so-called demand response. It is important from the standpoint of saving power and reducing carbon emissions, reducing customers' expenses, and decreasing the need for new generation capacity. While energy use is growing at a rate of 1.5 percent to 2.0 percent per year, peak load demand is increasing at a rate of 5–7 percent annually, forcing utilities to invest in generation and transmission capacity that is used only 5–10 percent of the time.[16] People have been observed to curtail their electricity use by 15 percent or more during peak pricing periods when they are able to assess the cost of electricity in real time. A 2008 trial by Baltimore Gas and Electric showed that customers with smart meters reduced their electricity consumption by up to 37 percent during peak periods. During a one-year pilot study carried out by Pacific Northwest National Laboratory (PNNL), consumers who installed smart meters reduced their electricity bill by 10 percent on average compared with the previous year. The modernization of America's power network must emphasize better use of available electricity. Smart meters are the cornerstone of better energy-efficiency. They track electricity use in real time and can transmit that information back to the power company, establishing a two-way data connection between the user and the provider. Smart meters will allow utilities to vary the price of electricity throughout the day, allowing people to avoid peak pricing and informing them or their appliances directly of cheaper pricing opportunities.

Installing smart meters for every American home will not be cheap. California's utilities alone will be spending $4.5 billion on smart meter installation in the next few years. They have plans to install 12 million smart meters. PG&E is installing 10,000 smart meters a day and wants to equip 4 million homes by the end of 2011.[254]

The United States is not leading the way in smart metering. Enel, Italy's main utility, has already deployed more than 30 million smart meters. Sweden has recently become the first country where all customers have smart meters.[254] The province of Ontario, Canada, told its utilities to install a smart meter in every household by 2010. Province wide, Hydro One had installed 1.2 million Smart Meters at the end of the year. In January 2011, five hundred thousand of its customers were already consuming power according to Time of Use pricing. Some 76 million smart meters have been installed worldwide, a number that is forecasted to double by 2013 and almost triple by 2015.

Another obstacle to the deployment of a smart grid is the reluctance of some utility companies to participate in a scheme that is certain to reduce demand for the product they sell. Smart meters that allow customers to monitor their consumption reduce total consumption. California has successfully addressed that issue by "decoupling" the relationship between electricity sales and profit. The result has been that electricity consumption per person has stayed essentially the same over the past thirty years while it has increased by roughly 50 percent in the rest of the country.

Future gains in energy efficiency may also be achieved by improving storage capacity and moving energy generation closer to the end-users. Electricity storage technology is mobilizing a lot of brain power and attracting a lot of venture capital because of the new emphasis on renewable energy, the main sources of which, solar and wind, are intermittent. The advent of electric vehicles is providing the other impetus for energy-storage research. Lithium-ion batteries, sodium-sulfur batteries and other types of batteries may eventually replace large-capacity schemes such as "pumped hydro," which consists of pumping water up when there is excess power and using the falling water to drive turbines during peak demand. Making ice at night and using it to cool buildings in the daytime is another means of storing electricity. Bank of America Tower at the corner of Sixth Avenue and Forty-second Street in New York City makes more than half a million pounds of ice at night, a source of a thousand tons of air conditioning the next day.

The ability on the part of the customers to own and operate their own devices to generate and even store power could eliminate much of the loss associated with long-distance transmission. Small-scale generators already exist in the form of photovoltaic panels and small wind turbines. Fuel cells, micro turbines, and other energy-generating systems offer some promise but at present they are not cost-effective measures for reducing carbon emissions. The price of reducing emissions using micro-generation devices is more than ten times the price of mitigating emissions through the European emissions-trading scheme.[259] Nevertheless, American Electric Power reports that some

---

259 The Economist, "Energy Policy. Efficiency Drive," July 31, 2010, 44

renewable sources of electricity generation owned by their customers have grown "by a factor of one thousand in a decade."[16]

Solar Energy

The sun is ultimately the source of all our energy. Crude oil and coal are residues from plants that grew using the sun's energy, a process called photosynthesis, before they were buried deep under the surface of the Earth two hundred million to five hundred million years ago. The solar heating of the earth's surface and oceans determine the earth's atmospheric temperature and fuels wind farms, hydroelectric-power generators and oceans' wave power. But when people talk about solar energy, they usually refer to one of three forms of solar power: passive solar heating, photovoltaic energy, or solar thermal devices.

Every day, the sun sends to the earth an unimaginable amount of energy from ninety-one million miles away.[257] We harvest only an infinitesimal portion of it. Scientists calculate that enough sunlight reaches the earth every hour to supply the world's electricity needs for a whole year.[260] Each year, the sun bathes the earth in 85,000 terawatts of energy. Here is how we can capture some of it.

Passive Solar Energy

Passive solar heating consists of the sun shining on an object that absorbs that heat. A house exposed to the sun's rays is warmer than one shaded from the sun. Some houses in cold climates are specifically designed to take advantage of the heat of the sun with a heat-absorbing floor that is exposed to solar rays shining through south-facing windows. The tile/concrete floors radiate heat for hours after sunset. Architects have started incorporating in building design decorative tubes filled with water positioned to absorb the heat of the sun. Deciduous trees are also used by landscape architects to shade buildings in the summer and expose buildings to the sun's rays during winter.

Photovoltaic Energy

In the 1800s, French physicist A. E. Becquerel discovered the phenomenon called photovoltaics.[257] Photovoltaic (PV) devices are solar cells that use the

260 David Roberts, Popular Science, "The Future of Energy. Solar Power," July 2009, 40

sun's energy directly to generate electricity. They consist of semiconductor materials, usually silicon. When sunlight is absorbed by these materials, the solar energy knocks electrons loose from their atoms. These free electrons then travel into a circuit built into the solar cell that uses the sun's energy directly to generate photovoltaic power.

Commercial application of this discovery is credited to a Japanese businessman, Tokuji Hayakawa, the Sharp company founder, who set out in 1959 to turn that discovery into a working reality. In 1963, Sharp installed photovoltaic-powered buoys in Yokohama Bay as an alternative to the impractical oil or gas buoys that required frequent servicing. In 1966, Sharp installed photovoltaic panels on the lighthouse located on Ogami Island.[257] It was then the largest solar-energy system in the world. In 2007, the worldwide installed photovoltaic capacity was estimated at 9.2 gigawatts, but it accounted for less than 1 percent of the world's electricity output. Photovoltaic energy is attractive from a business-opportunity standpoint. One only has to consider the fact that more than 1.6 billion people have little or no electricity, according to a 2005 United Nations' report. Photovoltaic energy offers the chance to bypass centralized grid systems and centralized power plants.[257]

Solar cells currently provide only a fraction of 1 percent of the U.S. electricity need but there are plans to foster the growth of PV energy. The United States has a large and mostly untapped photovoltaic capacity. On January 1, 2007, SB1 became a new California state law that provided $3.2 billion in funding to build a million solar roofs over the next ten years. Another driving force behind the push for renewable energy in California is the requirement that utilities purchase at least 20 percent of their power from renewable energy producers by 2010.[259] The city of Denver, Colorado, went one step further, investing in PV. Last summer the city inaugurated a 7.5-acre PV system at its International Airport. The system is expected to generate more than 3 million kWh of electricity every year.[257] The U.S. Air Force is also tapping solar energy. In 2008, it installed more than seventy thousand solar panels at its Nellis Air Force Base in Nevada on 140 acres of vacant land, creating a vast renewable source of energy, saving us roughly $83,000 on our military's monthly electric bill. The panels follow the movement of the sun for maximum effect.[261]

261 Anna Mulrive, U.S. News and World Report, "Green is More Than the Color of Camo," April, 2009, 42–43

Photovoltaic capacity is expanding in many countries. Germany is a country that enjoys little sunshine and is much smaller than the United States but has been installing an average of 750 megawatts of solar photovoltaic capacity every year since 2005. In 2009, it accounted for roughly half of new installations around the world.[262] At the beginning of 2007, it operated 2,500 megawatts of solar photovoltaic electricity-generating capacity.[257] China, not surprisingly, is the largest manufacturer of solar panels, followed by Japan and Germany.[18]

Thin-film technologies are seen as the next generation of photovoltaic technology. It is at the heart of many new solar applications, like building-integrated PV and other coatings. The thin-film panels use a fraction of the amount of silicone that crystalline panels do, reducing their cost. Thin-film panels make up about 15 percent of $28 billion global solar-panel market. Sharp's Sakai plant is expected to produce up to one gigawatt of thin-film solar panels annually.[257] First Solar, a Tempe, Arizona, company is the leader in the field with an output of about 1 gigawatt a year. Abound Solar of Loveland, Colorado, on the strength of a $400 million loan guarantee from the U.S. Energy Department, is another emerging player in the solar-panel industry with an annual panel production of 200 megawatts. Another innovation is solar panels using cadmium-telluride instead of silicone, which costs less than silicone-based panels.[262]

A nascent technology referred to as "concentrated photovoltaic" uses special mirrors and lenses to direct more sunlight on solar panels. The technology is presently generating only 10 megawatts of electricity worldwide, but it is projected to generate 6 gigawatts of electricity by 2020. Sol Focus, a Silicon Valley company, is supplying the technology to installations in Spain and Greece. Sharp is also testing concentrated photovoltaic but reckons that commercial applications are still a few years out.[263]

Solar-Thermal Energy

Solar-thermal energy has application for small domestic systems and large commercial operations. The domestic systems consist of solar water-heating systems that heat water directly or heat a "working fluid" that is then cir-

---

262 The Economist, April 17, 2010, The Rise of Big Solar, Growing Pains, 69–70

263 Justin Ewers, U.S. News World Report, "Keeping The Solar Dream Alive," April 2009, 21–22

culated through a system of tubes immersed in water to heat the surrounding water. Solar thermal energy is already popular in many countries. China has the largest number of solar-heated hot-water systems in the world. By 2006, at least 10 percent of households had them.[264] Germany's solar thermal capacity is more than double its photovoltaic capacity at 6,300 megawatts. Israel also derives a large percentage of its hot water using rooftop systems. Solar water-heating systems can be cost-effective nearly anywhere in the United States and offer the quickest return on capital investment of any solar energy system.

Solar water-heating systems - They can be cost-effective nearly anywhere in the United States and offer the quickest return on capital investment of any solar energy system. (Photo: IStock Photo #10091467)

Commercial operations take it a step further by focusing the sun's energy. Concentrating solar thermal (CST) technology consists of solar water-heating systems that use mirrors to concentrate the sun's rays to heat water. The modern solar-thermal power technology evolved as a result of the oil crisis of the 1970s. The first company to achieve a commercial-scale operation was Luz International of Israel, founded in1980. Luz built a se-

264 Bay Fang, U.S. News and World Report, June 12, 2006, 37–40

ries of power stations in California's Mojave Desert in the mid-1980s using parabolic troughs to focus sunlight into liquid-filled tubes. By 1990, Luz operated nine plants with a total capacity of 354 megawatts. Concentrated solar power (CSP) heats water to the boiling point. The resulting steam drives turbines similar to those found at power plants that run on coal or natural gas. Acciona, a Spanish corporation, has a plant near Las Vegas, Nevada, called "Nevada Solar One" that can generate up to 64 megawatts.[265] So far, about 500 megawatts of capacity has been built in the United States. The Solar Energy Industries Association claims that CSP plants in the pipeline in the United States have a total capacity of 4,000 megawatts.[265] According to New Energy Finance, 2,000 megawatts of concentrated solar-thermal power is in planning stages in Europe. One of CSP's advantages is that it does not require expensive photovoltaic cells to transform the sun's energy into electricity.[265]

Bill Gross, the CEO of e-Solar, a Google-funded start-up, believes that CST is "probably the only thing that can be done at a big enough scale to produce terawatts." At its first e-Solar power plant northeast of Los Angeles, twenty-four thousand mirrors direct sunlight on water-filled towers. The resulting steam spins turbines, generating electricity. In February 2009, e-Solar signed a deal to build eleven 46-megawatt plants in the southwest and is set to build one gigawatt worth of plants in India using small, flat mirrors attached to computerized sun-tracking scaffolding.[260] At least thirteen plants are in advanced planning stages in the United States.

BrightSource Energy, a start-up based in Oakland, California, is developing a variation of this technology. The company is gearing up to install thousands of small mirrors in a circle around a central tower filled with water. The sunlight is concentrated on the tower, heating the water into steam, which is then transferred to a power station where it spins a turbine.[266] The company already raised $100 million and in 2010 received government loan guarantees to help build its first 400-megawatt solar plant called Ivanpah at an estimated cost of $1 billion.[262] The company has plans to construct a series of fourteen solar power plants that will collectively produce more than 2,600 megawatts of electricity. Pacific Gas and Electricity (PG&E), the northern California utility company, has agreed to buy 900 megawatts

---

265 The Economist, "Solar-Energy. The Power of Concentration," February 23, 2008, 84

266 Justin Ewers, U.S. News World Report, "Keeping The Solar Dream Alive," April 2009, 21–22

from BrightSource. Southern California Edison has agreed to purchase 1,300 megawatts.[266]

Solar-thermal power stations have several advantages over solar-photo-voltaic ones. They usually have a much greater capacity. They are built at lower cost and are most efficient when it is hottest and demand is the greatest. Additionally, since they produce steam to generate electricity, most plans can be easily supplemented with natural gas. Both power-tower and parabolic-trough systems can store thermal energy in the form of hot, molten salt that can produce steam even when the sun in not shining.

A third solar-thermal technology uses a mirrored parabolic dish to collect and focus the sun's energy into a sterling engine, A sterling engine converts heat into mechanical energy by compressing and expanding a fixed quantity of gas. Sterling Energy Systems, based in Scottsdale, Arizona, has pioneered the design and development of this technology. In January 2010, the company announced the opening of its Maricopa Solar power plant in Phoenix, Arizona. It is the first commercial project of its kind.

Wind Energy

The U.S. government's goal is to generate 20 percent of our electricity from wind power by 2030. Currently, the United States derives about 2 percent of its electricity from wind. Ramping up wind-generated electricity to satisfy 20 percent of demand presents a serious challenge, especially since consumption in 2030 will be 25 percent over what it is today. Achieving the government's goal will require a commitment of the magnitude of President Kennedy's ten-year plan to put a man on the moon. In a May 2008 report entitled, "20 Percent Wind Energy by 2030," the U.S. Department of Energy envisioned increasing capacity by 16,000 MW per year by 2018 and continuing at that rate toward the goal of 20 percent wind-powered electricity generation by 2030. That represents about ten thousand new wind turbines each year. (The wind turbines erected at wind farms are typically rated at 1.5 megawatts.) The Department of Energy also concluded that meeting that commitment would require an investment of at least $60 billion in new transmission systems.

Land-based wind turbine – The United States is considered to have one of the largest wind potentials of any country in the world. Currently, the United States derives only about 2 percent of its electricity from wind. (Photo: IStock Photo #9458693)

There are encouraging signs. Wind is already the second fastest growing source of energy after natural gas. It accounted for 30 percent of all new capacity added in the United States in 2007. In 2008, the wind industry added 8,358 megawatts of capacity, raising the United States' total wind power capacity to 25,170 megawatts.[267] In 2009, roughly 9,900 megawatts were added, according to the American Wind Energy Association (AWEA), bringing the total wind energy capacity in the United States to 35,000 megawatts, enough energy to power approximately 9.7 million homes.[268] Figure 8 compares the wind-energy production of the ten states with the greatest capacity.[269]

---

267 Frederic Cote, Les affaires, May 30, to June 5, 2009, A15

268 Environmental Building News, "U.S. Wind Industry Breezes to New Heights in 2009," March 2010, 6

269 Kay Shipman, FarmWeek, May 4, 2009

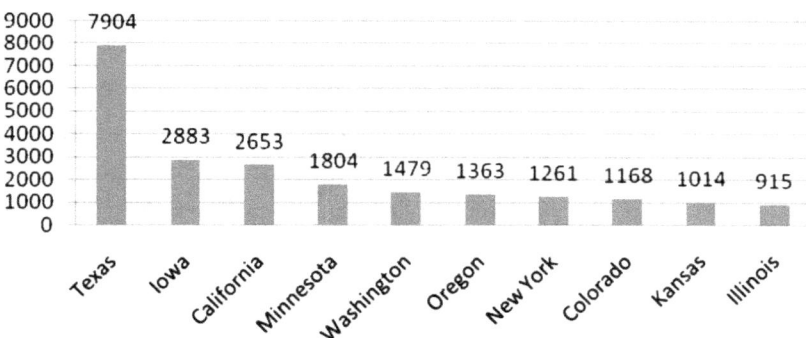

Figure 9: Top ten Wind Energy Generating States; Source: Kay Shipman, FarmWeek, May 4, 2009

Energy experts believe that wind power is capable of becoming a major contributor to the U.S. electricity supply. **The United States is considered to have one of the largest wind potentials of any country in the world after China.** "The United States' Great Plains are the Saudi Arabia of wind power," says Lester Brown of the Energy Institute. "Three wind-rich states, North Dakota, Kansas, and Texas, have enough harnessable wind to meet national electricity needs."

World wind power capacity is also growing at 30 percent a year, presenting great business opportunities for American companies. Worldwide in 2007, there were 97,200 turbines putting out 94,005 megawatts, triple the electricity generated in 2002. In 2008, there were 121,000 MW of installed capacity worldwide.[267] In 2009 the installed capacity had increased another 31 percent to 157,000 MW. That was still only a small percentage of the global electricity consumption of 15,000,000 megawatts. Some countries are far ahead of the United States in tapping wind for energy. Denmark draws more of its power from wind than any other country in the world at 20 percent. Germany, Spain, and Portugal draw significant amounts of power from wind, between 6 percent and 8 percent of their electricity. The United States draws only about 2 percent of its power needs from wind energy but is nevertheless the number one producer of total wind power, having leapfrogged Germany. Minneapolis-based Xcel is the largest U.S. wind-power producer.

Ocean Breeze

I f America is going to meet its 20 percent target for wind energy, wind
energy specialists feel it will need to look offshore to install giant wind
turbines. The challenge for the United States is the depth of the water off
our Pacific Coast. Present offshore wind operations are concentrated in the
North Sea and Baltic Sea in shallow water ranging from thirty to ninety feet
deep. With about one gigawatt of installed capacity, Britain has more turbines
around its coasts than any other country.[260]

Sea-based wind turbine – Wind energy specialists feel that if the United States is to reach
its target to generate 20% of its electricity from wind power by 2030, it will need to look
offshore to install giant turbines. (Photo: IStock Photo #10768231)

Some European firms have designed and are experimenting with floating
constructions, similar to those used in the offshore oil industry, which would
be appropriate for use in deep water such as that off our Pacific coast. Blue H
Technology BV of the Netherlands, Statoil Hydro of Norway, and Force Technology are leading the industry in developing floating construction. A pro-
totype called Submerged Deepwater Platform (SDP) for use in waters more

than three hundred feet deep is already in place off the coast of southern Italy. The technology uses platforms filled with ballast that extend several hundred feet below the surface of the water and are anchored to the bottom of the ocean.[260] This opens up new possibilities for our wind industry to harvest wind from the sea near our densely populated southern California coast; Portland, Oregon; and Seattle, Washington, from turbines typically rated twice as high as onshore turbines. Even though offshore wind energy production presents many advantages over onshore installations—such as higher wind speed, improved wind profile, and limited environmental impact—installation currently produces just over 1,000 MW, accounting for only 1.5 percent of the world's wind-generated electricity. Predictions are for offshore capacity to reach as much as one-third of the all wind energy produced by 2020. According to the U.S. Department of the Interior, seabound wind farms off the Pacific coast could generate 900 gigawatts of electricity every year.[260]

Shallower waters off the Eastern Seaboard present fewer technical challenges. On April 28, 2010, Interior Secretary Ken Salazar of the Obama administration approved what would become the nation's first offshore wind turbine operation, the Cape Wind's 130-turbine project. The wind farm to be built in Nantucket Sound will generate enough electricity to power more than two hundred thousand homes. The projects still faces financial and regulatory challenges. A coalition of opponents, including the Kennedy family, announced their intention to sue the Interior Department to block implementation.[270]Regrettably, people with narrow self-interest choose to ignore the greater good of the majority of people.

Wind Energy's Enviable Credentials

Wind power is one of the most environmentally friendly sources of power. The energy needed to build, install, operate, and maintain a modern turbine through its twenty-year design life is recouped within seven to nine months. After those first few months of operation, CO_2 emissions are effectively zero. Generating 20 percent of electricity by 2030 would reduce coal consumption by 18 percent and natural gas by 11 percent for a total CO_2 reduction of 825 million metric tons.[271] Congress in October 2008 took the im-

270 Stephen Power and Mark Peters, The Wall Street Journal, April 29, 2010

271 Dashka Slater, Sierra, "As the World Warms" September/October 2008, 24

portant step of extending the 1.9 cent per kilowatt hour federal wind power-production tax credit for another year. President Obama supports a five-year extension.

Wind power is homegrown. The United States is blessed with an abundance of wind capacity. Stiff winds blow across the Great Plains. The corridor that stretches from North Dakota to the Gulf Coast of Texas is particularly favorable for wind-power generation. Minnesota, Iowa, Kansas, Oklahoma, and New Mexico all have significant wind energy potential. The West Coast benefits from the Pacific breezes, accounting for California's high ranking in U.S. wind-power generation. Washington state and Oregon are also important producers.

Wind being free, the cost of electricity generation does not fluctuate with market forces. Coal and natural gas prices tend to move in tandem with crude oil prices. Natural gas prices tripled in 2008 while oil prices escalated to $147 a barrel and coal prices more than doubled. Many utilities put through some of the largest rate increases in decades, raising prices by double digits over the previous year in some places. The national average price for electricity reached 10.2 cents per kWh. Prices then came down as the price of crude oil retreated to $70 a barrel in October and $40 by November.

Wind has a number of other advantages. It meets the most stringent renewable criteria. **No water is needed to operate wind turbines and no waste is generated.** There are no serious health hazards associated with the operation of wind turbines and no noxious emissions. Wind turbines can be erected quickly. In large wind-energy projects, revenue can flow as each turbine is erected, an advantage over nuclear power plants that take many years to build and generate power only after completion.

Wind energy development also offers opportunities for growing the U.S. economy. Wind energy fuels the local economies by creating construction jobs and maintenance jobs. Farmers leasing land to "plant" turbines collect about $5,000 per tower per year. Yet each turbine takes only about one acre out of crop production. The broader economy stands to gain the most. Turbine components made in the United States have increased to about 50 percent of the market, up from less than 30 percent just three years ago. The extension of tax credits and the allocation of billions of dollars to upgrade transmission lines are certain to spur investments in wind energy. According to the Department of Energy (DOE) a 20 percent wind contribution to the U.S. electricity supply would support roughly 500,000 jobs and increase revenues to local communities by more than $1.5 billion by 2030. Germany, a much smaller country than the United States, employs 70,000 people in its wind energy industry. A thriving wind-turbine industry could also benefit America by exporting its expertise and manufactured products to the rest of the world at a time when wind energy is experiencing a worldwide boom. Europe, for one, has a binding target of 20 percent renewable energy by 2020. Britain has a target of 15 percent. China also has a very ambitious plan. The manufacture of wind turbines is one of Europe's fastest-growing industries. Three countries, Germany, Spain, and Denmark, which hold a near monopoly on the industry, have created an estimated 133,000 jobs. America should take note.

For all of its advantages it is surprising that wind does not account for more of the energy that we use. The main reason is that wind turbines generate electricity at a cost of a few pennies more per kWh than power plants utilizing coal or natural gas. Skeptics of the potential of wind power also argue that wind does not blow at the same velocity every day and every hour of the day so utilities cannot rely on wind as the sole source of power. They have a point, but there are ways to store electricity: batteries, compressed air, generated hydrogen, and stored hydropower. The reality is that few utility companies need to depend exclusively on wind energy.

Promoting Wind Energy

Corporations and even individuals can buy electricity from renewable sources as a means of fostering clean energy. For example, Baxter's 654,000-square-foot facility in Deerfield, Illinois, a suburb of Chicago, purchases Green-energy certified renewable energy certificates equivalent to 15.5 million kilowatt hours of electricity from Constellation New Energy, which in turn buys wind energy from a network of wind-power generators across the country. Baxter does not directly receive power supplied by those wind-power generators but the company's investment in renewable energy certificates provides an economic incentive for those power generators to increase the supply of clean, renewable energy to the electric grid in other parts of the country.[272]

More importantly, individuals and corporations need to support legislation to raise the cost of fossil fuel-generated energy. The drop in energy prices

---

272 Energy Market, Great Lakes Region, Issue 5, May 2007, 1-2

that occurred across the board in 2008 reinforced the need for a carbon tax to sustain incentives for investments in energy conservation, energy efficiency, and renewable energy. Duke Energy of North Carolina, one of the three largest utility companies in the United States, canceled a $400 million wind-power project and cut $50 million of its budget for solar power. Public Service Enterprise Group, New Jersey's largest utility, cut its 2009 capital expenditure budget—40 percent of the cuts coming at the expense of renewable energy. PPL Group Inc., one of the biggest producers of wind power, cut its 2009 capital spending for wind energy by nearly $1 billion. Florida Power and Light curtailed planned investment in wind power in 2009 by 400 megawatts.

Government subsidies should also be given consideration. Some people complain that many existing forms of renewable energy, including wind, rely on subsidies. That is true, but the whole energy sector is riddled with subsidies both explicit and hidden, most of which favor fossil-fuel-generated energy. It is estimated that global subsidies for fossil fuels amount to $557 billion annually, about twelve times more than the subsidies for renewable, which range from $43 billion to $46 billion.[273] Subsidies that foster the development of clean energy could be reduced or eliminated if a carbon tax were imposed on polluting industries.

Geothermal Energy

Geothermal energy is infinitely renewable, is available almost everywhere on earth, emits virtually no CO_2, flows uninterrupted, and exists in extremely large quantities. Yet it remains largely untapped in the United States and the world. According to the UN World Energy Assessment report, the geothermal resource is about 280,000 times the annual global consumption of primary energy.[274]

The United States is blessed with enormous geothermal resource. One of the hottest known geothermal regions on earth is located along the west coast of South, Central, and North America. California's North Coast region draws a substantial amount of its electricity needs from hot springs known as the geysers. The geysers generate about 1,000 megawatts of electricity, which

273 Newsweek August 16, 2010, The Index. Transportation, 12

274 The Economist, Technology Quarterly, September 4, 2010, 18–20

is below its peak production in 1987, but still enough to rank as the largest system of its kind in the world.

Large, commercial operations turn geothermal energy into electricity in two ways. One way is by venting steam, from depths reaching one mile underground, through a turbine that generates electricity. The other is by pumping water as hot as 390°F, so-called supercritical water, from wells as deep as 2.5 miles, to transfer the heat energy to clean water surrounding the coils through which the supercritical water is circulated. The clean water heats to a boil, releasing steam that drives a turbine. Used supercritical water is then driven back into the ground.

Iceland is the poster country for geothermal energy. It enjoys the highest per capita production of geothermal power but it actually ranks only fourteenth in the world for geothermal resources.[275] Geothermal power fulfills about 25 percent of the country's electricity consumption. Iceland's next frontier is known as Iceland Deep Drilling Project, which started ten years ago in Krafla. Engineers have already drilled two miles into the earth and are about three thousand feet from reaching a six-mile-wide caldera of supercritical water. The project is a high-stakes gamble. Success would go a long way toward solving Iceland's economic woes and reducing its consumption of fossil fuels.[275] Other countries with heavy reliance on oil or gas imports, Japan and Italy in particular, are considering their own potential to tap supercritical fluid. Italy has long been Europe's leader in geothermal power. The Larderello area produced 5.5 terawatt hours last year.

Geothermal energy can be used directly to heat buildings. Reykjavik, the capital city of Iceland, draws geothermal energy to warm most of its homes and commercial buildings. The advantage of heating buildings directly with steam is that it is done without incurring the energy losses associated with conversion of heat into electricity. We have such a system here in the United States, in Boise, Idaho. The state capital building and many other buildings are heated with geothermal hot water. The earth's crust needs to be thin, with high temperatures just below the surface.

Interest in geothermal energy is gaining momentum in the United States. The Department of the Interior recommended making available more than 190 million acres of federal land for development of geothermal energy sources. Its Final Programmatic Environmental Impact Statement anticipates a potential

275 Christopher Mims, Popular Science, July 2009, 50–53

5,500 megawatts of new electric generation capacity by 2015 from the twelve western states (including Alaska) and an additional 6,600 megawatts by 2025. Geothermal energy accounts for only 0.38 percent of the U.S. total electricity generation but ranks first in the world for total geothermal energy generation, producing 14.8 terawatt hours.[275]

Geothermal Power Plant, Italy – One of the hottest known geothermal regions on earth stretches along the west coast of the United States. Yet, geothermal energy generation accounts for only 0.38% of the U. S. total energy generation. (Photo: IStock Photo #6897582)

Other countries are drawing substantial amounts of geothermal power. Costa Rica draws 17 percent of its electricity from geothermal energy, and neighboring El Salvador and Nicaragua also benefit substantially from that energy source. The Philippines and Indonesia draw a significant amount of electricity from geothermal sources. East Africa also has geothermal potential. The United Nations Environment Program evaluates the Rift Valley potential at 14,000 MW. Currently only 200 MW is captured. Kenya also draws some energy from volcanic heat. Its geothermal station outside Naivasha produces 158 MW. The government's aim is to raise its geothermal capacity to 576 MW within a decade.

Geothermal energy is also available to homeowners. There is a source of energy in the ground under our feet anywhere we stand that has domestic applications. At a depth of around 150 feet, the temperature of the ground is about 55 degrees Fahrenheit. That's only a 15 degree differential to a comfortable 70 degrees in the winter months and more than enough to keep you cool in the summer months. That 55-degree air can be brought into homes by drilling a few holes in the ground at depths of 150 to 300 feet and inserting pipes through which air is circulated. The outside air is warmed in the winter months and cooled in the summer months before it reaches your home heating/cooling unit. In the summer months, it is ready to cool your house. In the winter months, the air needs to be warmed by a few degrees to produce a comfortable environment. Retrofitting existing homes with the system is cost-prohibitive, but it can be cost-effective for new construction.

Nuclear Power

"Nuclear has to be part of the energy mix." Claude Mandil, the head of the International Energy Agency [276]

Nuclear power is touted as the only alternative to fossil fuel that can produce electricity on a vast scale when "the sun isn't shining and the wind isn't blowing." Michael Grunwald, Time, January 12, 2009

The world's first civilian nuclear power stations appeared in the United States, the United Kingdom, and Russia in 1950 following the discovery of nuclear fission in the 1930s. In 1953, President Dwight Eisenhower gave his famous "Atoms for Peace" speech before the United Nations General Assembly, calling for the controlled application of nuclear energy in a civilian context. Several reactors were built in the ensuing two decades. At the end of 2007 there were 439 reactors in 39 countries generating 15 percent of the world's electricity. The United States ranks number one in total nuclear-generated electricity, accounting for 31 percent of the world's total but France gets more of its electricity from its fifty-nine nuclear plants than any other country at 78 percent. France's reliance on nuclear energy stems from its determination to drastically

276 The Economist, "Nuclear Power. Half Life", November 11th 2006, 71-72

reduce its dependence on imported fossil fuels following the oil crisis of 1973. Other countries derive a substantial amount of their electricity from nuclear plants. Sweden derives 50 percent; the Ukraine 45 percent; Japan 34 percent; Germany and Finland about 25 percent each.[277] The United States' 104 nuclear reactors generate 19 percent of U.S. electricity. Other countries with significant total output are Russia, South Korea, Canada, China and India.

Nuclear Power Plant – The United States' 104 nuclear reactors generate 19% of its electricity. A full 21% of active reactors are over 20 years old. (Photo: IStock Photo #12069377)

Most of the nuclear plants in operation today in the world are old. The sentiments against nuclear power generation that resulted from the 1979 Three-Mile Island incident near Harrisburg, Pennsylvania and the 1986 meltdown of Ukraine's Chernobyl plant became a major headwind for the nuclear industry, especially in the United States. A full 81 percent of active nuclear reactors in the United States in 2011 are over 20 years old, more than half being between 25 and 40 years old.[278] The only reactor to start operation in the United States

---

277 The Economist, "Energy in Germany. Nuclear Fallout", August 8th, 2007, 43-44

278 Brendan Greeley with Nicolas Comfort, Alan Katz and Dexter Roberts, Bloomberg Businessweek, March 21-March 27, 2011, 13-14

in more than two decades is the Watts Bar Unit 1, located on the Tennessee River, which came on line in May, 1996 after being under construction for twenty-three years. Work suspended in 1988 on Watts Bar Unit 2 resumed in 2007. Completion date on the 1,180 MW reactor is scheduled for 2012.

Until the Fukushima Daiichi Nuclear Power Plant tragedy of March 2011, sentiments against nuclear power generation had softened considerably in the United States and abroad. An industry poll conducted in 2008 found that new reactors were supported by most Americans, including 80 percent of those who live near one. "There is only a very small minority in Congress that still opposes nuclear power," said Alex Flint, the top lobbyist at the Nuclear Energy Institute (NEI). In 2008 Senator John McCain called for the United States to build forty-five new nuclear reactors by 2030 to break America's dependence on pollution-generating fossil fuels. **"Every year, nuclear reactors spare the atmosphere from the equivalent of nearly all automobile emissions in America," McCain said at Missouri State University in June 2008.** [279]

A shift in sentiment was also taking place across Europe, according to Ian Hone-Lacey, spokesperson for the World Nuclear Association based in London, England.[280] In Europe, support for nuclear power was a reaction to high energy prices and the specter of energy insecurity following two recent interruptions in the flow of Russian natural gas, which is so vital to Europe's energy security.

The change in attitude also reflected concerns about the global warming consequences of burning fossils fuels. The operation of nuclear power plants generates essentially no greenhouse gases, although detractors of nuclear energy disagree. They make the point that when the entire lifecycle of a nuclear power plant is taken into consideration—the construction of the plant, the mining and milling of the uranium fuel, the transportation and storage of nuclear waste, and the eventual decommissioning of the plant—nuclear energy produces many times more CO_2 than energy generated by wind or solar power. Still, it emits much less CO_2 than natural gas and many more times less than coal.[16] Another attraction is the perception that nuclear is a renewable source of energy. The reality is that uranium, the power source of nuclear power plants, is not a renewable resource but it is abundant and it is available in large quantities in stable countries like Canada and Australia.[276]

279 Laura Meckler and Rebecca Smith, The Wall Street Journal, June 19, 2008

280 Elizabeth Rosenthal, Chicago Tribune, May 2008

Nuclear power plants also have the advantage of producing energy on a vast scale at competitive costs. The Nuclear Energy Institute claims that the average operating cost of America's nuclear power plants was 1.7 cents per kWh in 2005 when the average wholesale price of electricity was around 5 cents per kWh, affording the plants a large profit margin. Nuclear wattage is considered cost-competitive even when compared to electricity generated by coal and natural gas, and is expected to gain a price advantage over fossil fuel-generated power when carbon-taxing schemes are implemented. Firms have also gotten better at managing the plants, producing power 90 percent of the time as compared to 50 percent of the time in the early 1970s.[280] They have also improved the efficiency of the non-nuclear aspects of their operations, such as the steam turbines. All in all, the improved efficiency of the American nuclear plants was the equivalent of adding about five new reactors.

Fading memories of nuclear accidents, the specter of climate change and the increasing demand for energy all contributed to the renewed interest in nuclear power generation. As a result more than fifty reactors are under construction worldwide and at least fifty in planning stages. In the United States, ten fully completed applications to build nuclear reactors have been submitted to the Nuclear Regulatory Commission and applications are in progress for seven other plants.[173] The country with the greatest number of plants under construction is China with 28, accounting for almost half of the reactors being built worldwide.[278] China's energy planners say they expect to have forty reactors by 2020 and enough additional reactors by 2030 to generate more power than all 104 reactors presently in operation in the United States. Zhao Chengkun, vice president of the China Nuclear Energy Association, said, "Developing clean, low-carbon energy is an international priority." Other countries with several reactors under construction include Russia, India, and South Korea.

Suddenly, in March 2011, the world's third strongest earthquake on record and the catastrophic tsunami that followed led to radiation leak from the Fukushima Daiichi Nuclear Power Plant in Japan prompting a reassessment of risks and rewards of the reliance on nuclear fission for electricity generation. On May 6th, Japan's Prime Minister Naoto Kan called for temporary closure of the Hamaoka nuclear power plant, an aging facility. According to the report "Japan Unplugged", published in the May 4th, 2011 issue of The Economist, Kan announced on May 10th, his intention to rewrite the blueprint, scarcely a year old, that planned to roughly double nuclear power's contribution to Japan's energy mix by 2030. Switzerland shelved plans for new reactors and Italy is holding off on its newly launched nuclear program.[170] Angela Merkel, Germany's chancellor, under pressure exerted by tens of thousands demonstrators, agreed to power down five of Germany's oldest reactors. Earlier, Merkel had reversed her predecessor's plan to end the country's nuclear programs by 2022.[278] The U.K. , Germany and our own government have announced nuclear safety reviews. The International Energy Agency, before Fukushima, had predicted that 360 gigawatts of nuclear generating capacity would be added by 2035. The agency now expects only half that amount.[281] Some governments are unphased. The Chinese Communist Party, unburdened by the need for social consensus has no plan to change course. Abu Dhabi confirmed it would proceed with plans for a civilian reactor despite the Japan disaster.[282]

Consumers of energy must realize that most forms of energy generation come with risks. If we are not willing to accept the risks associated with nuclear energy, we need to explain what low-carbon alternative would replace them. The 104 nuclear power plants in operation in the United States generate more than seventy percent of our carbon-free electricity. As Duke Energy CEO Jim Rogers pointed out during an interview by Charlie Rose, we are going to need nuclear power. "As we look out 20 years from now, we will start to retire that nuclear fleet, and we need to start building now, not only to meet the growth in demand but also because we foresee that a significant number of old coal plants will be retired as a result of environmental regulation – and that as a consequence we're going to have to replace them".[283]

For the sake of safety, the United States needs to accelerate the replacement of the oldest and most vulnerable nuclear plants using the safest technology and design. Capital investments required for new plants are certain to go up with added new safety measures. The first detailed cost estimate filed by Florida Power and Light for a plant south of Miami ran around $15 billion. Progress Energy announced a $17 billion plant, also to be built in Florida. The cost is triple the estimate just one year earlier. According to Michael Grunwald, a reporter for the *Washington Post*, Amory Lovins, chairman and chief scientist of the Rocky Mountain Institute, has calculated that overall electricity from

281 The Economist, Gauging the Pressure, April 30th, 2011, 70

282 Antony Di Paola, Bloomberg Businessweek, April 4-April 10, 2011, 62

283 Charlie Rose, Bloomberg Businessweek, March 21-March 27, 2011, 26

new nuclear plants will cost more than twice as much as electricity generated from coal or gas.[284] That is in sharp contrast with the cost of producing electricity from existing nuclear plants.

A looming limitation to the expansion of nuclear energy generation may be the availability of water. Nuclear plants require more water than any other type of power plant, twenty-five thousand to sixty thousand gallons for each megawatt-hour of electricity produced by a plant using an "open-loop" cooling system.

New Generation Nuclear Reactors

For a long time, France has been at the forefront of nuclear technology. It is promoting a new generation of reactor referred to as the European Pressurized Reactor or EPR, three of which are currently under construction, one in Perly in northern France, one in Flamanville in the Normandy region, and another in Olkiluoto, Finland. The new reactors will be more powerful than any currently in operation while consuming 15 percent less uranium. They are being promoted as safe, owing to an advanced safeguard system that cools the heart of the reactor, and to a shell of reinforced concrete that can withstand the impact of a wide-body jetliner. Environmentalists, however, point to the fact that their waste will be considerably more radioactive than that produced by conventional reactors. The spent fuel recovered from those reactors still contains around 96 percent of the original uranium and some plutonium.

Other countries are making their presence felt in the nuclear industry. A new design that is close to commercial energy generation is the Pebble Bed Modular Reactor (PBMR). It was under development in Germany for decades then in South Africa.[285] The nuclear fuel in the PBMR is encapsulated in rugged "pebbles" the size of tennis balls. The pebbles which are cooled by helium gas are designed to withstand a loss of coolant without disintegrating, making them extremely safe. The South African government was at the forefront of developing this new nuclear technology until it canceled the project in September 2010 for lack of investment capital. China, which took over where the South Africans left off, is close to commercializing the PBMR. The Mas-

---

284 Michael Grunwald, Time, January 12, 2009, 32-36

285 Peter Coy with Dinakar Sethuraman and Rakteem Katakey, Bloomberg Businessweek, March 28-April 3, 2011, 70-77

sachusetts Institute of Technology, the University of California at Berkeley and the Idaho National Laboratory are also working on this new type of reactor. The American companies General Electric, in cooperation with the Japanese firm Hitachi, and Westinghouse, with its parent company, Toshiba, are designing the next-generation nuclear plants that they hope to build in the United States. Between them, these two consortia have nine reactors under construction worldwide. Westinghouse's design, referred to as AP1000, "rely on natural forces like gravity, rather than engineered safety features like pumps, to deliver cooling water to the reactor core".[283]

The United States needs to look at nuclear generation as a source of clean energy and also as another way to project American technological know-how around the world. In September 2009, the Obama administration announced $40 million in funding for research and development of a reactor based on a promising new design using water at a much higher temperature and pressure, referred to as supercritical water. In his fiscal 2012 budget request, Obama asked for $36 billion in government backed loan guarantees for new nuclear reactors. He also asked for $125 million for research in Generation IV nuclear reactors. [285]

The challenges facing the U.S. nuclear industry are still daunting. The American people need to be confident of the safety of nuclear power to create a favorable legislative environment. Streamlining the permitting process, safer designs, improved construction techniques, heightened awareness of the environmental impact of burning fossil fuels, and the impending cost burden of a carbon tax on competing coal-powered plants are all positives for the nuclear industry. The industry also stands to benefit from government subsidies, such as guaranties for part of the construction loans (The Energy Policy Act passed by Congress in 2005), insurance against regulatory delays, limited liability in the event of an accident, and tax credits. A negative that is not going away is the issue of nuclear waste.

Nuclear Waste

Most reactors in operation today are thermal reactors operating on enriched uranium, which consists of two types of uranium, U-235 and U-238. Those reactors cannot extract all of the energy from a given amount of nuclear fuel. After about three years of use, the fuel is depleted of most fissionable uranium but still retains long-lived radioactivity that cannot be burned in conventional reactors. At the present time, nuclear waste is stored near the plant until it can be moved to a permanent facility. The Department of Energy, the agency that regulates the management of spent nuclear fuel, is supposed to provide a permanent repository but no country is yet operating such a facility. Yucca Mountain in Nevada is a projected site but local opposition has prevented its use until now and many speculate that it will never be built.

Another concern is the use of by-products of uranium's nuclear fission to make weapons. One of those by-products is a form of plutonium, plutonium-239, an isotope that can be isolated and used to make nuclear bombs.

Thorium, a cousin of uranium has been promoted as an alternative to uranium. Kent Garber, in the April, 2009 edition of *U.S. News & World Report*, discussed the advantages of thorium over uranium as a fuel for nuclear reactors. Garber made the point that thorium fuel rods could stay in the reactor twice as long as uranium rods. He also emphasized the fact that thorium waste products would be safe from terrorists since "it would be incredibly challenging, if not impossible, to isolate its plutonium to make a bomb." Thorium Power, a company based in Virginia, is one of the leading companies working on the commercialization of thorium and has plans to test the fuel in a commercial reactor. Like Uranium, thorium is available in countries that could provide a reliable source. Australia, India, Norway, the United States, and Canada have the world's largest thorium reserves. There has been little enthusiasm for thorium in the United States where the industry is mainly focused on reprocessing unconsumed uranium and plutonium from spent fuel and reusing it. Unfortunately, the process involves separating plutonium from the spent uranium, a procedure that has been banned in the United States since the 1970s.

Terra Power, a company funded in part and chaired by Bill Gates, Microsoft's co-founder, and headed by a former Microsoft chief scientist is using massive computing power to design a reactor that could run for decades on an isotope of uranium that is considered waste. So far the company has not found a production partner or a host country.[285]

Hydroelectric Power

Conventional hydroelectric generators consist of dams that store water to be used to spin electricity-generating turbines.

Hydropower is the largest renewable energy source in the world. Fifteen percent of global electricity is generated by hydroelectric facilities. Brazil relies on hydropower for a full 80 percent of its electricity and most Latin American countries draw a considerable amount of their power from hydro sources. Paraguay gets 100 percent of its electricity from hydropower.

The world's largest generator of hydroelectric power is Hydro Quebec, wholly owned by the province of Quebec, Canada. The world's biggest publically traded hydroelectric generator is RusHydro, a partly state-owned company that operates most of Russia's hydroelectric plants. Its combined 25,000-megawatt capacity is Russia's largest source of electricity. The world's number one electricity generating dam is the Three Gorges erected on China's Yangtze River. That project, completed in 2006 at a cost of $30 billion, generates 22,500 megawatts of electricity annually, boosting the country's hydroelectric capacity to 17 percent of its total electricity generation.[286]

Grand Coulee Dam   Hoover Dam
The United States draws 7.3% of the electricity from hydropower, its largest renewable energy source. Analysts claim that the current capacity could double by 2040. (Photos: IStock Photo #7381160, 14080840)

286 David Biello, Scientific American Earth 3.0, Volume 19, Number 1, 2009, 34–41

The United States gets 7.3 percent of its electricity from hydropower, making it its largest truly renewable energy resource. The Grand Coulee Dam on the Columbia River in the state of Washington, completed in 1945, is the largest hydropower generator in the United States. Its 21,000 megawatts of annual electricity generation ranks it the fifth-largest in the world. The Hoover Dam, named after President Herbert Hoover, was the largest generator of hydroelectricity in the world until it was dethroned by the Grand Coulee Dam. The Hoover Dam on the Colorado River is now ranked thirty-eighth in the world.

The United States has a lot of untapped hydropower resources. Analysts claim that the current capacity could double by 2040. The Federal Energy Regulatory Commission is reviewing more than 30,000 megawatts of new projects, equal to one-third of all existing hydropower capacity. Existing dams hold promise according to Linda Church Ciocci, executive director of the National Hydro Power Association. **Only about 3 percent of the country's eighty thousand dams generate electricity. Power-generating turbines could be added to many of those dams. Some are urging the federal government, which owns most of those non-improved dams, to begin assessing their potential.**[287]

There are also less awe-inspiring ways of producing hydroelectric power. Any movement of water has the potential to generate electricity. Wave energy is harnessed using the up and down movement of the surface of large bodies of water, mainly the oceans. Norsk Hydro, a Norwegian company, is involved in a Portuguese wave farm project producing 2.25 megawatts of electricity. Tidal power projects have been in place for decades in China, Russia, and France. In 1984, Canada established a tidal research station in the Bay of Fundy, New Brunswick. Ocean Power Delivery, a Scottish company operating off the coast of Portugal, started operating a power station providing 2.25 megawatts of electricity.

New technologies are enabling ways to generate electricity in all kinds of waterways. Turbines shaped like windmills are submerged in rivers and aqueducts or other locations where free-flowing water causes them to spin. Ciocci is of the opinion that the country's waterways could provide much more clean renewable energy.

---

287 Linda Church Ciocci, Scientific American Earth 3.0, Volume 19, Number 1, 2009, 19

Biomass

B iomass from dedicated crops, such as miscanthus and switchgrass, and other forms of biomass, such as wood residues, woody materials, brush, and trees, have been touted as good sources of cellulose for the production of the second-generation ethanol. A new perspective coming out of former Vice President Al Gore's research is the notion that solid forms of biomass from dedicated crops as well as from construction debris and forest waste could be effectively used in the generation of electricity, rather than being transformed into transportation fuels through expensive and wasteful processes.[16] Researchers from Michigan State University, the University of Minnesota, and the Swedish University of Agricultural Sciences published the results of a study that found that more than 30 percent of the energy contained in cellulosic biomass is lost during the recovery of fermentable sugars. Another 27 percent of the energy contained in the sugars dissipates during fermentation. To top it all, about 75 percent of the energy remaining in the liquid fuels, ethanol and biodiesel, is then lost when the fuels are burned in inefficient internal-combustion engines.[16]

Granted, conventional power plants lose an average of 65 percent of the energy in the fuels to wasted heat when producing electricity, but that electricity displaces significantly more petroleum than is displaced by ethanol and biodiesel when it is used to power the more efficient electric vehicles. When power plants become more efficient, combining heat and electricity generation (cogeneration), less than 40 percent of the energy contained in biomass will be lost, further increasing the recoverable energy of biomass. According to Gore, "Many energy experts have come to believe that, in most cases, the most efficient use of biomass is a fuel for direct combustion to create thermal energy for the space heating and cooling of buildings and for the making of steam-to-power electricity generators."[16]

The main obstacle to the expansion of biomass electricity generation is the inferior energy density of biomass when compared to coal and oil. The required large volume of feedstock presents a logistical challenge when it comes to transporting large enough volumes of biomass material to generate electricity in large quantity, thus the importance of locating bio-refineries near the source of feedstock. At present, Europe is the largest producer of biomass electricity, mostly from wood pellets. In 2006, electricity generation from biomass accounted for approximately 7 percent of global production of renewable electricity, wood accounting for slightly more than half of all the biomass energy generated.[16]

Another form of biofuel that has potential for displacing fossil fuels is waste, mostly in the form of landfill gas. Currently, it contributes only a fraction of total U.S. biomass energy, 0.531 quadrillion BTU, much less than the 2.041 BTU yielded by ethanol and biodiesel.[288]

Because of Americans' profligate consumption, the United States emits more than two and a half times the amount of landfill gas as the next-largest national source, China. **Methane, the main gas that emanates from municipal landfills, could be a significant source of energy.** The technology for capturing methane from landfills is mature and cost-effective. It can be burned to produce electricity, used in boilers for space heating, or collected to power vehicles modified to run on natural gas. Approximately 37 percent of U.S. landfills are now regulated by the Landfill Rule enacted in 1966, but about half of them flare the gas they collect instead of using the gas productively.[16]

Some companies have already established mutually beneficial partnerships with landfill operators. The BMW plant in Greer, South Carolina, meets 70 percent of its energy needs using landfill gas to generate heat and electricity, saving almost $1 million a year in energy costs.[16]

Sewage is also attracting interest as a source of biogas. Capturing methane from human excrement has the double benefit of yielding energy and preventing potent greenhouse gases from being released into the atmosphere. Technological improvements allow for the extraction of even more biogas from human excrement. Heating the sewage to speed up the digestive process of fecal material into methane has proven beneficial. Stirring the sludge allows the methane to bubble to the surface faster, promoting better bacterial contact with the substrate for quick digestion. Such technical advances are resulting in ever-larger proportions of sewage being used as raw material for energy generation. Germans already derive energy from about 60 percent of their human excrement, and the Czechs, British, and Dutch are not far behind.

The large amount of waste food, food that has not been eaten, still contains all its energy and is an even more promising source of biogas. In the United States in particular, numerous sewage plants have begun processing undigested food in large quantities over the course of the past year, as a result

288 Mark Jenner, FarmWeek, September 21, 2009

of a cooperative effort between the Environmental Protection Agency and the Department of Energy.[24]

■ Chapter Five: What You Must Do For Your Country

❋ Support legislation that mandates minimum renewable energy standards

❋ Embrace nuclear power

❋ View higher electricity pricing as an incentive for energy conservation

Part Three:
The American Life-style:

Chapter 6: The Unsustainability of the American Life-style

A life-style that consumes an inordinate amount of natural resources, which accounts for roughly one-third of total global consumption spending, and has a disproportionate environmental impact, is not sustainable. Enlightened thinkers have warned about the unsustainability of the American life-style.

"If everyone on Earth enjoyed a North American life-style, it would take up to five planet Earths, owing to the increasingly consumptive U.S. life-style." Charles Kibert, Sustainable Construction

"Suburbs represent the greatest misallocation of resources the world has ever known." James Howard Kuntsler, The Long Emergency

"Today's land-grabbing, auto-dominated, fuel-inefficient metropolises have evolved into parasitic black holes, sucking in excessive megatons of energy and materials from all over the globe and spewing out volumes of (often toxic) waste." William E. Rees, urban planner.

"The vast and amusing game called the American life-style has limits after all." Andres Duany, foreword of Sustainable Urbanism by Douglas Farr.

The lingering economic crisis that started in 2008 lends credibility to those views. A great number of Americans are unemployed, 4.2 million having lost their jobs in the fifteen months preceding May 2009, 8.5 million as of February 2010, and 14.6 million by the end of August 2010. More than 15 percent of the workforce is jobless or underemployed.[10] Many people have lost a great portion of their assets, from the loss or the devaluation of their home. In 2008, 2.3 million Americans lost their homes or faced foreclosure and about as many suffered the same fate in 2009. The value of Americans' homeowner equity slumped from a peak of $12.5 trillion in 2005 to $8.5 trillion at the end of 2008, putting roughly 10 million Americans in negative equity, a situation in which the amount of their mortgage exceeds the value of their homes. The value of their portfolio of securities has also plummeted. All told, household net worth fell $11.2 trillion in 2008. Personal debt exceeds $10 trillion.[289] Real median household income dropped 7 percent between 2000 and 2009. More than 17 percent of Americans live below the poverty level, the highest ratio in more than fifteen years.

The housing debacle that caused the worst recession since the Great Depression stems from policies that lowered the threshold for home ownership – subprime lending – instead of addressing the causes of poverty that prevented so many Americans to afford a home. It was also brought on by policies aimed at stimulating the economy by making it easy for individuals to move into homes that were larger, more expensive to acquire and maintain than they needed or could afford. Both groups of homeowners acceded to a lifestyle that was unsustainable. Furthermore, policies that fostered the use of homes as ATM machines – tax-deductible interest payments on home equity loans – increased the vulnerability of homeowners to cyclical downturns in housing values.

Measures to support the value of the housing stock, applied early in the downturn, would have mitigated the effects on the broader economy of the misguided policies that led to the over-building. A three-to-five year moratorium on new single family homes or the adoption of other measures – prohibitively restrictive financing requirements – to effectively dry up new supplies would have gone a long way to stop the decline in prices.

The impact on the construction industry could have been mitigated by implementing measures to improve the energy efficiency of the 144 million existing homes and the five million commercial building. Those investments would have assured long-term savings and generated a healthy return on investments. Former President Bill Clinton was reported to have lobbied the Obama administration in 2009 for an energy-efficiency loan-guarantee program. According to Jonathan Alter, writing for Newsweek on October 4, 2010, Clinton presented a detailed program outlining "a plan that would use $9 billion from the Treasury to leverage $67 billion in financing to retrofit offices and residential buildings." Alter added that this "would create hundreds of thousands of new green jobs in construction and manufacturing that can't be exported." Stemming the decline in home value would have protected the equity of 144 million home owners. The banking industry could have been

289 George F. Will, Newsweek, February 8, 2010, 20

spared most of the losses that resulted from the housing debacle, and Washington, the cost of bailing out the banks and the mortgage insurance providers. Raising the bar on new construction could still afford significant benefits. It would help dry up foreclosures and would have a much-needed wealth effect by raising the value of existing homes.

The quality of life of Americans is also threatened by the escalating public debt. The federal deficit for the 2009 fiscal year was $1.4 trillion. The 2010 budget deficit totaled $1.3 trillion and the 2011 deficit is projected to rise to $1.5 trillion. The projected ten-year deficit stands at $9 trillion.[289] **For the past half century, federal spending has averaged about 20 percent of GDP and federal taxes about 18 percent of GDP, leaving a budget shortfall of around 2 percent of GDP. In 2009, the federal government took in revenues amounting to about 15 percent of GDP while expenditures reached about 25 percent of the economy, an unsustainable imbalance.** By all accounts, closing that gap will be difficult. [290] Assuming "normal" employment figures, the Congressional Budget Office (CBO) projects spending for 2020 at 26 percent of GDP, and tax revenues at around 19 percent, leaving a deficit of 7 percent of GDP. The federal debt averaged 37 percent of GDP between 1960 and 2000. In 2011 it is $14.3 trillion, about 90 percent of GDP. It is projected to reach $18.5 trillion by 2020, about 78 percent of projected GDP. Former White House Budget Director Alice M. Rivlin and former Senator Pete V. Domenici, who co-chaired the Bipartisan Policy Center Commission, reported the findings of the group's nineteen experts on November 17, 2010. They warned that letting deficits continue unchecked would make the United States increasingly vulnerable to the dictates of its creditors, some of which don't have our interest at heart.[290]

States are also facing budgetary crises. With the sole exception of Vermont, state governments are not allowed to operate at a deficit. Yet every state but two faced a deficit in 2009. California's budget gap was the worst at $19.1 billion. Illinois, New Jersey, and Florida had operating deficits of $12 billion, $8 billion, and $6 billion, respectively, and there are other states with billion-dollar deficits. The projected aggregate state deficits for 2010 stood at $166 billion, according to the Center on Budget and Policy Priorities, a research group based in Washington, D.C. It estimates that by the end of the fiscal year 2011, the cumulative fiscal deficit of the fifty states will exceed $350 billion.

---

290 Peter Coy and Heidi Przybyla, Bloomberg BusinessWeek, November 22–November 28, 2010, 14–16

Cities are struggling to balance their budgets. According to the National League of Cities, in 2011, U.S. cities face a collective deficit of $14 billion.[291] New York City faces a $4.9 billion shortfall for 2011. When states and cities can't make ends meet, services are trimmed and jobs are cut. New York Mayor Michael Bloomberg wants to reduce the city payroll by 4,286. Earlier, the mayor had painted an even bleaker picture when he testified before the state finance committee on the impact of the state's cuts on New York City's share of state revenues. Mayor Bloomberg said he would be forced to lay off as many as 19,000 city workers, including 8,500 teachers and 3,100 police officers and that many other services would be trimmed. Chicago's projected budget deficits for 2011 stands at $654 million. Chicago's Transit Authority cut its commuter train and bus services February 7, 2010, to help trim a $95 million budget deficit, laying off hundreds of employees. Discontinued or reduced services and job cuts are painful consequences of unsustainable fiscal policies. The combined weight of federal, state, and municipal debt, which is projected to reach 110 percent of GDP in 2020, is imperiling America's ability to support the lifestyle of its people in years to come. America finds itself on an unsustainable path at all levels.

Lessons to be Learned

The debt crisis that Greece faced at the beginning of 2010 offers a small window on the situation that the United States could face in the future. Decades of fiscal irresponsibility and lopsided import-export balances brought Greece to the edge of bankruptcy. Its fiscal deficit for 2009 amounted to 13.6 percent of its GDP and its debt 115 percent of GDP. Its current account deficit for 2009 was more than 8 percent of GDP. The deterioration of Greece's public finances came to the fore when lenders downgraded the country's credit rating ahead of a €8.5 billion debt repayment scheduled for May 19, 2010, sending Greece's two-year bond yields on a steep climb to over 15 percent before Greece's partner in the euro zone agreed to a financial rescue package worth €110 billion ($145 billion) to stave off default.[292] The financial aid package came only after the Greek parliament agreed to austerity measures amid rioting in Athens and following weeks of begging by Prime Minister Papandreou. The

291 Christopher Palmeri, Bloomberg Businessweek, April 18-April 24, 2011, 31–32

292 The Economist, "Financial Fortress Europe," May 15, 2010, 61

conditions for assistance were aimed at slashing the country's budget deficit below 3 percent of GDP by the end of 2012. They included public-sector wage cuts, a higher value-added tax, excise duty increases for alcohol and cigarettes, adjustments in retirement age benefits, and promises of other austerity measures for 2011 and 2012.[293]

Decades of overspending by Greece offers a cautionary tale for politicians in Washington; Sacramento, California; Springfield, Illinois, and for other state and local politicians. There should be concern that the European nation's problems with heavy debt load and deteriorating bond ratings will be replicated here as international lenders become less tolerant of the high levels of our public debt. **The United States is on track to join Greece as a nation overburdened by debt. The United States projected deficit for 2011 is only slightly less than Greece's at 11.1 percent of GDP, and the nation's total public debt will exceed 90 percent of GDP before 2012. The United States is already the most indebted nation in the world.**

Bold Course Corrections

O ur federal government and many of our state and local governments find themselves on an unsustainable course. Mounting debt cripples their ability to carry out their functions. If Americans want to receive the most benefit, over time, from their taxes, they must demand fiscal responsibility from their elected officials. Interest payments on public debts is money that is not available to improve the quality of life of taxpayers. Debt service obligations reduce governments' ability to fund social programs, invest in infrastructure projects and respond to a crisis.

The burden on taxpayers of public debt service is staggering. In 2009, interest payments just on the federal debt totaled $383.1 billion in a historically low interest rate environment. Erskine Bowles, President Clinton's former White House chief of staff, stated in *Bloomberg Businessweek*, November 22-November 28, 2010, that the consequences of the national debt are frightening:" **We'll be paying a trillion dollars in interest costs in 2020."** Another concern is the fact that much of the debt is owed to foreigners. At the end of July 2010, $4.07 trillion of U.S. government debt was in foreign hands. China and Japan each

---

293 Nick Skrekas and Alkman Granitas, The Wall Street Journal, May 7, 2010

held more than $800 billion. Interest payments to foreign lenders are a drain of American wealth and a boon for America's competitors.

Containing the debt must be a priority. It will require spending cuts and measures to increase revenue. Growing the economy will make it easier to service the debt.

Cost Cutting Measures

S pending cuts must target the most expensive programs. **The three big entitlement programs, Social Security, Medicare, and Medicaid, consume 41 percent of federal spending. On the current trend, that figure is expected to rise to 60 percent in 2030.**[294]

The U.S. Social Security program was instituted in 1935. The official pensionable age was then sixty-five, three years beyond the lifespan of Americans at that time. In 2011, the retirement age is still sixty-five even though Americans sixty-five years of age can now expect to live an additional sixteen years. The age of which benefits can be claimed was recently raised to sixty-six and is due to go up to sixty-seven in 2026.[295] Those adjustments are deemed inadequate by many economists.

Another strain on the Social Security program is the fact that baby-boomers – those born between 1946 and 1964 – started to turn sixty-five in 2011, swelling the ranks of retirees.[295] This is coming at a time when following generations are smaller. Since the American system is a pay-as-you-go scheme, fewer wage earners are paying into the fund that supports the retirees.[296] In 2010, payroll taxes provided only 91 percent of the retirees' benefits, which totaled $700 billion, a situation that is expected to worsen as the ratio of retirees to workers widens.[296] By 2050 there will be just 3.6 workers supporting each pensioner.[297]

Congress has the power to change Social Security. "The right to alter, amend or repeal any provision of this Act is hereby reserved to Congress" is part of the Social Security Act of 1935. In a 1960 decision, the court expressly

---

294 David Brodeur, Investor's Business Daily, February 4, 2010

295 The Economist, Pensions. Falling short. April 9th, 2011, 3-16

296 Robert J. Samuelson, Newsweek, March 14, 2011, 25

297 The Economist, 70 or Bust!, April 9th, 2011, 13

rejected the argument that people have a contractual right to Social Security.[296] Congress has repeatedly altered benefits. From 1950 to 1972, Congress increased benefits nine times! Congress must now act responsibly by adjusting the benefits of future retirees.

The best way of assuring the sustainability of the Social Security program is for future retirees to work longer. Retiring later reduces the length of time for which benefits need to be paid and extends the time that workers contribute to their retirement. It also boosts national output. With rising life expectancy the pension age should be raised to 70.[295] Another measure is to halt the widespread practice of retiring before the official pension age. More than half of the workers stop at age sixty-two, the age at which they can start drawing Social Security, albeit at a reduced rate.[295]

Unfunded public pension systems are becoming a major concern. Taxpayers face as much as $3 trillion in unfunded benefits, according to a study by Northwestern University and the University of Rochester reported in the October 18 – October 24, 2010 issue of *Bloomberg Businessweek*. Governments need to trim benefits of public employees. Public-sector employers should not be retiring earlier than private-sector ones. They should be asked to contribute more to their retirement plans. A most effective change would be to enroll workers into defined-contribution plans.

Some consideration should be given to making all retirees' benefits less generous. Generally, pensioners need less to live on. They don't have the expenses of dependent children, they mostly have paid-off mortgages on their house, they no longer need to save for retirement and avoid the expenses associated with going to work. Limiting inflation-linking has been proposed. Only since 1972 have benefits been indexed to inflation. Sweden, Germany and Japan are dealing with their deteriorating pension finances largely by making the inflation-linking less generous.[295]

One solution that is rarely considered is growing the labor force. Demographically the United States is in a better position than most other countries but that edge could be more fully exploited. Let's take advantage of the fact that the United States is still a magnet for immigrants by being more welcoming to foreigners. After all, in 2011, the United States had 3.2 million job openings, according to the Bureau of Labor Statistics. Most of those are unfilled for lack of qualified workers. We need to make it easier for talented foreigners to come here and hire them. There are also twelve million undocumented

immigrants already within our borders that could be contributing to the Social Security fund if they were given some sort of legal status.

Healthcare is a burden on the public and the private sectors. In 2011, total
healthcare expenditures will reach $2.7 trillion, 17.4 percent of G.D.P.. Govern-
ment actuaries have calculated that healthcare spending will increase to $4.6
trillion or 19.6 percent of G.D.P in 2019.

In 2009, the federal government spent $836 billion on healthcare. Rising
healthcare costs are projected to be the main contributor to widening budget
deficits. Medicare, the program that currently covers fifty seven million elderly
Americans at a cost of $519 billion a year, is projected to drain $929 billion from
the federal budget in 2020.[298] Medicaid, the program for the sixty three million poor Americans accounts for about one-sixth of the country's healthcare
spending. Its cost is expected to rise by eight percent each year for the next
decade.

Providing health care for civil servants is onerous. Defense secretary
Robert Gates complained that health care costs are "eating the Defense Department alive". Since 2000, the Defense Department's healthcare bill has increased from $17 billion to $49 billion in 2010 and is expected to reach $65
billion by 2015, according to a report published in the May 28, 2011 issue of *The
Economist*.

Healthcare is a burden to state and local governments. In 2020 they are
expected to shoulder 18 percent of the total healthcare burden. Healthcare expenses are also taxing households and businesses. It is forecasted that in 2020
households will account for twenty six percent of healthcare expenditures and
business eighteen percent.

Healthcare costs adversely affect the competitiveness of the United States
in world markets. The country spends far more per capita than any other industrial nation on healthcare yet scores below many other countries in acces-
sibility of care and quality of care than countries that spend much less. Billionaire philanthropist Bill Gates, during an interview conducted by Charlie Rose
for *Bloomberg Businessweek* remarked: "We spend 17.8 percent of our GDP
on healthcare ... just mind-blowing". Gates pointed out that the next highest is at 12 percent. "The British spend 9 percent of their GDP on healthcare
and our outcomes aren't much better", added Gates.[299] Americans, on average,

---

298 Heidi Przybyla, Bloomberg Businessweek, October 25 - October 31, 2010, 31-32

299 Charlie Rose, Bloomberg Businessweek, February 7-February 13, 2011, 40

die three years younger than the average citizen of France or Israel, four years younger than Australians and five years younger than the citizens of Japan.

There are many claims of cost-saving opportunities in healthcare delivery. The U.S. Centers of Medicare and Medicaid Services estimates that as much as $500 billion is "wasted on duplicate processes, bad coordination and out-of-date scheduling".[300] *The Economist* reported in its June 18, 2011 edition that more than $300 billion is spent on "unnecessary care". Elizabeth A. McGlynn, director of Kaiser's Center for Effectiveness & Safety Research, submits that as much as one third of healthcare spending, around $900 billion a year, is for "ineffective or unnecessary care".[301] There is also the issue of appropriation of healthcare dollars.In 2008,

a full twenty eight percent of Medicare expenditures were devoted to recipients' final year of life.[302]

Sharon Begley, writing for Scientific American, suggests greater use of comparative effectiveness and cost analysis data. The Patient Protection and Affordable Care Act that was signed into law in March 2011 bars Medicare from using comparative effectiveness research to decide what to pay for but there is no provision preventing Medicare from using research data to set payment rates in a way that would encourage providers to deliver the best care for a given price, a system called "equal payments for equal results". Cardiologist Steven Nissen of The Cleveland Clinic said "its safe to say that the United States has the least-cost-effective medicine in the world. If there is any country in the world that needs comparative effectiveness research, it's the United States". Other countries are embracing comparative effectiveness research. For many years the U.K. has been incorporating such data into decisions about what its National Health Service will cover.[301]

Individuals must also realize that much of healthcare expenses are spent treating conditions brought about or aggravated by poor lifestyle choices. Emphasis must be placed on preventive medicine, on educating people about the benefits of not smoking, about proper nutrition, good hygiene and exercise. Many medical problems can be traced to cigarette smoking. We need to do more to dissuade people from smoking. Obesity-related problems account

---

300 Rachel Layne, Bloomberg Businessweek, April 18-April 24, 2011, 24-25

301 Sharon Begley, Scientific American, July 2011, 50-55

302 Mary Meeker with Peter Coy, Bloomberg Businessweek, February 28-March 6, 2011, 49-56

for 9.1 percent of all medical expenses.[131] Fred Krupp, co-author of Earth: The Sequel, concluded that 13 percent of the weight gain of Americans is attributable to low gas prices.[90] We need to more appropriately tax gasoline. Nutrition should make up a bigger part of the curriculum in grade school. More emphasis needs to be placed on physical education. "Mens sana in corpore sana" is an old adage that still holds true today.

Discretionary programs also offer opportunities for spending cuts. The Department of Defense, which eats up $708 billion of the country's $3.52 trillion proposed spending for 2011, accounts for half of all discretionary spending. The importance of Pentagon budget restraint was made clear by Admiral Michael E. Mullen, Chairman of the Joint Chiefs of Staff, who warned in February 2011 that **"debt is the greatest threat to our national security"**. [303] Slashing defense spending was part of the recommendations of the Simpson-Bowles National Commission on Fiscal Responsibility and Reform released December 1, 2010.[290] The commission had an important ally in Robert Gates, the former secretary of defense, who targeted twenty high-profile weapons for cuts or elimination, averting some $330 billion in future spending. The next challenge is to convince legislators to agree to cuts that will affect the flow of federal funds to their districts. The secretary also intended to disband the Joint Forces Command based in Norfolk, Virginia, eliminating thousands of jobs.[304]

The issue is much bigger than canceling a few weapon systems or streamlining the Pentagon's bureaucracy. The president, congressional leaders, and Americans need to decide how large a military force the country requires to protect its global economic interests and prop up its geopolitical stature. The U.S. Department of Defense budget is as big as those of the world's next 20 highest military spenders combined. It looms exceedingly large over China's $60 billion defense spending and Russia's $40 billion budget. Gates asked sardonically, "Is it a dire threat that by 2020 the United States will have only twenty times more advanced stealth fighters than China?"[304] Our elected officials should recognize that the era of geopolitical power expansion, driven by the geniuses of generals and the strength of their armies, has passed. The demise of the Soviet Union in spite of its military might, the decline of U.S. global influence in the face of its vast military advantage, and the rise of China, India,

---

303 Roxana Tiron and Kevin Brancato and Rochel Layne, Bloomberg Businessweek, February 28-March 6, 2011, 28-29

304 John Barry and Evan Thomas: Newsweek, September 20, 2010, 30-33

and Brazil on the strength of their economic expansion should send a clear message that a vibrant economy trumps firepower as a means of achieving geopolitical preeminence.

The cost of providing public services at the federal, state and local levels must be trimmed. Public workers are better off than the people they are serving. The American Bureau of Labor Statistics estimates that public-sector workers earn, on average, a third more than their private-sector counterparts! Governments could provide the same services and benefits for less money. Productivity in the state sector has lagged behind the private sector. Barry Bluestone, an economist, cited in the January 8, 2011, edition of *The Economist*, calculated that the cost of America's public service increased 41 percent between 2000 and 2008 while the price of private services rose 27 percent.

Revenue Generation

B alancing the budget will require more than spending cuts. Revenue-generating measures will need to be the part of the process. Federal revenue in 2011 is expected to be only 14.4 percent of G.D.P, the lowest level in sixty one years. It is also low when compared to other industrialized nations.

We need to set a tax policy that raises the necessary revenue in a way that is fair and simple and encourages work. America taxes income too heavily and consumption too little compared with other countries. A value-added tax (VAT) should be a part of an overhaul of the tax system. Former President Bill Clinton, who presided over federal budget surpluses, advanced the idea of a value-added tax in an interview conducted by Maria Bartiromo on *CNBC* on May 17, 2010. The Domenici-Rivlin report suggested a 6.5 percent national sales tax. The implementation would have the added benefit of reducing consumer discretionary spending that aggravates the country's current account deficits. A meaningful increase in gasoline tax would have countless benefits. A tax of $1 on every gallon of gasoline and diesel fuel would generate more than $175 billion in revenue. The ultimate goal should be a tax of $3.50 per gallon.

We need to eliminate tax loopholes – what economists call tax expenditures. Peter Coy, referring to a report from the nonpartisan Joint Committee on Taxation, wrote in the February 14-February 20, 2011 edition of *Bloomberg Businessweek*, "If left untouched, tax expenditures of various kinds will reduce the federal government's revenue by about $5 trillion between 2010 and 2014 from what it would have been with no such breaks. "Tax deductions for mortgage-interest payments need to be phased out for existing homes and eliminated for homes yet to be built. Phasing out preferential tax treatment for mortgage-interest payments is one of the measures put forth by the Simpson-Bowles Commission. Eliminating those deductions would raise tax revenues by $131 billion in 2012, according to a White House estimate. Preferential tax treatment for mortgage interest payments and home equity loans is a perverse incentive for building expensive homes and for excessive consumer spending. Furthermore, the deduction applies only to about one-third of taxpayers who itemize their returns, typically those with higher incomes. Special interest groups are not taking lightly the prospect of losing this cherished U.S. government subsidy. The National Association of Realtors, whose 1.1 million members donated $3.9 million to candidates in the November 2010 election cycle, the American Bankers Association, who spent $6.2 million on lobbying in 2010, the National Association of Homebuilders and other special interest groups are forming a powerful coalition to oppose any change. The President and CEO of the National Association of Homebuilders declared "We're preparing for one hell of a fight."[305]

Widening income inequality is an issue that deserves more attention. According to a January 22, 2011, "special report on global leaders" published in *The Economist*, in 1997 the top one percent earners received 12.3 percent of all the pre-tax income. In 2007, their share had almost doubled at 23.5 percent. Not only have those top earners appropriated for themselves a greater share of the wealth, they have managed to keep more of it. Jesse Drucker reported in the April 11-April 17, 2011 edition of *Bloomberg Businessweek* that the approximately 1.4 million Americans who make up the top 1 percent of taxpayers paid an effective federal income tax rate of 23 percent in 2008 down from 29 percent in 1995 according to the IRS. Those at the very top of the food chain, the 400 U.S. taxpayers with the highest adjusted gross income, paid an effective rate just under 17 percent in 2007, down from almost 35 percent in 1995.

Wealthy Americans need to shoulder a greater share of the burden of funding government programs. The Bush tax cut for the wealthy cost $1.5 trillion in lost revenue over ten years according to an estimate by the Congressional Budget Office. The portion of the Bush tax cut that benefited earners of more than $250,000 a year should have been allowed to expire as planned at

---

305 Lorraine Woellert, Bloomberg Businessweek, February 7-February 13, 2011, 33-35

the end of 2010. Rolling back the estate and income tax cuts for the wealthiest would increase revenue by $807 billion over the next decade.[306]

Taxing income from all sources at the same rate would help raise the effective tax rate of high income earners. Capital gains were taxed at a rate of 28 percent in the 1990s, then to 20 percent during Bill Clinton's tenure and further reduced to 15 percent by President George Bush. Raising rates back to 20 percent just for those earning $250,000 or more, would increase federal revenue by $12 billion in 2014.[307] Taxing capital gains and dividends at lower rates than earned income is the main reason why billionaire Warren Buffet claims his tax rate is less than that of his secretary.

Corporate taxes also need to be reformed. The U.S. statutory corporate tax rate is the highest in the world at 35 percent (Japan's 39.5 rate is higher but the Japanese government has plans to reduce its rate to 35 percent in April 2011). When state taxes are added, the U.S. combined federal-and-state tax rate reaches 39.2 percent. The United States is staying on the sideline of a global trend. From 2000 to 2010, the average statutory corporate tax rate of the OECD member countries dropped from 32.8 percent to 25.7 percent, putting the United States at a disadvantage. There is also the issue of industry-specific loopholes. Those special deals that lower some corporations' tax burden cost the treasury about $102 billion each year according to the Tax Foundation, a non-partisan group in Washington.[308] Even with a high top rate, U.S. corporate tax revenue as a share of the gross domestic product has declined since the 1950's from 4.7 percent of GDP to an average of 1.9 percent from 2000 to 2009. Corporate taxes accounted for 30 percent of federal revenue in the 1950's and only 11 percent in the last decade.[309] Rachelle Bernstein, tax counsel to the National Retail Federation favors lowering the tax rate and broadening the base.

Introducing those and other revenue-generating measures now could reduce or eliminate the need for more painful and more stifling measures later. Robert J. Samuelson, author of *The Great Inflation and Its Aftermath* and a contributor to *Newsweek*, pointed out that "Balancing the federal budget in

---

306 Mike Dorning, Bloomberg Businessweek, February 21-February 27, 2011, 28-31

307 Gary Rivlin, Newsweek, May 9, 2011, 17

308 David J. Lynch, Bloomberg Government Insider, Spring 2011, Too Many Modest Proposals, B2-B3

309   Alison Fitzgerald and Catherine Dodge with Rich Miller and Richard Rubin, Bloomberg Government Insider, Spring 2011, Wanted: A Tax Code for the Digital Age, B4-B7

2020 would require a tax increase of almost 50 percent from the past half-century's average." He further warned that the consequence of future tax increases is "probably a less robust economy." The CBO noted that unprecedented tax burdens could "slow growth in the economy, making the government's spending burden harder to bear."[310]

Cities also need more revenue. A progressive real estate tax rate should be applied to homes. As homes get more expensive, the tax rate should be adjusted upward. This would have the benefit of discouraging the building of McMansions.

Americans need to realize that their federal government's mounting debt, their state and local governments' escalating deficits and their personal indebtedness are serious threats to their future standard of living.

Growing the Economy

An effective and painless revenue-generating measure is growing the economy.

Investment capital and employment opportunities go hand-in-hand when it comes to growing the economy.

The economic crisis that started in 2008 drained much needed investment capital from the economy. By the end of 2008, homeowners had lost $4 trillion in home equity from the peak of $12.5 trillion in 2005.[289]

Policymakers do not seem to grasp the importance of shoring up the value of the housing stock. In 2011, there is still a need for bold action. Roben Farzad, writing for *Bloomberg Businessweek* in the July 11-July 17, 2011 edition, quoted Jonathan Smoke, head of research for Hanley Wood, a housing data company. Smoke said "it's still a vicious cycle of foreclosures, price falling and buyers sitting on the sidelines". In the same article Farzad quoted Scott Simon, who heads real estate analysis for bond giant Pimco, who said: "there are still 6 million to 7 million more foreclosures yet to come".

Lawmakers must take measures to reverse a trend that could take additional trillions of dollars from the economy. Smoke calculates that the nation still has 1.6 million more homes than it needs. Legislators must implement polices to stop the building of new single-family homes for the benefit of homeowners, banks, other mortgage holders and mortgage insurance providers.

---

310 Robert J. Samuelson, Newsweek, July 20, 2009, 26

It is arguable that more jobs would be created than would be lost by instituting a three-to-five year moratorium on new single-family homes. Drying up the supply of new homes would lure potential homeowners to enter the market. New homeowners buy furniture and appliances and often remodel their new homes. Existing homeowners, feeling more secure about the future value of their houses, would be incentivized to start long-delayed improvements. Tax credits could be used as catalysts to prompt investments in energy-sparing retrofits. Fixing some of the 144 million existing houses has the potential to generate more constructions jobs than building less than half a million new homes each year.

Small businesses would also benefit from higher home prices. Forty million Americans are self-employed. Ninety-four percent of small employers own their homes and a quarter of owners of small companies borrow against their houses for business purposes according to market data provider Barlow Research Associates. Entrepreneurs whose houses have lost value are prevented from raising money by mortgaging their homes. Measures to support the value of existing homes would provide investment capital for small businesses. Small businesses have historically played an important role in job creation.

A sure way to increase the available capital is to keep more in this country. We must focus on redressing our long-standing trade imbalances that result from oil imports and consumer goods imports by properly taxing gasoline and applying measures to dampen the enthusiasm of free-spending consumers. Our financial institutions would greatly benefit from the trillions of dollars that we exported to Asian countries and oil-rich countries. Those U.S. dollars have been fueling their economic boom and expanding their international presence. How much more vibrant would our economy be if those trillions of U.S. dollars were available to our financial institutions and our corporations?

America needs to promote manufacturing. In 1979 U.S. manufacturing employed 19.5 million Americans. In 2009, with a larger population, only 11.7 million Americans were earning a living in manufacturing. In only nine years, between 2000 and 2009, 6 million manufacturing jobs were lost. As a consequence, just over 80 percent of "prime age" men, those aged between 25 and 54 have a job, the lowest rate of the Group of Seven (G-7) economies. In the late 1960s, 95 percent of those men had jobs.[311] The share of American males aged sixteen to sixty-four who are employed has fallen from nearly 85 percent

---

311 The Economist, "Decline of the working man", April 30th, 2011, 75-77

in the early 1950s to less than 65 percent in 2010.[312] This segment of population is expected to grow by 42 percent between 2000 and 2050. "Male worklessness has economic, fiscal and social costs. It reduces America's economic potential."[311]

Andy Grove, former CEO and chairman of Intel, points out the limitations of a society that "consists of highly paid people doing high-value-added work and masses of unemployed". Grove is of the opinion that innovation and new technologies create an insignificant number of jobs. Job creation comes with what he calls "scaling up", the phase where companies work out design details, build factories, and start the manufacturing process.[313] He cites the example of the computer manufacturing industry in Asia, which employs about 1.5 million workers versus the approximately 166,000 employees of the U.S. computer industry. One company alone, Foxconn, employed 800,000 people with revenues of $6.2 billion in 2009.[313]

There is more at stake than exported jobs. Grove said industries are not benefiting from the accumulated technical know-how that comes with manufacturing, "the chain of experience that is so important in technological evolution." Grove warned of another consequence of outsourcing. "Abandoning today's commodity manufacturing can lock you out of tomorrow's emerging industries. Without scaling, we don't only lose jobs; we lose our hold on new technologies." Grove also deplores the loss of relationships that develop between manufacturers and suppliers.[313] Gary Pisano of Harvard Business School believes this has already occurred. In a May 14, 2011 report in *The Economist*, he argues that in some areas, such as consumer electronics, the United States no longer has the necessary supplier base or infrastructure to bring jobs back to the country.

Individuals have a lot of power when it comes to creating jobs for fellow citizens. Americans consume almost 30 percent of the world's goods. We must make an effort to purchase products manufactured in this country, from toothpaste to cars. If all of us made a concerted effort to support our manufacturers, we would create job opportunities for many and improve the country's current account balance. It would boost the value of U.S. companies.

Many jobs are already created but remain unfilled for lack of qualified applicants. Bill Clinton, writing in Newsweek's June 27, 2011 edition, pointed out

---

312 Peter Coy, Bloomberg BusinessWeek, April 11-April 17, 2011, 7-8

313 Andy Grove, Bloomberg BusinessWeek, July 5 - July 11, 2010, 50-53

that, even with unemployment at more than 9 percent, there are 3 million posted job vacancies. He favors special programs involving companies, community colleges and vocational programs to teach people the skills they need to fill those jobs. The former president is also a proponent of immigration reforms to make it easier for talented foreigners to come to the United States and work.

The global emergence of the green economy is an opportunity for job creation that America risks missing if it doesn't get its act together soon. The global shift to a more environmentally considerate life has become a major driver of economic growth worldwide. The International Energy Agency estimates that $33 trillion of investments will be needed by 2030 to support the shift to low-carbon energy production and infrastructure in the developed world and the emerging economies. Gordon Brown, former prime minister of the United Kingdom, estimated that as early as 2015, the global environmental sector could be worth $7 trillion and sustain tens of millions of jobs.[314]

World leaders are trying to position their countries to lead the transition to a greener global economy. Gordon Brown said, "The economies that embrace the green revolution earliest will reap the greatest rewards."[314] Angela Merkel, Germany's chancellor, declared, "Whoever is first to conquer green-tech markets will have an enduring export advantage and create jobs." [315]

Respected thinkers in this country see the benefits for the United States of embracing renewable energy. Jim Meacham, a respected journalist and editor of *Newsweek*, said, "Energy technology could well be the successor to information technology as the next great engine of economic growth and we surely need that engine."[315] Tom Friedman, author of *Hot, Flat and Crowded*, offers even more compelling reasons for America to transition to a more carbon-benign economy. He said, **"The country that owns green, that dominates that industry, is going to have the most energy security, competitive companies, healthy population and, most of all, global respect.** I want that country to be the United States of America."[316] Friedman claims that energy technology, which he calls ET, will be the IT of the twenty-first century.

314 Gordon Brown, Newsweek, September 28, 2009, 56

315 Jim Meacham, Newsweek April 13, 2009, 5

316 Tom Friedman, Newsweek, April 13, 2009, 50

Bill Clinton sees green technology as an important driver of job growth. He is of the opinion that the refusal of the United States to sign the Kyoto protocol was a misguided decision. He points to the fact that, before the financial meltdown, the four countries that are on track to meet their Kyoto greenhouse-gas emissions targets were outperforming the United States with lower unemployment, more business formation and less income inequality.

Investment in renewable energy is important to engage the United States in one of the world's fastest-growing segments of the world economy. Costs to the consumer of legislation to promote renewable energy should be viewed as a small price to pay to engage the United States in an emerging global industry of major proportion. Many studies conclude that carbon caps could bring overall benefits by stimulating investments in clean energy—wind, solar, nuclear, ocean waves, geothermal, biofuels, etc.—creating many more jobs than would be lost as a result of imposing carbon caps. Thirty states have developed or are developing comprehensive climate action plans and most project net economic benefits driven by fuel-cost savings and overall economic development, creating new jobs.[317] A 2009 study commissioned by the U.S. Green Building Council concluded that the green building trend alone will support or create 7.9 million jobs between 2009 and 2013 and contribute $554 billion to the economy.[318]

The federal government needs to create a safe environment for entrepreneurs who are willing to invest in ways to reduce our dependence on fossil fuel and its inherent ills. In a featured article titled "From Geeks to Greens," *The Economist* chronicled examples of executives pursuing opportunities in clean energies. [85] It underscored the fact that **the private sector creates jobs, but private enterprise depends on public policies to create a stable environment for investors.** When it comes to green investing, public policy risk may matter as much as technology risk.

The push to develop renewable energy should not overshadow plans to reduce energy consumption. Energy efficiencies are a major component of the green economy. Incentives for U.S. manufacturers to develop energy-efficient technologies are needed to grow our export market. Energy efficiency is also important from the standpoint of improving U.S. competitiveness in world markets. Opportunities for substantial gains abound in every sector of the economy—residential, commercial, industrial, transportation, and power generation.

---

317 Michael Northrop and David Sassoon, Environmental Finance, October 2008, 18-19

318 College of Lake County Classes, Fall 2010 (www.clcillinois.edu/gogreen

The industrial sector is rife with opportunities for efficiency gains. Replacing old, inefficient electric motors with more efficient motors has been singled out as one of the areas offering great benefits. According to the Department of Energy's Office of Energy Efficiency and Renewable Energy, "Motor-driven equipment accounts for 64 percent of the electricity consumed in the U.S. industrial sector." Amory Lovins calculated that industrial motors use more primary energy than highway vehicles. Lovins added, "A comprehensive retrofit of the whole motor system typically saves about half its energy and pays back in around sixteen months."[16]

Measures to improve energy efficiencies can greatly reduce the need for more energy generation, advancing the goal of the country to reduce its carbon emissions in the process. The International Energy Agency (IEA) reported, **"On average, an additional $1 invested in more efficient electrical equipment and appliances avoids more than $2 in investment distribution infrastructure."**[16] The energy saved from the 150 million more energy-efficient refrigerators in use today than those used in 1974 is more than all the wind and solar energy now being generated in the country.

Building a modern, efficient infrastructure is the foundation to a competitive economy. In 2009, the American Society of Civil Engineers gave the U.S. infrastructure an overall D rating. The report noted a downward trend since 2005 in transit, aviation, and roads. Dams, hazardous waste, and schools got a D, while drinking water got a D-minus. Leaking pipes lose some seven billion gallons of drinking water each day. Many reservoirs and pumping stations are nearing the end of their "design life." Air-traffic control needs to be modernized from a ground-based radar system to a satellite system, allowing more efficient routing of planes.[319] According to the American Society of Civil Engineers, the United States would need to invest $2.2 trillion through 2014 to bring our existing infrastructure up to a passable level.[320]   Roads and bridges need an estimated $930 billion. The potable water infrastructure requires about $255 billion. Aviation needs an estimated $87 billion. Felix Rohatyn made an important point in *Bold Endeavors: How our Government Built America and Why it Must be Rebuilt Now*: "The aging of our nation's infrastructure has lessened our ability to

---

319 Bloomberg BusinessWeek, November 1 - November 7, 2010, 14

320 Arianna Huffington: Third World America, 2010

compete in the global economy, shaken our perceptions about our own safety and health, and damaged the quality of American life."[321]

Cities must be at the center of any plan to improve the competitiveness of the American economy through efficiency measures. **The largest one hundred "metros" account for 65 percent of the population and 75 percent of economic output.** Moreover, much of the population growth is expected to take place in urban areas. By 2050, it is estimated that 70 percent of the population, projected to reach 420 million, will live in urban settings.[9] Federal and state governments must address the needs of the cities to insure that those areas, first of all, have the infrastructure they need to thrive. "Make no little plans," said Daniel Burnham, a leading U.S. urban architect.[9] America has a tradition of grand national planning. It's time to think big again.

Civic leaders around the world are improving the sustainability of their cities. Transport officials in Singapore; Brisbane, Australia; and Stockholm, Sweden, are using computer systems to reduce congestion. Singapore leads the pack. It charges drivers for using much traveled streets and will soon introduce real-time pricing on its roads using a satellite-based system. It collects data to measure the average speed of traffic so it can adjust traffic lights to accommodate the flow of vehicles. It is developing a parking-guidance system after studies revealed that drivers looking for parking spaces account for a lot of congestion. Seoul, South Korea's capital, and the home of 10.4 million inhabitants, began its civic reinvention a few years ago. It was awarded the top prize of World Design Capital 2010 by the International Council of Societies of Industrial Design in a competition that promotes the creation of livable cities through smart, innovative design. Seoul earned the distinction thanks to its plan to use high technology to create a new urban environment that is user-friendly for its citizens, its businesses, and its visitors, and above all, is "planet-friendly." New York, Los Angeles, Chicago, Houston, and all major U.S. cities should strive to emulate Singapore and Seoul.

For cities to become truly efficient, technology and urban development must come together. "Smart city" projects are sprouting around the world. Masdar, a no-car city near Abu Dhabi that welcomed its first of forty-thousand residents in 2010, is being built on a raised platform under which its smart infrastructure is deployed. Above, it is a showcase of green technology. Some of

321 Felix Rohatyn, Bold Endeavors: How Our Government Built America, and Why it Must Rebuild Now, 2009

America's leading companies are at the forefront of high-tech urban develop-
ment. Cisco is providing all the digital technology for Songdo City near Seoul,
South Korea. The city is considered the most ambitious smart-city project yet.
It is expected to cost $35 billion and be home for sixty-five thousand people.
Accenture, McLaren Electronic Systems, and Cisco have been enrolled by Liv-
ing PlanIT to provide sensor technologies for a planned smart city in Portugal.
IBM is also engaged in efforts to introduce smart features in a variety of sec-
tors to better manage the urban environment.[322]

Since many of our corporations are at the forefront of futuristic cities,
funding should be made available in this country to develop those models
showcasing American vision, entrepreneurship, and technological know-how.

Stop Empowering U.S. Competition

U.S. consumers are responsible for 28 percent of total global consumption.[323]
Such profligacy grants them enormous power to drive economic expansion. Regrettably, they have used their power to fuel the growth of foreign
manufacturers. In 2006, 40 percent of the consumer goods they purchased
were manufactured in China alone.The result is that trillions of American dollars are now fueling the growth of foreign corporations. The McKinsey Global
Institute reported that Asia's sovereign assets stood at $4.6 trillion at the end
of 2007. Predictions called for Asia's foreign assets to rise to $7.7 trillion by 2013
and possibly to $12.2 trillion, if its economic growth—mostly fueled by its ex-
port business—continues at the fast pace of the last seven years.

Asian countries have used U.S. dollars to build their infrastructure, invest
in R&D, and expand their manufacturing base to make products for global
consumption, increasing competition for U.S. companies and empowering
their citizens. The Chinese middle class is now larger than the entire U.S. population. While the Chinese were improving their quality of life, the quality of
life of Americans was deteriorating. The Chinese have smartly used American
wealth to invest in their future. Chinese scientists and researchers are return-
ing home to conduct research at well-funded institutions. China has become
the most important state supporter of green technology. It is the world leader
in solar- and wind-energy hardware. It is conducting cutting-edge research in

322 The Economist, November 6th, 2010, A Special Report on Smart Systems, p 3-18

323 Robert J. Samuelson, Newsweek, "A New Economic Order", May 10, 2010, 24

energy-storing devices and their application in electric vehicles. Already China has the largest fleet of clean-energy vehicles in the world and is eyeing a world market for its car industry.

America's imperiled economy has far-reaching geopolitical consequences. **The United States will not retain its influence on the global stage without a competitive economy. "From the Spanish Empire of the sixteenth century to the British Empire of the twentieth century, great global powers have always found that their fortunes begin to turn when they get overburdened with debt and stuck in a path of slow growth. Unless the United States gets its act together, and fast, the ground will continue to shift beneath its feet slowly but surely",** warned Fareed Zakaria in 2009.[324] The ascent of China in the last twenty years has been fueled by the unprecedented expansion of its economy, which has been growing at a rate of about 10 percent a year for two decades, raising its international profile at the expense of the United States. China has plans to launch a space module for docking exercises in 2011 in preparation for a scheduled moon landing in 2013. [325]

American consumers are building another competing power center: the oil-rich countries. The power wielded by the member countries of the Gulf Cooperation Council (GCC), Bahrain, Kuwait, Oman, Qatar, Saudi Arabia, and the United Arab Emirates, is anchored by their oil and gas receipts and the size of their hydrocarbon reserves.[326] In 2007 the GCC took in $407 billion in hydrocarbon receipts, $381 billion from oil, and $26 billion from gas. The sovereign wealth funds of the oil-rich states already stood at $4.6 trillion at the end of 2007. Researchers at McKinsey & Company recently concluded that the economies of the GCC could bring in as much as $9 trillion in oil-export earnings by 2020, assuming average oil prices at $100 a barrel—a large amount of wealth, especially considering that the GCC has a population of only 35 million people. The director of international affairs for Abu Dhabi, Yousef al Otaiba, felt the need to write to America's treasury secretary saying, "It is important to be absolutely clear that the Abu Dhabi government has never and will never use its investment organizations or individual investments as a foreign policy tool." It is telling that Abu Dhabi, that little country which, before 1961 lacked

---

324 Fareed Zakaria, Newsweek, June 8, 2009, 26

325 Rana Foroohar and Melinda Liu, Newsweek, March 22, 2010, 36-39

326 Chip Cummins and Alistair MacDonald: The Wall Street Journal, June 19, 2009

even a paved road, felt the need to reassure the United States that it would not use its wealth or our dependence on its oil to dictate our policies. Fouad Ajami, discussing the power of petrocracy, made the point that the modern global economy "has been restructured in favor of the oil producers" and that their newfound wealth "sustains adventures abroad beyond the limits of their societies."[58] When are we going to wake up to the new realities stemming from our reckless transfer of wealth to foreign countries either in payments for oil or in payments for Asian consumer goods? Not so long ago, in 1980, America had a positive current account trade balance equal to 0.4 percent of its GDP. In 2006 the current account balance was negative by almost 6 percent of GDP.[327]

The balance of power is not going to shift in our favor anytime soon. We depend heavily on China's trillions of dollars to finance our national debt. This dependence mortgages our sovereignty and grants China new-found international clout. China's foreign currency reserves are allowing the Chinese to scour the world, securing business partnerships and making acquisitions of prized assets. Rana Foroohar and Melinda Liu warned Americans that China has aspirations to dominate the world for the benefit of its people. Already Beijing is enjoying some success advancing its currency, the yuan, as a rival to the dollar. The yuan has become an official trading currency between Southeast Asia and China. Foroohar and Liu echo the prediction by Gu Xiaosong, director of the Institute of Southeast Asian Studies in Nanning, that "the yuan will next be used as a trading currency with India, Pakistan, Russia, Japan, and Korea."[325]

OPEC controls over 40 percent of the world's stated oil reserves and over 22 percent of the world's natural gas reserves. It has more pricing power now than it enjoyed in the 1980s because non-OPEC production is in decline after peaking in 2002. By contrast, in the early 1980s, non-OPEC producers in places such as Mexico and the North Sea were ramping up production. The GCC governments realize that even if the rich countries can curtail their oil use, their own oil production is likely to decline even more. Currently, the OECD's share of world oil consumption stands at 58 percent while its oil production accounts for only 23 percent of global output, leading to a huge transfer of wealth from consumers to producers. The OECD's share of natural gas consumption outstrips production 50 percent to 38 percent. Those imbalances are the most compelling seller's market in the history of capitalism, providing an uninterrupted transfer of wealth to suppliers of hydrocarbons. Russia's rising power also is underpinned

327 The Economist, "Rebalancing Global Growth. A Long Way to Go", July 25th, 2009, 12-13

by its riches in natural resources, mostly oil and natural gas. Russia earned $166 billion from oil/gas exports in 2007 and accumulated $560 billion in foreign reserves from 2000 to 2007, almost all petrodollars.

It is not enough to stop the outflow of U.S. dollars. Targeting the country's export business is important. The countries that have been growing their economies all have positive trade balances. At the end of 2007, the previous twelve months' current-account balances of China, South Korea, Taiwan, Singapore, and Hong Kong were, respectively, $259.8 billion, $17.4 billion, $17.6 billion, $37.4 billion, and $24.9 billion, accounting for a large percentage of their GDP.[328] The current-account balances of the oil exporters, Saudi Arabia and Russia, were $99 billion and $73 billion, respectively, thanks to their oil and gas revenues. Those positive trade-balances were in stark contrast with the U.S. balance, which stood at a negative $793 billion! The "Economic Report of the President" released February 11, 2010, by the Council of Economic Advisers made the point that it is not enough for the economy to start growing again. Rather, "the composition of spending needs to be re-oriented giving smaller roles to housing and consumption and bigger roles to savings, investments, and exports."[329] Almost coincidentally, in his 2010 state of the union address President Obama called for a doubling of exports in five years.

Latin American Opportunities

Improving trade and diplomatic relationships with Latin America would serve the United States and all the American countries well.

Latin America is endowed with remarkable human and natural resources. Human resources are 580 million strong, of which 40 million were lifted out of poverty between 2002 and 2008, thanks to an economic growth averaging 5.5 percent a year. If the region keeps up the rate of the past few years, the income per person by 2025 is expected to double to $22,000 a year. By then, Brazil may be the fifth-biggest economy of the world. Brazil's scientists are conducting world-class research, especially in agriculture, leading to a 150 percent increase in production over the past thirty years with only 20 percent more land in

---

328 The Economist, "Economic and Financial Indicators", December 15th, 2007, 106

329 The Economist, "Mixed Message", February 13th 2010, 78

production. Embraer, its aircraft-maker, is a strong player in the international market for medium-size jets.[330]

Buenos Aires

BRAZIL

Rio de Janeiro

Sao Paolo

Santiago

South America – Latin America's approximately 580 million people and its immense natural resources present the United States with mostly untapped economic and geopolitical opportunities. (Photos: IStock Photo #15110299, 12769748, 14187722, and 12485261)

The region's natural resources are among the richest in the world. Brazil holds 15 percent of the world's oil reserves. Recent discovery of offshore oil gives it claim to reserves twice the size of the U.S.'s. Brazil has a large stock of minerals, and a full quarter of the world's arable land, much of it still virgin, and 30 percent of all the fresh water in the world. Brazil, by itself, is the world's largest exporter of coffee, sugar, beef, chicken, tobacco, and ethanol, and the second-biggest source of soya products. It expects to be the world's leading food exporter by 2025.[330]

---

330 The Economist, September 11th, 2010, A Special Report on Latin America, 3-18

The natural resources of South America are among the most diverse and the most plentiful of any continent. (Photos: IStock #12909965, 12900298, 12097669, 12936398, 5471116)

In 2010 the economy of more than half a billion of our Latin American neighbors grew about 6 percent presenting obvious opportunities for the United States. The $300 billion in annual trade with Latin America already supports 900,000 plus U.S. jobs. More than a quarter of those resulted from trade with Brazil. The United States needs to build a framework for future cooperation. Brazil holds $300 billion in reserves and plans to spend $200 billion on infrastructure projects in the next 3 to 5 years. Hosting the World Cup in 2014 and the Olympics in 2016 will raise Brazil's international profile and fuel its economic growth for years. Brazil is already attracting investments from United States' rivals China, India and Russia. In 2009 China displaced the United States as Brazil's top trading partner.[331]

It behooves the United States to improve diplomatic and trade relationships with our neighbors to the south in order to create business opportu-

331 Nicholas Johnston and Julianna Goldman with Randy Woods, Bloomberg Businessweek, March 21-March 27, 2011, 40-41

nities for our multinational companies. The more open the United States is toward Latin America, the greater the chance of creating prosperity, which is "the best protection against conflict and disorder."[330] Prosperity in countries that are already important trading partners of the United States offers some of the best opportunities to increase exports of U.S. goods and services. Already Latin America takes a quarter of the total U.S. exports and around one-fifth of its outward flow of portfolio investments.[330]

■ Chapter Six: What You Must Do For Your Country

* Adopt a more frugal life-style; reduce your credit card balances
* Choose American-manufactured products over foreign-made goods
* Adopt a healthier life-style
* Support legislation to increase the eligibility-age for social security benefits
* Lobby your elected officials for spending cuts at all levels of government; Demand salary freezes for federal, state and local public employees until their remuneration adjusts to that of private-sector workers
* Lobby for reductions in Pentagon spending
* Support the phasing out of special treatment for mortgage interest and home equity loan payments
* Support a national consumption tax and an appropriate fuel tax
* Lobby for the adoption of measures to stop the construction of new single-family homes.

Part Four: America's Trump Card

Chapter 7: People are America's Greatest Asset

The future of the United States rests with its people. Americans have the ability to reinvent themselves. They have the will to rise to the occasion. They see opportunity in every difficulty and they are not above learning from their rivals. Americans are remarkably good at embracing new ideas and encouraging entrepreneurial spirit.

The size of the U.S. population is an undeniable asset. Americans rank third in the world in population and are on a trajectory to gain demographically over their main competitors. The U.S. population is projected to top 400 million by 2050. According to Joel Kotkin, author of *The Next Hundred Million: America in 2050*, **the U.S. population aged fifteen to sixty-four will grow 42 percent between 2000 and 2050.** That contrasts with declines of 10 percent in China, nearly 25 percent in Europe, and 44 percent in Japan. Russia's total population, which is shrinking by eight hundred thousand a year, is projected to drop a full 30 percent by 2050. The U.S demographic advantage will rest not only with the ability of its workers to meet the needs of its retirees but with the economic expansion driven by a growing workforce.[332]

Americans enjoy another enviable advantage: the size of their country. The United States has the fourth-largest landmass of the globe, after Russia, Canada, and China, and it is barely edged in size by the last two countries. Americans can keep reproducing and welcome immigrants without the country feeling crowded.

America has always been a magnet for talented people from around the world. Unfortunately, the insecurities that followed the 9/11 events resulted in the erection of barriers to immigration and travel to the United States. A nation built on immigrants is building a fence to keep them out. America needs to embrace immigrants. They have served the United States well in the past. Some seventy of the three hundred Americans who have won Nobel prizes since 1901 were immigrants. According to the Kauffman Foundation, 52 percent of Silicon Valley start-ups were founded by immigrants. Iconic American companies like Intel, Google, and Sun Microsystems have immigrants among

---

332 Joel Katkin, Newsweek, May 10, 2010, 46

their founders. About one-quarter of information technology (IT) firms in Silicon Valley were founded by Chinese and Indians. A quarter of U.S. engineering and technology firms founded between 1995 and 2005 had immigrant founders, according to Vivek Wadhwa of Harvard Law School. Some 40 percent of American doctoral degrees in science and engineering go to immigrants. About 40 percent of all the patents filed in America are filed by foreigners. Immigrants energize our economy. It is estimated that for every foreigner who comes to America on an H1B visa, five jobs are created. Vivek Wadhwa estimated that in 2005 immigrant-founded engineering and tech companies employed four hundred fifty thousand people and generated $52 billion in sales.[333] An H1B visa allows companies to sponsor highly educated foreigners to work in America for three years. The number is so low—eighty-five thousand—that the annual allotment is taken up as soon as applications open April 1. Then officials deal with the mismatch between supply and demand by allocating the visas by lottery. The result is that hundreds of thousands of highly qualified people—doctors, scientists, and entrepreneurs—are denied a chance to work in the United States.

Immigrants have played an invaluable role in the advancement of science and technology in America. Silicon Valley start-ups are populated by immigrants. The medical profession owes a lot to doctors and other medical scientists who came here to train and stayed, and professionals who received their education elsewhere and are working side by side with native doctors. The United States must see as an asset the children of immigrants who grow up with the knowledge of Spanish, Mandarin, Polish, Russian, German, French, and other foreign languages in a world ever more interconnected. The heterogeneity of the U.S. population has been responsible in great part for the global reach of America. Immigrants, foreign faculty members, and foreign students are ambassadors of the United States in their native countries. They encourage a two-way flow of people, products, and ideas and help develop ties with people around the world. The United States cannot afford to pass up opportunities to expose foreigners to our culture and our language.

Comprehensive reforms are needed to facilitate immigration. Immigrants keep America young and growing and could stretch the preeminence of the United States for longer than many people predict. Visas should be readily available for students and the most talented and educated individuals. Sena-

---

333 S.S.: Newsweek, "Immigrants Make More Jobs Than They Take," August 24–31, 2009, 66

tors Chuck Schumer and Lindsey Graham, as part of a multifaceted immigration reform, proposed granting automatic green cards for students "who earned advanced degrees in science, technology, engineering, or math in America, and an elimination of country quotas on green cards." The proposal went nowhere, leaving backlogs of eight to ten years for applicants from China and India.[334] We are giving up economic growth by not addressing that issue.

America's rivals for talented immigrants are taking advantage of America's restrictive ways. At a time when America is competing with emerging economies for skilled, highly educated immigrants, its immigration process is hobbled by its paranoia toward foreigners. Technology companies are being forced to set up offices abroad. Microsoft opened a software development center in Canada in part because Canada's more liberal immigration policies made it easier to recruit people from around the world. **The Labor Department projects that by 2014 if immigration restrictions are not eased, there will be more than 2 million job openings in science, technology, and engineering at a time when the number of Americans graduating with degrees in those subjects is declining.** America needs all of the world's brightest people that it can get. Otherwise, we will lose the global talent war with grave long-term consequences. Michael Bloomberg, mayor of New York, pointed out that America's broken immigration system is hurting our ability to attract top talent. He said, "We must at least bring service improvements to our customs and immigration departments, so that all visitors are treated as guests, not potential terrorists."[335]

Granted, the United States needs to take advantage of the global talent pool, but it should turn its attention to improving education of its own people. As Jeffery Joerres, CEO of Manpower, Inc., put it: "As the global recovery gathers pace, cultivating future talent and alleviating the shortage of skilled workers is becoming vital to ensure economic growth."[336] The College Board reported an "alarming decline in young American adults who have completed college; once a global leader, the United States now ranks twelfth in the world by that measure." Education Secretary Arne Duncan said, "The country that out-ed-

---

334 The Economist, "Green-Card Blues," October 30, 2010, 33

335 Michael Bloomberg, The Economist, The World in 2008, "The City Club," 42

336 The Business Ledger, "Manpower Survey Cites Shortage of Skilled Workers," September 16, 2010, 3

ucates us today will out-compete us tomorrow."[337] A recent study by McKinsey & Company showed that **the growing gaps in educational achievement between the United States and other leading nations "impose the economic equivalent of a permanent national recession, one substantially larger than the deep recession the country is currently experiencing."**[337] Americans, collectively, must make whatever sacrifices are needed to assure a world-class education for all children. Failure to properly educate our children will have profound consequences on American corporations' competitiveness in world markets, the ability of American workers to afford a high standard of living, and the country's ability to maintain its prestige.

Immigration reform cannot ignore the undocumented immigrants already within our borders. We need to take advantage of the human capital that numbered an estimated 11.9 million undocumented immigrants in the United States at the end of 2008. It is in America's interest to embrace them. We need them to support the population expansion that will fuel our economic growth. We need them to create jobs. Maureen Rimmer and Peter Dixon, economists studying immigration issues for the Cato Institute, found that "even low-skilled immigrants expand the economic pie and create jobs further up the ladder."[333] We need them to fill the void in our workforce as baby boomers retire. Those twelve million young immigrants constitute a mostly untapped asset for the United States. They are the ones with the fertility rate that will help offset the negatives of the aging American population.

An asset embedded in this group of potential new citizens that is not appreciated is their knowledge of another popular language in our hemisphere, Spanish, which is spoken by 108 million people in Mexico, 47 million in Columbia, 40 million in Argentina, 29 million in Peru, 28 million in Venezuela, 16 million in Chile, and tens of millions of other South and Central Americans. What an advantage to have tens of millions U.S. citizens who can speak the language and have some understanding of the culture of the many people who live in our hemisphere in countries that have enormous potential for growth. Some people argue that English is the language of business in most parts of the world and that it is good enough for American businesspeople to speak English. There is also a point to be made that to penetrate the masses, to go beyond those countries' elite, one needs to speak the local language. Raising a crop of Americans who speak the language of hundreds of millions of people

---

337 Michael Hirsh, Newsweek, August 23 & 30, 2010, 40–42

with whom we want to do business presents a significant economic and political advantage. **A young, working population and a bilingual population is an asset of great value for America's future, an important potential for deeper economic integration within the Americas. The result could be a common market and trading block 900 million people strong with enormous land mass and tremendous natural resources.** The United States must make it a priority to resolve the issue of undocumented immigrants and prepare them and their descendants to play a bigger role in the integration of all the American nations. The United States needs to do it all can to promote trade within the Americas to strengthen the economies of our neighbors and raise the standards of living of our natural trading partners.

■ Chapter Seven: What You Must Do For Your Country

* Insist on the implementation of measures to provide the best possible education for American children
* Embrace a more welcoming immigration policy
* Support the legalization of undocumented immigrants

EPILOGUE

"Doing what's right isn't the problem. It is knowing what's right." Lyndon Johnson, *July 1968*

I hope this reading has shed some light on what's right. I trust that individuals will have the discipline to do what is right and our leaders, the fortitude to implement policies that will sustain the right behavior.

LIST OF ACRONYMS

AC	Alternative current
ALERTS	Automated Land-Change Evolution, Reporting and Tracking System
ANWAR	Arctic National Wildlife Refuge
API	American Petroleum Institute
ATM	Automated teller machine
AWEA	American Wind Energy Association
BMI	Body mass index
BTU	British thermal unit
CAFE	Corporate average fuel efficiency
CDM	Clean development mechanism
CEO	Chief executive officer
CFL	Compact fluorescent light
CH_4	Methane
CIA	Central Intelligence Agency
CNG	Compressed natural gas
CNOOC	Chinese National Offshore Oil Corporation
CO_2	Carbon dioxide
CO_2 eq	Carbon dioxide equivalent
CRI	Container Recycling Institute
CRP	Conservation Reserve Program
CST	Concentrated solar power
Cuss	Carbon capture and storage
DDG	Dried distillers grain
DOE	Department of Energy
E.U.	European Union
ECAD	Energy Conservation Audit and Disclosure
EPA	Environmental Protection Agency
ETS	Emission Trading System
EUETS	European Union Emission Trading System
E-waste	Electronic waste
FAO	Food and Agriculture Organization

FOB	Forward operating base
GCC	Gulf Cooperation Council
HERS	Home energy rating systems
HFC	Hydrofluorocarbon
HVDC	High-voltage direct current
ICSU	International Council for Science
IEA	international Energy Agency
IMF	International Monetary Fund
IPCC	Intergovernmental Panel on Climate Change
IT	Information technology
KEPCO	Korean Electrical Power
Kwh	Kilowatt hours
L.A.	Los Angeles
LED	Light-emitting diode
LEED	Leadership in Energy and Environmental Design
LNG	Liquefied natural gas
LPG	Liquefied petroleum gas
mpg	miles per gallon
mph	miles per hour
MW	Megawatt
N_2o	Nitrous oxide
NASA	National Aeronautics and Space Administration
NEI	Nuclear Energy Institute
NRC	Nuclear Regulatory Commission
OCO	Orbiting Carbon Observatory
OCS	Outer Continental Shelf
OECD	Organization of Economic Cooperation and Development
OMB	Office of Management and Budget
OPEC	Organization of Petroleum Exporting Countries
PFC	Perfluorcarbon
PG&E	Pacific Gas and Electric Company
PHIUS	Passive House Institute U.S.
PNNL	Pacific Northwest National Laboratory
ppm	Parts per million
PV	Photovoltaic
R&D	Research and development

RFS	Renewable fuel standards
RPA	Regional Planning Association
SDP	Submerged Deepwater Platform
SF6	Sulfur hexafluoride
SUV	Sports utility vehicle
TARP	Troubled Asset Relief Program
TES	Thermal energy storage
U.K.	United Kingdom
U.N.	United Nations
U.S.	United States of America
UAE	United Arab Emirates
UNDP	United Nations Development Program
UNEP	United Nations Environmental Program
UNFCC	United Nation's Framework Convention on Climate Change
UPS	United Parcel Service
USDA	United States Department of Agriculture
USGBC	U.S. Green Building Council
USGRP	U.S. Global Change Research Program
VAT	Value-added tax
WTO	World Trade Organization

www.ingramcontent.com/pod-product-compliance
Lightning Source LLC
Chambersburg PA
CBHW062134280526
45788CB00001B/163